THE
EVERYTHING

GUIDE TO STARTING AND RUNNING
A RESTAURANT

2ND EDITION

Dear Reader,

If you're thinking about starting your own restaurant (well, you must be if you just picked up this book!), you should know that it is a great way to make a living. I grew up in the restaurant business, and I love it. Sure, it's hard work, the hours are long, and weekends and holidays are usually when I'm busiest. But I wouldn't trade it for any other business in the world. Where else can you express creativity and passion for food, meet lots of people, and make money doing so?

It isn't a walk in the park, not even for someone like me. I started my own restaurant when I was twenty-five. As a teenager, I worked at my parents' restaurants. After college, I thought I knew everything I needed to go on my own, but I soon discovered that it was a whole new ballgame. Fortunately, it worked out, and my restaurant is still going strong after seventeen years, although I learned a few lessons along the way.

After reading this book, you will be much more prepared than I was when I started out. If you have the passion and the drive, there's a good chance you'll succeed.

Good Luck!

Ronald Lee

Welcome to the EVERYTHING Series!

These handy, accessible books give you all you need to tackle a difficult project, gain a new hobby, comprehend a fascinating topic, prepare for an exam, or even brush up on something you learned back in school but have since forgotten.

You can choose to read an Everything® book from cover to cover or just pick out the information you want from our four useful boxes: e-questions, e-facts, e-alerts, and e-ssentials.

We give you everything you need to know on the subject, but throw in a lot of fun stuff along the way, too.

We now have more than 400 Everything® books in print, spanning such wide-ranging categories as weddings, pregnancy, cooking, music instruction, foreign language, crafts, pets, New Age, and so much more. When you're done reading them all, you can finally say you know Everything®!

QUESTION

Answers to
common questions

FACT

Important snippets
of information

ALERT

Urgent
warnings

ESSENTIAL

Quick
handy tips

PUBLISHER Karen Cooper

DIRECTOR OF ACQUISITIONS AND INNOVATION Paula Munier

MANAGING EDITOR, EVERYTHING® SERIES Lisa Laing

COPY CHIEF Casey Ebert

ASSISTANT PRODUCTION EDITOR Jacob Erickson

ACQUISITIONS EDITOR Kate Powers

DEVELOPMENT EDITOR Meredith O'Hayre

EDITORIAL ASSISTANT Ross Weisman

EVERYTHING® SERIES COVER DESIGNER Erin Alexander

LAYOUT DESIGNERS Erin Dawson, Michelle Roy Kelly, Elisabeth Lariviere, Ashley Vierra, Denise Wallace

Visit the entire Everything® series at *www.everything.com*

THE
EVERYTHING®
GUIDE TO
STARTING AND
RUNNING A RESTAURANT
2ND EDITION

The ultimate resource for starting a successful restaurant!

Ronald Lee

Adamsmedia
Avon, Massachusetts

To my children, Alice Ai Chiotti Lee and Henry An Chiotti Lee

An Everything® Series Book.
Everything® and everything.com® are registered trademarks of F+W Media, Inc.

Published by Adams Media, a division of F+W Media, Inc.
57 Littlefield Street, Avon, MA 02322 U.S.A.
www.adamsmedia.com

ISBN 10: 1-4405-2685-0
ISBN 13: 978-1-4405-2685-5
eISBN 10: 1-4405-2783-0
eISBN 13: 978-1-4405-2783-8

Printed in the United States of America.

10 9 8 7 6 5 4 3 2 1

Library of Congress Cataloging-in-Publication Data
is available from the publisher.

This publication is designed to provide accurate and authoritative information with regard to the subject matter covered. It is sold with the understanding that the publisher is not engaged in rendering legal, accounting, or other professional advice. If legal advice or other expert assistance is required, the services of a competent professional person should be sought.

—From a *Declaration of Principles* jointly adopted by a Committee of the American Bar Association and a Committee of Publishers and Associations

Many of the designations used by manufacturers and sellers to distinguish their products are claimed as trademarks. Where those designations appear in this book and Adams Media was aware of a trademark claim, the designations have been printed with initial capital letters.

This book is available at quantity discounts for bulk purchases.
For information, please call 1-800-289-0963.

FEB 1 7 2012

Contents

Acknowledgments

A special thanks to Kate Powers, Meredith O'Hayre, and the whole team at Adams Media, for the opportunity to write this book; to my staff at Spice Island Tea House for their hard work; and to Danielle Chiotti, my love and inspiration, for her support, wisdom, positive attitude, and putting up with me in general.

Top 10 Lingo
in the Restaurant Business

1. **Top:** A group of customers at a table, used in conjunction with a number. A table of two is a two-top (also know as a deuce), a table of four is a four-top, a table of six is a six-top, and so on.

2. **On the fly:** To need something quickly, as in "I need the order for Table 9 on the fly!"

3. **Full house:** All tables are taken, either reserved or currently occupied, as in "We have a full house until 10 P.M." A.k.a., "Music to a restaurateur's ears."

4. **Jumpin' (or hoppin'):** A term describing a very busy restaurant but under control, as in "The place is jumpin'!"

5. **Slammed:** To have orders all coming in or going out at the same time. "The night started off slow, then we got slammed!"

6. **In the weeds:** To be so busy it seems you'll never catch up to your orders.

7. **Fire:** To start cooking now. For example, "Fire Table 8!" means "Start cooking Table 8's order."

8. **Weedwacker:** Someone who comes in and bails out the person who is in the weeds.

9. **86:** To be out of something, or to throw out an unsatisfactory or unpopular item. For example, "The chef didn't like the soup he made today so he 86'ed it."

10. **Yesterday:** Urging someone to hurry up, as in, "Water at Table 6, yesterday!"

Introduction

OWNING A RESTAURANT HAS a great many benefits. Of course, being your own boss is a tremendous incentive, but the main reason so many restaurateurs find it rewarding is because it is an exciting, energetic business that utilizes their creativity, business acumen, marketing and social skills, and passion for food. A well-executed restaurant can be a profitable business, but it can also establish itself as an endearing institution within the community. People get excited when a new restaurant opens in their neighborhood. Even if you're just running a hot dog stand or pizza joint, you are still trying to sell a product that pleases your customer. It is one of the few industries in which you can have an immediate reaction from your customers. Nothing is more satisfying to restaurateurs than people enjoying themselves at their restaurants. In a nutshell, restaurant owners love being in the business because they love pleasing people.

That being said, getting into the business is not something to enter into lightly. Opening a restaurant requires substantial capital, effort, and planning. Essentially, the process of starting a restaurant can be divided into three stages: the planning, the set-up, and the opening. This book will guide you through each stage and help you evaluate your ideas and make the best decisions. During the planning stage, you will develop your business plan. You will decide the type of restaurant to open, define your concept, choose your target market, analyze your competition, and research your preferred location. You will project start-up costs and revenue and consider your financing options.

Next is the set-up. During this stage, you will put your business plan to work. You will secure a location and begin construction. On the legal front, you will set up a business structure and obtain the proper permits and insurance. You may also plan a menu, research your purveyors, and install the proper cooking equipment.

The third stage, the opening, is the point in which your restaurant transforms from a plan into reality—you are ready to open for business. You have hired and trained a staff, your kitchen is stocked, and your publicity and marketing plans are firmly in place. All that's left is to open your doors, and meet your customers.

Once your restaurant is up and running, you must keep it on the path of success. That includes listening to customer feedback and reviews, keeping up with your competitors, and remaining open to change while staying true to your vision. You may also begin thinking about future developments, such as catering services, expansion, franchising and merchandising.

The restaurant business is dynamic and fascinating. Every day people from all different backgrounds are opening restaurants across the world. It could be a diner, a French bistro, a taqueria, a burger joint, a sushi bar—the varieties are endless. No other industry has the diversity that the restaurant industry has. The possibilities are constantly growing, and with *The Everything® Guide to Starting and Running a Restaurant, 2nd Edition*, you are on your way to turning the possibility into a reality.

CHAPTER 1

Preparing for the Challenge

People love restaurants. Many people eat out about three times a week. Because we love to go to restaurants so much, it is only natural that so many of us have the desire to start our own. However, most people tend to focus on the fun aspects of the business without acknowledging the challenge involved in starting and running a restaurant. This chapter will prepare you for the challenge ahead.

Why Do You Want to Run a Restaurant?

In many cases, running your own restaurant gives you the chance to express your creative side, show off your culinary flair, meet interesting people, and garner praise from your customers as well as respect in the community. A few restaurateurs go on to become local or even national celebrities, authoring cookbooks, hosting cooking shows, and hobnobbing with Hollywood stars. These are some of the financial and social benefits that attract people to the restaurant business. While these benefits are good reasons for getting into the restaurant business, they should not be the only reasons. Your motivation for getting into the business must come from something more than just a desire to make money and gain social status. Here are some questions you may ask yourself:

- Do you enjoy a challenge?
- Do you like a potentially fast-paced, changing work environment?
- Are you passionate about food—not just eating it, but studying it, creating it, presenting it, promoting it?
- Do you enjoy being in a restaurant atmosphere?
- Do you like juggling many tasks on a daily basis?
- Do you enjoy talking with customers and addressing their needs and expectations?

If you answer all these questions with an emphatic "yes," you probably have the drive to survive in the restaurant business. If not, there are many other good reasons to start your own restaurant. The important thing is to be honest with yourself about identifying them. The best way to find out whether you have the interest is to get a job in a restaurant. If your personal and financial situations do not allow you to go that route, you'll need to take a step back and look at the business from a different perspective. Instead, try dining at several different restaurants on various busy weekend nights. Observe each restaurant, not through the eyes of a customer, but through those of a potential restaurant owner. Pay attention to the atmosphere, the clientele, the staff, and the pace of the restaurant.

Make a list of things that interest you about working in this environment and a list of things that don't. If the things that interest you outnumber the things that don't, that's a good sign you might enjoy being in the restaurant business. At this point you've only begun to scratch the surface. Nevertheless, it's a good start.

ALERT

Before you decide to invest time and money into a restaurant venture, remember—the restaurant business is a business—and it is a tough business. Getting to the point where you reap the financial and social rewards takes long hours, lots of hard work, patience, commitment, and a little luck.

A Day in the Restaurant Manager's Life

The duties of a manager vary from restaurant to restaurant. If it is a large establishment, a restaurant may have one or two general managers and assistant managers on staff to share responsibilities. In a small start-up restaurant, the owner may be the manager or the executive chef who probably also makes most, if not all, of the administrative, personnel, and purchasing decisions.

A typical manager's day at a restaurant open for lunch and dinner can be divided into five parts: opening duties, lunch rush, the mid-afternoon break, dinner rush, and closing duties. Certain tasks and duties are routinely done during each period, along with tasks that may need to be done throughout the day, at any time.

The restaurant environment changes practically every minute. The manager has to respond at a moment's notice to resolve various pressing matters. The lists of duties that follow are by no means comprehensive, but they should give you a good idea of the multitasking, detail-oriented nature of running a restaurant.

Opening Duties

Opening duties are the work the manager does before the restaurant opens. Some opening duties for managers may include checking the previous day's sales and preparing for the daily bank deposit. After checking inventory of food and other supplies, the manager may negotiate prices and place orders with purveyors (restaurant-speak for supplier). If the employees' payday is coming up, the manager may prepare for payroll. In addition, he probably has to reconcile other accounts payable to suppliers, utility companies, the landlord, and other creditors. Equipment sometimes needs maintenance, so it helps if the manager is a handyman as well. The manager typically holds meetings with the staff to inform them of the day's specials and to brief them on the business and their performance. He oversees the opening duties of the staff to make sure that the restaurant is prepared when the first customers of the day arrive.

The Lunch and Dinner Rushes

The lunch and dinner rushes are the busiest periods of the day, and if order is not maintained, these times can become quite chaotic. The lunch rush usually occurs between 11:00 A.M. and 2:00 P.M. The most popular dinner hours occur between 5:00 and 10:00 P.M., depending on the kind of restaurant. During these rushes, the manager usually bounces back and forth between the kitchen and dining room, and at any time she may be doing one or more of the following: greeting and seating customers, monitoring quality and service, supporting the staff where needed, addressing customer questions and complaints, or assisting in some food preparation.

The manager may also assure that menu items are prepared expeditiously and taken to the correct tables. Throughout all of this, she maintains order in the restaurant, anticipating any problems that may arise.

The Mid-Afternoon Break

The mid-afternoon break is the slow-down period of the day between lunch and dinner rushes. Many restaurants use this time to make the transition from lunch to dinner mode. Changing staff, altering place settings for dinner service, and preparing the kitchen for the dinner menu are some of the operations that occur at this time. Some restaurants may be closed during the afternoon, while others choose to remain open. This may be the time when the manager can resolve some less pressing matters and even be able to take a break and eat. Some typical matters he might address at this time may include planning new menus or specials, working on a promotional campaign, preparing work schedules, placing ads with newspapers and magazines, calculating lunch sales, and reconciling the cash register. He may also interview potential new staff or meet with sales reps during this break.

Closing Duties

Closing duties are the work that a manager does to prepare for closing the restaurant for the night. The closing hour varies from restaurant to restaurant, especially if the restaurant has a late-night bar operation. At the end of the evening, the manager must tally and reconcile the sales and secure the cash in the restaurant's safe if there is one. She also might calculate tip-outs for bussers, bartenders, or hosts and oversee the staff's closing duties. She might do an inventory of food and other supplies, especially if the restaurant serves alcohol. The end of the night is also a good time for the manager to address an employee about performance if necessary. Finally, before she leaves, the manager should make a safety check of the building and lockup after all employees vacate the premises.

ESSENTIAL

Performing all these duties is quite mentally and physically demanding. The manager must manage her time efficiently. When situations arise that seem to throw the restaurant into chaos, the manager must keep her composure while working quickly to calm the storm. Moreover, the manager also has to maintain a pleasant demeanor in front of the customers. Running a restaurant is inherently stressful work, but many people thrive in this environment and do very well.

Do You Have What It Takes?

If running a restaurant is so difficult, why do new restaurants open all the time? Starting a restaurant presents the kind of challenge that many people thrive on. Despite its unusual demands, the restaurant business has a tremendous upside. Though it requires financial risks and personal sacrifices, many people find the business exciting, and they want to see their creation grow and enjoy the fruits of their labor. With that in mind, only you can decide whether the restaurant business is right for you.

Are You Willing to Take the Financial Risks?

Like most businesses, starting a restaurant has its share of risks. There is no guarantee you'll be successful even if you've done your homework and planned your operation well. A poor economy, inclement weather, and other unforeseeable circumstances may affect the likelihood of your success. Unless you can seek out investors or secure a business loan from a lending institution, you may have to use your own savings, borrow from friends and relatives, or take out a home-equity loan. Your personal liabilities could set you back financially until your restaurant is off the ground. However, if you do plan your operation well, you can cut down on the risks and avoid going over budget.

Can You Handle Life Without a Paycheck?

Not only might you finance your venture by putting up the money you've saved or borrowed, it might take a little time initially before you can give yourself fair compensation for your work. Depending on your initial operating budget, you may have to forgo paying yourself until the restaurant gets off the ground and can generate significant cash flow.

Can You Make the Tough Decisions?

Along with making the fun and creative decisions, such as naming your restaurant, planning a menu, and designing your space, you will face situations that call for the hard decisions—such as firing an employee, cutting costs, or dropping longtime suppliers. As the owner, you have to make decisions based on what is best for the business, and sometimes your decisions may not sit well with everyone involved, perhaps even your family.

Can You Withstand Growing Pains?

External factors can affect the success of a business. There may be times when business slows down regardless of how well you planned and organized your restaurant. You must be just as ready to brave the storm when the restaurant hits a downturn as you are to bask in the light of its success when it thrives. You must keep yourself and your staff motivated so that the quality of your product and service will not drop off and cause your business to suffer as a result.

Can You Adapt to a Major Lifestyle Change?

This may be one of the most important questions to ask yourself, especially if you have a family. As you probably already know, restaurant hours, although somewhat flexible, are not like the hours of a typical office job. During its infancy, the restaurant schedule may require you to work ten to twelve hours a day, sometimes seven days a week. On weekends, while most people are relaxing or taking short trips, you are probably the busiest you've been all week. You will probably be working during the holiday season, which may be one of the most profitable times of the year. You may not be able to take a vacation while the restaurant gets off the ground.

Assess Your Abilities

There is more to running a successful restaurant than just providing good food and good service. Before deciding on starting a restaurant, you should take a moment and assess your abilities. The following list includes skills and characteristics that a successful restaurateur should possess. As you read through the list, determine whether or not you are proficient in that area. Be honest with yourself. If you don't think you have all the skills or characteristics listed, don't worry. In time you will develop them. The important thing is that you are aware that developing these characteristics will help you become successful.

- **A mind for business:** Are you a smart buyer? Do you know how to get the most for your money in any situation? Do you have the organizational skills to mind complex financial records? Can you play the negotiation game? Can you think on your feet and lead a dynamic group of people in stressful situations?
- **Good social skills:** Restaurateurs are generally sociable people. You must be good at making your customers feel welcome and at ease so they keep coming back.

- **Food service skills:** Whether it is table service, kitchen service, café service, bar service, or even retail service, it helps if you have some experience in the service industry. Not only will you be able to get a better grasp of running the restaurant, but you might relate to your employees better because you've "worked in the trenches."
- **Leadership:** As a leader, you must find a way to make your employees feel they are a team with a purpose—to sustain the restaurant's success. You'll need to know when to be flexible and when to be firm, when to be a coach and when to be a counselor, but you should always manage your staff with fairness and respect.
- **Creativity:** The need for creativity underscores all areas of the restaurant business. Creativity is not limited to the design of your restaurant and the preparation of your food. It includes the way you choose to serve your customers, promote your restaurant, and maintain a positive work atmosphere.
- **The ability to handle pressure:** The nature of the restaurant business is fast-paced and sometimes chaotic. When faced with a stressful situation, whether it's a customer complaint, disgruntled employees, or malfunctioning equipment, you must stay cool and handle the situation rationally.
- **Flexibility:** In this business, you can't get too wrapped up in your ideas or the usual ways you operate. Sometimes you must make adjustments in situations even though these changes may not have been in your initial plan.
- **Stamina:** Running a restaurant can be quite physically demanding. You'll face long days, late hours, and being on your feet most of the day.
- **Love for the business:** You have to love the business. If you don't, your restaurant won't last long. Passion is what keeps you and your restaurant running.

Why Some Restaurants Fail

Although it is not as high as commonly believed, the restaurant failure rate is a daunting and hard fact. Various social and economic factors can contribute to these failures, including some extenuating circumstances such as a recession or natural catastrophe, but most restaurant failures can be attributed to two causes: inadequate planning and inadequate management.

One of the telltale signs of inadequate planning is inadequate budgeting. Poor budgeting doesn't necessarily mean the restaurateur didn't raise enough capital. It could mean that he spent too much on the construction and didn't have enough initial operating capital leftover to pay expenses; or perhaps he grossly underestimated the start-up and operating costs. Another sign of inadequate planning is insufficient research into the market. Inadequate target marketing, poorly constructed concepts, and haphazard location-scouting all indicate lack of research. A restaurant may never overcome the struggles created by such deficient planning.

FACT

It is commonly believed that restaurants fail at a rate as high as 90 percent in the first year. However, according to a study done at Ohio State University, only 26 percent of restaurants fail during the first year of business. The rate of failure for restaurants during a three-year period is about 61 percent for independent restaurants and 57 percent for franchised chains.

Even if an entrepreneur has adequate resources to open the restaurant, it doesn't make turning a profit any easier. The restaurant must be managed properly in order to build a steady revenue stream and maintain a reasonable profit margin. Lack of quality control, wasteful spending, poor relations between partners, poor employee morale, and unsound policies are just a few signs of an inadequately managed restaurant. There are many details of the restaurant that require supervision. If sufficient steps aren't taken to address them, the restaurant incurs losses and eventually fails.

You have to have a solid plan, and you have to manage the restaurant well. Without these two factors you'll be hard pressed to succeed. This book guides you through all the stages of planning and management so you can put your plan in motion with confidence and keep your business profitable and running efficiently.

CHAPTER 2

Taking the Plunge

If you are thinking about opening a restaurant, you probably already have an idea of the kind of restaurant you want. However, it is important that you understand all your options. You need to know the types of restaurants available for you to consider and the different ways to get into the restaurant business. Once you have a clearer picture of what you want, you can develop a concept for your restaurant that will take you to the next stages of research and planning.

Types of Restaurants

The world of restaurants is incredibly diverse. The options for today's consumer can be a bit overwhelming. For a group of people deciding on where to dine, it can sometimes end up being a lengthy debate. Despite the numerous styles of food and service that restaurants create to appeal to customers, there are essentially three ways to categorize restaurants: quick service, casual dining, and fine dining.

Quick Service

Quick-service, also known as fast-food restaurants refer to establishments whose menu items are priced relatively low and are already prepared or can be prepared quickly. Customers usually order and receive their food at the counter, or they may serve themselves, as in a cafeteria. The seating area is very casual, either benches or basic chairs and tables. Hamburgers, pizza, french fries, and tacos usually come to mind when people think about quick-service restaurants. McDonald's, Wendy's, and Taco Bell are a few well-known examples. However, as the market responds to the growing demand for more variety and fresher ingredients, food-on-the-fly has evolved to new levels over the past few years. Gourmet breads and sandwiches, health-conscious options, ethnic foods such as Chinese and Indian, and even sushi have entered the realm of the quick-service restaurant. Places such as Panera Bread, Au Bon Pain, Chipotle, Panda Express, and Sarku Japan are some examples of a growing marketplace for quick service. Many of these restaurants are either chains or franchises, but an independent fast-food restaurant can be successful in this market as long as it can establish an edge in quality and service while staying close to the competition's prices.

FACT

The phrase "turnover rate" refers to the time it takes the customers occupying a table to leave in order to accommodate the next party. Quick-service restaurants normally have the fastest turnover rate, while fine-dining establishments are the slowest. Turnover rate may become an issue if the restaurant's waiting list and the duration of the waiting period are long.

Casual Dining

Casual dining lies in the middle area between quick service and fine dining. It can encompass a wide range of food and styles of service. Typically, atmosphere and service are the factors that separate casual dining from the other two groups. The atmosphere is generally comfortable, perhaps even hip and modern, but it's not posh or sleek like the more sophisticated fine-dining establishments. Like quick-service restaurants, the dress code is consistently casual. The menu items are generally reasonably priced, ranging from inexpensive (around $5 per entrée) to moderately expensive (usually under $20 per entrée), with different levels of service. Customers generally order and receive their food at the table, or they may go to a buffet station or salad bar.

Because of its broad spectrum of food and styles of service as well as its relative good value for the price, casual dining has a tremendous appeal to a huge segment of the population. As is the case for quick-service restaurants, chain restaurants such as Applebee's, P. F. Chang's, Denny's, and The Cheesecake Factory have a large share of the market in casual dining. However, many independent casual-dining restaurants are also very successful because they can provide a level of service and food quality that surpasses the chains and still maintains good value for the money. The average charge per customer at a casual-dining establishment may be higher than that of quick-service, but the food and labor costs are likely to be higher as well. Furthermore, customers at casual-dining restaurants tend to linger longer, meaning an increase in time to turnover a table for the next customer.

Fine Dining

Fine-dining restaurants are the most expensive type of eating establishment. That means the clientele expects the highest quality in food, service, and ambiance. The decor may be modern and hip or more traditional, but every aspect of the establishment should be top-notch, including the tableware, linen, and the service. The waitstaff should be knowledgeable in proper fine-dining service etiquette, such as serving plates from the correct side of the customer and replacing silverware after each course. Reservations are often required for fine-dining restaurants, perhaps to project an air of exclusivity but more often for the purpose of managing table flow. The menu may not be extensive, but the food in these establishments should be prepared with high-quality gourmet ingredients and presented with panache. Most likely, there is a wine list that complements the menu items, with prices ranging from moderate to very expensive. Restaurants of this caliber call for a connoisseur's palate as well as extreme attention to detail. They require a well-trained and organized staff that knows the intricacies of the culinary arts. The average check per customer may be much higher than a casual-dining restaurant, but the cost of the whole service will be higher as well. While on a busy night, casual restaurants might average five to six seatings per table (that is, the number of times the same table may turnover), fine-dining restaurants might not have more than three seatings per table.

Franchises

You know you want to run a restaurant, but where do you start? Essentially, there are three ways to get started in the restaurant business: purchasing a franchise, purchasing an existing restaurant, or building from the ground up. Buying a franchise means purchasing the license to use the name, brand, and logos to market and sell the products and services of an established company.

From Whom Can You Buy a Franchise?

There are hundreds of companies on the regional and national level that offer franchise opportunities ranging from full-service to fast-food establishments. Quite simply, you can buy a franchise from anyone willing to sell you one, whether they be an independent owner of one or two restaurants or a multibillion-dollar company like McDonald's. Buying a franchise may be the least risky way to get into the restaurant business, especially if the franchise has a well-known brand. However, purchasing the license to use the name may cost you $250,000 and up for nationally recognized brands like Burger King or Wendy's. You then will have to tack on the normal start-up costs of building the business. Along with the high price tag, some larger companies are very selective in selling their franchises and prefer individuals or companies who have significant capital to operate multiple locations.

On the other hand, it may be easier and less costly to purchase a franchise from a smaller, emerging company that might be more motivated to work with individual franchisees. There may be more risk involved because smaller companies may not have the brand identity or the professional support that larger companies have.

The Pros and Cons of Buying a Franchise

Buying a franchise means entering a business partnership with another company. There are advantages and disadvantages to this relationship. Here are some of the advantages of buying a franchise:

- Buying into a franchise allows you to purchase a proven brand. Brand recognition and a loyal customer base are all established without the growing pains of a new restaurant. You will have a consistent product and a menu that customers already expect.
- Franchises generally come packaged with information systems and proven methods for market research and analysis, sales projection, cost controls, and other management operations.
- Franchisers offer thorough training programs for management teams and provide their own forms and policies for hiring, handling employees, and scheduling.
- You will get support from the franchiser as the brand evolves. New menu items and designs, as well as updated marketing and management techniques, are some of the ways the franchiser may help the business keep up with the competition.
- To help protect your investment (and their brand name), franchisers often address quality control issues through franchise visits and meetings with the principal owner of the franchise.

Buying a franchise saves you a lot of the legwork in the planning and management aspects of the restaurant. You have a business model that has been proven to work, a product that is already established, and a support system to ensure your restaurant's productivity. However, there are always two sides on every coin. Despite all the advantages that come with buying a franchise, doing so has its disadvantages, including the following:

- You have the franchiser's brand, its product, and its customer base, but you also have to follow its policies, meet its expectations, and serve its menu.
- There is no room for creativity. When you buy into the franchiser's concept, you give up the right to modify it.
- Not only do you have to pay for the license to use the franchiser's name, you may initially have to pay some high set-up fees and franchise fees, usually a portion of your sales each month.

There is no right or wrong decision when deciding on whether to choose the franchise route. Like any other business, there is no guarantee you'll succeed.

ALERT

Franchisers want to protect their brand name and product. That is why they make routine quality assurance checks to monitor franchisees' operations. If the operations do not perform up to their standards, there may be some serious consequences.

Buying an Existing Restaurant

Another way to get into the restaurant business is to take over an existing restaurant. There are two ways this can be done: first, to purchase the entire business—concept, location, and all assets—or second, to purchase the assets only, usually the location and equipment. Look for restaurants for sale in the newspaper's classified section or scope out "For Sale" signs in windows of restaurants. Perhaps the most effective way to find an existing restaurant for sale, however, is to hire a restaurant broker. The broker will help you locate a restaurant that might be right for you and may assist in the negotiation of the sale. You may have to pay the broker a commission upon closing, usually about 6 percent of the sale price. Hiring a broker lets you spend the time you would have spent searching for a restaurant on planning your restaurant and handling other details instead. Regardless of how you find a restaurant to purchase, be sure that you retain the services of a good attorney specializing in business and liquor laws, especially if the sale of a license to sell alcohol is involved.

Purchasing the Business

One of the advantages of purchasing an existing business is that you can eliminate the construction time it would take to build from the ground up and start to generate revenue almost right away. When purchasing an existing business, you must look closely at the financial viability of the existing business, including its profits, losses, and debts if any, as you may be assuming responsibility for these matters once you take over. Through this purchase, you gain not only the building and equipment, but also the name, reputation, concept, menu, and in some cases, even the staff. You can choose to run it as it was before, or you can make changes as you see fit.

If the restaurant has a good reputation, you might also inherit the clientele. However, as a restaurant's image is intrinsically tied to the owner, there is no guarantee that the success will carry over after you take charge. Nevertheless, it is an option for you if you want to save some time and money.

If you find a restaurant that you'd like to buy, you must inspect the operation thoroughly and figure out why the owner is selling. The best scenario is that the owner wants to retire or is moving, and the restaurant has a good reputation and has been a success. More often, however, the owner is selling because the restaurant has some difficult problems or is failing. You'll have to do some detective work to discern which of these scenarios seems more likely.

Start by asking the owner to show you the restaurant's financial records. There is the possibility that the owner's books aren't accurate, so be sure to request to see tax returns from the previous two or three years. Have a reputable contractor inspect the equipment and structure of the restaurant. Has the equipment been well maintained? Is the building structurally sound? Does the restaurant have a pest problem? Besides figuring out why the owner is selling, knowing these issues may also be used as a bargaining chip if you are making an offer to purchase.

It is possible that the owner is selling due to an increase in the rent. More than likely, you'll be assuming the lease or agreeing to a new lease before closing the deal. In either case, have an attorney read the lease carefully and determine that the terms are fair.

Is the restaurant in a good location? Do your research so you can thoughtfully determine whether the space you may be taking over is right for you.

Purchasing the Assets Only

In most instances, purchasing assets means acquiring tangible property the business may own, but not the business itself. This includes the equipment, the built-in fixtures, and possibly the inventory. The price may also include goodwill, which covers intangibles such as the right to the location and transference of lease. It may even include real estate if the owner of the restaurant also owns the building. However, in the restaurant business, the value placed on a restaurant's assets is somewhat arbitrary and is based on how the seller perceives their worth on the market. Certain intangibles such as location, architectural or historic significance of the building, design and layout of the restaurant, and terms of the lease can raise the perceived value of the restaurant's assets. The assets of a restaurant in a great location can command a much higher price than those of another business of equal or even higher quality that happens to be in a mediocre location. In this way, valuating the assets of a restaurant works in the same fashion as it does in real estate—you can't really compare apples to apples. You may be paying a higher price tag for the assets of a restaurant because you want to do business in a better location, not necessarily because the equipment and whatever goes along with it are worth more.

When your purchase consists solely of the assets of a restaurant, you will have to address many of the issues associated with a new start-up restaurant, but you will have to work with the space and the used equipment you just purchased. You still have to develop a concept, set up a business structure, plan your menu, project sales, hire and train staff, and market your restaurant. You still have to change the decor and maybe even update the furniture to make your dining room match your concept. Doing major renovations could wipe out the time and money you saved by purchasing the assets. So what are the benefits of purchasing only the assets of a restaurant? Here are a few:

- Most of the hefty costs of construction—the electrical, plumbing, heating, ventilation, air-conditioning, and structural work—are already done. Unless you're planning to change any of this, or dramatically alter the floor plan, you probably won't be required to get a permit.

- You don't have to worry about occupancy or zoning law discrepancies, since the space was already set up as a restaurant.
- You can open your business in a relatively short amount of time despite having to make changes to your space.

Building from the Ground Up

You are working with a blank slate. Everything you do to create your restaurant is all up to you. Despite the limitations you may have once you find a location, you get to put everything together. If you like to be creative, and you have the financial capabilities to make it happen, building from the ground up is a very exciting way to get into the business. But it can also be very nerve-racking—with creative freedom come many responsibilities. You have to address all the same issues associated with starting a new restaurant that you would have purchasing a franchise or an existing restaurant. Beyond that, you also have to develop your concept, design your floor plan, your menu, and your decor, as well as work with zoning laws and building-code issues, construction issues, equipment purchases and placement, and so on.

Taking this approach requires organization and discipline. A disorganized approach could cost you a lot more time and money than you anticipated before you make even a dime in profit. You have to be persistent, but you also have to be flexible and willing to make compromises. You need to decide when and where to control costs and avoid cutting the wrong corners. Essentially, you are swimming in uncharted waters. The upside you must always remember is that everything you do will be done your way. As long as you map out your strategy carefully, you will increase your success significantly.

Develop Your Concept

When you go to a restaurant, you don't simply expect to be fed. You expect a satisfying experience. Even in a fast-food restaurant, you expect your service to be fast and courteous, your food to be of acceptable quality, and your surroundings to be relatively pleasant, even if basic. Furthermore, you don't just want to have the same experience over and over. As a consumer, you want variety. You want to go to places that are interesting, and you want to feel you are getting your money's worth. As a potential restaurateur, you need to come up with a concept for your restaurant that meets or exceeds the consumers' expectations.

What Is a Concept?

"Concept" refers to the overall approach you take to packaging your restaurant. Your concept encompasses your restaurant's food, menu, prices, design, atmosphere, style of service, and everything else about the restaurant that conveys your message to your potential customers. If you have considered starting a restaurant, you have probably already started thinking about the concept, but you may not have all the pieces for the whole puzzle. This is one of the fun parts of planning a restaurant because at this stage, you can go wherever your imagination can take you.

There are thousands of concepts, ranging from lunch carts to multilevel seafood restaurants, and luckily there are some fundamental rules you can use as a base for your concept. Type of cuisine is perhaps the most obvious way to build a concept. Some examples of cuisine types are New American, French bistro, and Cajun. Specialty dishes can also be another way to focus on the concept. For example, The Cheesecake Factory has a variety of items on its menu, but the differently flavored cheesecakes are fundamental to its concept.

Ethnic themes are another cornerstone on which to build a concept. When you walk into a Thai restaurant, not only will you find that it serves Thai cuisine, you will also discover an ambiance and decor that likely reflect the styles of Thailand. A concept can convey an attitude. A restaurant with sleek, modern furniture and chic design may suggest an urbane, artsy attitude whereas a restaurant with portraits of Marlon Brando and James Dean on motorcycles may project a rebellious image. Concepts revolving around sports are very popular. Typical sports bars and grills might feature barbeque ribs and hot chicken wings on their menu, but they are flexible enough to also be able to focus on specialized deli sandwiches and hamburgers.

Naming Your Restaurant

Just as you do with your concept, you should give your restaurant's name some thoughtful consideration because it will help convey your message to your targeted customers. The name of your restaurant can identify the kind of restaurant it is and even where it is located. It should be unique, easy to remember, and above all, legal. (You don't want to use a name that's already trademarked.) If you are having trouble deciding on a name for your restaurant, here are some ideas to get your creative juices flowing:

- **Location of the restaurant:** This is a very popular method for naming a restaurant; the name will be easy to remember and says where the restaurant is located. Eleven Madison Park (Manhattan), Tremont 647 (Boston), and Seventh Street Grille (Pittsburgh) are examples.
- **Foreign words and ethnic names:** Obviously this method suggests an ethnic concept or menu, but it doesn't necessarily have to. If you are using foreign words in the name, make sure they aren't too hard to remember. Buca di Beppo, for example, is a chain restaurant serving family-style Italian cuisine.
- **Food represented in your menu:** It could be an ingredient or a spice you use, a food that is indigenous to a certain region, or a dish you specialize in. Sage, Olives, Figs, Cilantro, and Tamarind are just a few restaurants that use food as their names.
- **Plays on words and puns:** These are fun, humorous ways to name your restaurant. Just be careful that the name doesn't offend anyone. Wok N' Roll and Once Upon a Tart are some good examples.
- **Landmarks:** If your restaurant is located at or near a landmark or a famous public structure, use it as part of your name. For example, the Carnegie Deli is located near Carnegie Hall in Manhattan.
- **Your own name:** Unless you have the same name as Mario Batali or some other celebrity chef, why not? It's your restaurant. Keep in mind that you want the name of your restaurant to be easy to remember. So it's probably not a good idea to name a restaurant after yourself if your name is difficult to pronounce or is very long.
- **Someone else's name:** Naming the restaurant after someone is always a good idea. It can attach a homey, personal feeling to the restaurant, or it may have some meaning or story behind the name. It can be someone significant to you, or a historical figure, or even a fictional character.

Don't limit yourself to just these ways of naming your restaurant. Brainstorm. Be creative. Come up with a list of names. Say them out loud to yourself and to others. Just don't put too much emphasis on the name. The name can say a lot about your restaurant, but it doesn't say everything about your concept. Your restaurant's name can catch people's attention and stick in their minds, but remember that you're selling the whole package. If your restaurant doesn't live up to your customers' expectations, they may still remember your restaurant's name. They'll just remember not to go back. So keep in mind what's important.

CHAPTER 3

Exploring Your Market Potential

Now that you have your concept, you have to figure out how your restaurant might do in the competitive market. You'll need to explore the market, identify your competitors, figure out their strengths and weaknesses, and position your concept against theirs. Your research in the market helps you identify who your customers will be, what the competition holds, and what you need to do to hold on to your competitive advantage and keep up with trends.

Who Will Be Your Customers?

The first stage of research is determining who will be your customers. To begin, look into the demographics. Demographics refer to the statistics that group people into various categories such as age, gender, income, education, marital status, occupation, race, religion, and ethnicity. You must determine which demographic group you want your concept to attract.

Determine Your Demographic Group

In order to determine the demographic group likely to be your clientele, start by asking yourself whom you want to be your customers. The list below provides just a few ways to get started:

- In what age range do you want the bulk of your clientele to be? Twenty-one to thirty-five? Or over fifty?
- Do you want to attract more families, or are you interested in drawing couples and single people?
- Do you see your customers being more white-collar or blue-collar?
- Do you plan to cater more to people who live and/or work in the city or people who live in the suburbs?
- Do you envision your concept targeting more male clientele than female? Or is gender not an issue?

ESSENTIAL

Every product has a target consumer, just as every film or song has a target audience. Restaurants are no different. Focusing on a demographic group doesn't mean you are limiting your clientele to just that group. You are simply determining the clientele most likely to dine at your restaurant and then gearing your concept to their expectations.

Once you've determined a target demographic group, you need to figure out what motivates its purchasing decisions—such as where it dines out, shops, and finds entertainment, and how your concept can satisfy its wants and needs.

Determine Your Target Group's Wants and Needs

When you determine whom you would like as your demographic group, you'll need to recognize what it might want as diners. Here are some tips on where you may focus your research:

- **Convenience:** How much importance does your target group place on convenience? Location near work, residence, public transportation, or other businesses can be a factor, as can your hours of operation and parking availability.
- **Value:** How much value does your clientele expect for the price they pay? Do they generally perceive value more in terms of quantity or quality? How much is too much to pay?
- **Service and food quality:** What type of service and food quality will your targeted customers expect with respect to your concept?
- **Menu:** Does your potential clientele prefer an expansive menu with many options or do they prefer a shorter, well-conceived menu? If your concept is ethnic, does your clientele expect your menu to be authentic or more adapted to their tastes?
- **Atmosphere:** What kind of atmosphere makes your desired clientele feel comfortable? A casual atmosphere? An urban chic, modern atmosphere? Or a more traditional setting?
- **Trends:** Is your potential clientele likely to follow trends in lifestyles? Trends such as popular diets and new foods can influence consumers' eating decisions.

Where to Find Information

Once you determine what characteristics you want your demographic group to have, you need to research all the information you can find pertaining to this group. Where can you find this information? There are several good ways to find sources for consumer demographics, at least on a broad national or regional scale. You will have to investigate more local channels to get details about the demographics in your community.

National trade publications and restaurant associations routinely put out information on trends, business tips, demographics, and new products.

Local business and civic associations and chambers of commerce may provide some valuable information about the demographics of their respective communities. These organizations may also provide information on the types of businesses in the area that allows you to gauge the consumer market.

Fee-based market research companies may be an option if you are willing to spend the money to purchase their services. They can provide you with specific data about consumers in a particular area and customize the research to suit your concept. You can use the Internet to find any number of market research firms that might fit your bill, but as always, investigate the company's reputation before you purchase its service.

FACT

The Food Network on cable television has had a strong impact on the way consumers perceive food. Creative cuisine that may have once been limited to large cities or specific regions has found its way to the television sets of consumers across the country and, consequently, to the menus of restaurants as well. The Food Network is continually gaining popularity, educating viewers, and helping them become savvier and more discerning.

Food magazines such as *Food and Wine*, *Saveur*, and *Bon Appetit* provide good information on the kinds of cuisine your potential customers may be looking for in restaurants. Even your local newspaper may feature articles on restaurants and foods that people currently find interesting. Watch television cooking shows as well as programs that feature restaurants to get a sense of what is shaping the American palate.

Be a consumer yourself. You might receive great information from reading trade journals, magazines, and demographic reports, but the best way to research your market is to go out and see for yourself where people are eating. Go to several busy restaurants whose concepts are similar to yours or that attract the clientele you are targeting. Make notes of the customers' ages, attire, whether they are there with their families, whether the place is attractive to couples, and anything else that you can use to describe the clientele. Visit these places at different times of the day to see if the clientele changes.

Ask the servers which menu items are popular. Ask your friends, family, and associates about what they liked or didn't like about the places you've been. This will keep you ahead of the trends rather than behind them.

Scope Out the Competition

You know the group that is likely to be your customer base, and through your research you have figured out what motivates their decisions as diners. Now you have to find out who your competitors are. Determining whom you are directly competing with can be easy if you are trying to penetrate the market by offering products and services that are similar to those of other businesses. For example, if you want to open a pizza shop with free delivery, you are obviously in direct competition with every other pizza shop offering free delivery. Even if your concept is unique to the geographical market, you may still have direct competition. You may have a style of food that is different from other businesses, but consumers may view your restaurant as similar to another. For example, say you want to open the only Spanish restaurant in town featuring paella (a seafood-and-rice dish). True, there are no other Spanish restaurants competing against you, but the Mexican restaurant a couple blocks away may be considered your direct competition because consumers may perceive the two as similar based on similar cultural associations.

You also have to keep in mind your indirect competitors. Indirect competitors may not share the same type of food (as far as the consumers perceive it), but they have similar prices, style of service, or atmosphere. For example, if you own an Italian restaurant that serves various pastas at moderate prices, the Chinese restaurant next door with the same price range and similar style of service is an indirect competitor.

ALERT

Competition is becoming a more significant market factor now. This is not only because there are more restaurants available, but because other forms of business such as supermarkets and movie theaters have expanded their services to include a food court or café that may take away some market share from restaurants.

To begin, you should make a list of restaurants that your research has indicated are your competitors. Dine at these restaurants and take notes on their food, menu, prices, service, location, and anything else that might factor into your analysis. Determine what works for each restaurant and what works against each restaurant, and write these factors down in an organized manner so you can use the information as a reference. The following list shows an example of how you can organize the information noted about a competitor. Along with some of the criteria presented in the example, try to come up with some of your own.

GIORGIO'S PASTA HOUSE
- **Location:** City, near university, street parking only, bus stop nearby
- **Hours of Operation:** 11 A.M.—midnight (seven days a week)
- **Menu:** Broad menu featuring pastas, pizza, typical Italian fare, salads
- **Price/Value:** Entrées $7–$12; value based on quantity not quality
- **Food Quality:** Large portions, preparation unremarkable, standard quality
- **Service:** Table service, friendly and expeditious, attractive female servers
- **Atmosphere:** Kitschy, 1950s diner motif, blue and red neon, loud rock music
- **Demographic Group:** College students, 18–25 years old
- **Gimmick:** Half-priced food after 11 P.M., daily blue-plate special
- **Final Word:** Works because large portion is good value as perceived by college students on tight budget. Attractive female servers help draw in young male clientele. Loud rock music not appealing to older clientele. Half-priced food is good motivation but is deceiving because the portions are cut down as well.

After you do the same kind of analysis on a few other competitors, you can position your concept against your competitors and figure out what you can do to gain a competitive advantage.

Do a Competitive Analysis

Consider our example of Giorgio's Pasta House. Suppose you want to open an Italian restaurant nearby that focuses on fresh ingredients and quality pastas. You plan to have better food, but in order to control costs your portions will also have to be smaller. Given your location in an urban university setting, you know your demographic group will be largely college-aged. So how can you play up your strengths to compete against Giorgio's, a popular place with the college crowd?

This is the point where you need to determine what you do well and how you can differentiate yourself from the competition. To do a competitive analysis, you will need to weigh the things you do well against the things your competitors do well. Furthermore, you will also have to recognize areas that need improvement while playing up your strengths and exploiting the competition's weaknesses.

Suppose you have determined that the following things will differentiate your restaurant from Giorgio's: fresh ingredients, quality pastas, homemade sauces, Italian-style desserts, cappuccino and espresso service, creative menu with seasonal specials, and a rustic decor with muted lighting. Next, you should list the points that differentiate you from Giorgio's and compare them to what works for Giorgio's, as in the table shown here.

Giorgio's Pasta House	Your Restaurant
Large Portions	Advantage
Price/Value	Advantage
Fresh Ingredients	Advantage
Broad Menu	Advantage
Creative Menu	Advantage
Half-priced Food	Advantage
Location	Even
Atmosphere	Even
Desserts/Coffee	Advantage
Menu Special	Advantage
Attractive Servers	Advantage
House Sauces	Even

When you measure your strengths against your competitors, you must consider what matters to your potential customers. For example, even though your food quality is better than Giorgio's, college students on a tight budget might perceive Giorgio's as a better value because of the large portions. At the same time, you also have to consider factors within that demographic group that will have an effect on its preferences. For instance, even in the college-student demographic group, people still differ in economic background, ethnicity, religion, and gender. Furthermore, you may also have a smaller, yet significant, nearby clientele who are faculty members, university employees, and area businesses. These potential customers may favor higher quality and an atmosphere suited to their more mature tastes. Ultimately, you have to decide what course of action you want to take to improve upon any factors that you may perceive as a disadvantage. At the same time, you have to emphasize your strengths and exploit your competitors' weaknesses.

Hold On to Your Competitive Advantage

The face of the restaurant market has changed drastically over the last few years. In seeking continual growth, larger companies are focusing on strategies and concepts that might expand their clientele base. As an independent restaurant owner, you might feel you'll get swallowed up in a market full of companies with better name recognition, larger advertising budgets, and more resources to secure good real estate.

True, the market share of chain restaurants has grown tremendously in the last decade, but many independent restaurants are surviving and doing extremely well. They remain successful because they are able to hold on to their competitive advantage. Independent restaurant owners can respond to specific needs of their target market on a very local and personal level. While many chain restaurants can provide very personal service, they are not able to respond to customers in the same way an independent restaurant owner can. When chain restaurants react to market conditions, they must react with uniformity across national or regional levels. They do not have the flexibility to do something different in one operation simply because that local market demands it.

Study your local market. Be part of the community. Get to know the people in the area and what motivates them. Sample the local flavors. The more you learn about the people in the community, the better you are able to assess what they want and how you can satisfy that need.

Keep Up with Market Trends

Stay tuned to current events and what's happening to other consumer-oriented industries aside from the restaurant industry. You might have to make some temporary adjustments if current events or trends alter consumer tastes and perceptions in ways that might work against your plans. For example, say you were planning on having a grand opening of your new gourmet hamburger joint, but new rumors of mad cow disease have caused the market's demand for beef to dip significantly. You may then want to delay your grand opening for a few weeks until the fear blows over.

Of course, the above example may seem a bit extreme, but it does happen. More often, trends in the market involve changes in consumer culture and lifestyle. Some trends may sustain and become part of the mainstream. Sushi, for example, a hot ethnic-food trend in the 1980s has endured and incorporated well into American culture. Yet many hot trends quickly saturate the marketplace and eventually fizzle out.

FACT

Fad diets also affect food trends, positively and negatively. At its peak popularity in 2003–2004, the Atkins diet prompted the industry to produce more low carb items, while at the same time, diminished the appeal of high carb products, such as the famous Krispy Kreme Doughnuts.

Concepts built around a hot food trend are not a formula for success because there are always others on the same bandwagon. You still have to differentiate yourself from your competitors. Furthermore, identifying the trend is only half of the marketing picture. Determine what factors in the community or the culture in general have shaped the current trend. Understanding what motivates consumers to buy into a trend will help you stay on top of the current market.

Create a Niche with Unconventional Concepts

If you focus on a specific need or desire of your target consumer, you may be able to find a subgroup or a niche within the market that your competitors may overlook or choose to ignore. On the other hand, your restaurant can also specialize in a niche product that isn't overexposed in the marketplace.

Focusing on Special Needs

One way to gain a competitive advantage is to focus on a specialized need of your target customers. For example, say you want to open a gourmet pizza restaurant with a focus on fresh ingredients, but several well-established places already have that same concept. How do you compete? In researching your target market, you discover that about 8 percent of the people a have gluten intolerance. Moreover, you find that a growing number of people are reducing their wheat consumption for dietary reasons. You know that your competitors are famous for their traditional pizzas and wouldn't even bother with a gluten-free pizza. So you try out several recipes for gluten free dough and develop a gourmet gluten free pizza restaurant. By going against the convention of a traditional pizza restaurant, you have gained a competitive advantage since your competitors choose to ignore this need.

Focusing on Niche Product

Eateries specializing in a single, specialized item may be referred to as a niche concept. The restaurant industry continues to grow with concepts that feature a single, well-made product—taco trucks, Belgian waffle stands, and fondue restaurants are just a few examples. If you want to develop an unconventional niche concept, be sure your product is well-made and something your target consumer would want. Furthermore, even if you're specializing on one kind of product, you should lend your product some sense of variety. For example, breaded chicken livers are a southern delicacy, but would the dish create enough buzz to stand on its own? Perhaps, but it would make for a stronger product if the breaded livers come with a variety of dipping sauces. This gives your niche product a level of options, something that consumers like.

CHAPTER 4

Business Plan Basics

If you want to accomplish a complex project, you need to have a plan. Starting a restaurant is no quick and easy task. Going in blind and resolving unexpected issues as they arise will cost you more time and money, to the point that you may never get to reach your goal. That is why a business plan is crucial to the start-up process. It lays out all the issues you may have to confront before they occur, guiding you along the way.

Why You Need a Business Plan

A business plan is your blueprint to building your business. It maps out all your ideas, your research, and the profitability of your proposed restaurant in an organized manner. Without a business plan, you'll be more likely to make bad decisions when problems arise. That lack will cost you more money and time in the end. A business plan can help you achieve several objectives:

- Finding financing from banks and investors
- Explaining your vision and goals
- Measuring your performance
- Keeping you focused on your project

Finding Financing From Banks and Investors

If you are trying to get financing from bank loans and/or investors, a business plan is a must. Without one, you'll be hard pressed to convince banks and potential investors to give you the money you need. A business plan proves that you've done the sufficient research in the market, accurately assessed the costs of start-up and operations, and set realistic projections of your restaurant's profit potential in a detailed, convincing manner.

ESSENTIAL

Though many people hire someone to write their business plan, it is important to remember that no one knows your ideas better than you. As intimidating as writing a business plan may seem, you should still write your own. A business plan is not just a package that explains why your restaurant can succeed; writing it is also an exercise in putting your mind in the proper perspective. The writing process makes you think about your restaurant in ways you might not have otherwise.

Even if you're not looking for loans and outside investors, you still have to explain your vision to people who are going to be working with you, whether they be your chef, your partners, or your managers. Everyone involved in the management of the restaurant has to understand what the business is to become. A plan can clearly define your concept, the customers you have targeted through market analysis, and the financial goals of the operation.

You can also review your business plan to track the performance of your business to see if you have met or surpassed your goals. In your business plan, you define set expectations in future growth, profits, sales, and costs. You can measure your performance with the goals set in the business plan and see what needs to be done better. You can also use your plan to revise your concept or expand the scope of your business. It is essentially a measuring stick for your restaurant's success.

When completed, a good business plan lays out all the issues you'll have to confront in your start-up process and keeps you on the right track. You cannot blindly go into the restaurant market without a clear vision of what you want to accomplish and how you intend to achieve it. You must stay on course and tweak or expand your ideas as issues arise that may affect their implementation.

What to Include in a Business Plan

Business plans vary in length and format. Provide as much detailed information as possible, but also keep the language relatively simple and concise. As long as your plan communicates your ideas clearly and effectively in an organized manner, it doesn't need to be a large document. The basic parts of a business plan are these:

- **Cover page:** Identifies the legal name of the business and the names and office address of the people submitting the plan.
- **Table of contents:** Lists the contents of the plan and their page numbers.
- **Executive summary:** Generally a one-page overview of your plan.
- **Mission statement:** One or two sentences describing your restaurant and its long-term goal.
- **Business concept:** Describes your restaurant in detail, including the size, hours of operation, style of service, pricing strategy, ambiance, decor, and menu.
- **Market analysis:** Identifies the market that currently exists for your restaurant and describes how your restaurant is different from your competitors' businesses.

- **Target demographics:** Describes your customers, their education, income bracket, consumption patterns, needs and wants, and so on.
- **Marketing strategy:** Describes how you intend to market your restaurant, whom you are trying to reach, and what sales and advertising tactics you plan to use to accomplish your goals.
- **Management team and personnel:** Identifies the management personnel, their qualifications, personal histories, and experience in the field.
- **Financial projections:** Describes the start-up and operating costs, source of funding, forecasted sales, cash flow, and other financial analyses.

There are a number of ways you can organize your information, including charts, diagrams, or graphs. Just make sure you have the necessary details to support why your restaurant will be successful.

ALERT

Investors and loan officers generally aren't interested in business plans longer than fifty pages. Your plan should be concise and accurate, not verbose and laden with jargon. Not only is jargon difficult to understand, it may make the reader suspicious of your plan, as if your ideas aren't convincing enough and you are hiding behind a bunch of trendy words.

Describe Your Business Concretely

In general, a business plan is divided into two sections: the business section, which contains the descriptive aspects, and the financial section, which includes the numbers. In the business section, you have to articulate the vision and goals of your restaurant in detail, such as concept, market, marketing strategy, and the management structure.

The Mission Statement

The mission statement describes exactly what your business is and what the overall goal of the business is for the long term. The mission statement should be brief, usually one or two sentences. Your mission statement should address what the restaurant does for its customers and perhaps the community. Don't state "making money" as part of your mission statement. Profit is already understood as a reason for going into business. If your proposed restaurant is an upscale French bistro named Pierre's, and you are targeting affluent couples thirty-five to fifty-years of age, your mission statement might read: "Pierre's is an elegant, romantic bistro serving regional French cuisine creatively prepared with the highest quality ingredients. Pierre's seeks to be consistently among the city's best upscale restaurants in terms of food quality, service, and atmosphere." In just a couple of sentences, the mission statement communicates the restaurant's concept, what it provides for the customers and community, and its goal for the long term. Having a mission statement not only defines your business in a nutshell, it also communicates the general direction of your business to your investors, partners, and associates.

The Business Concept

Your business concept defines how you package your restaurant as a whole. Here, you have to articulate what your restaurant is, what it will be serving, how it serves your customers, and where it will be located. This section also includes your menu, pricing, atmosphere, service style, decor, and location if applicable. Each part of the concept should be described separately and in detail. Stress the factors that differentiate your restaurant from the competition and the ways your restaurant offers the things your targeted customers want and need.

Here are some items you should mention in your business concept:

- **Menu:** Describe what you will be serving. Even if you don't know exactly what menu items you will be serving, you should have some idea of what the menu will include. If you already have a menu, attach a copy as an appendix to the plan.
- **Pricing:** Explain how you will price your menu in relation to costs. Establish the fact that your prices are competitive. State the proposed check average (the amount spent per individual), and explain the profit potential based on the revenue projected.
- **Service:** Describe the level of service your restaurant is going to provide, whether it's counter service, table service, buffet, or a combina-

tion. Explain how the type of service fits with your targeted customers' expectations as well as the pricing and menu.

- **Decor:** Describe the decor you will choose to match your concept, and explain how that appeals to your market.
- **Location:** If you've already chosen a site, explain why this location is right for your restaurant.
- **Atmosphere:** Describe the kind of atmosphere you want to create, whether it's fun, kid-friendly, exotic, romantic, or something else.

Other pertinent information in your business concept includes the size of the operation (number of seats), the hours of operation, and the number of days opened during the week.

FACT

In order to protect their concepts, ideas, and other secrets, some restaurateurs request that prospective investors and bankers sign confidentiality agreements before they receive the business plan. The agreement usually states that the reader is not to disclose any parts of the business plan and is to return (or delete, if sent electronically) the document upon request.

Market Analysis

Your business plan should include a market analysis that clearly defines the market in which your restaurant will be competing. The market analysis may include the following:

- Current economic conditions and market trends
- Demographics of the market area and the growth potential
- Competitors in the area and their strengths and weaknesses
- Comparison of the strengths and weaknesses of competitors to yours
- Niche markets (markets that have been ignored or unrealized)

In this section, you explain how your concept is right for the market conditions and how your restaurant's location will benefit your business. You should also stress the strengths of your restaurant against your competitors, as well as address any weaknesses you could improve upon. Your analysis should leave little room for doubt that your restaurant will do well in the market.

Target Demographics

Once you've defined your concept and your market, you should define the likely demographic group of your customers. There are a number of ways you can describe your target customer. Age group, gender, marital status, income bracket, and education are among the more common ways to determine demographic groupings. Describe your target customers' consumption patterns, their motivations for making purchases, and their wants and needs. You might consider using some charts to illustrate the percentage of the market in your area that fits into your demographic group. Explain why your concept will attract customers and how your restaurant can meet or surpass their expectations.

Marketing Strategy

In the marketing section of your business plan, you describe how you intend to market your restaurant to customers. You should lay out your advertising and sales strategy and pinpoint the clientele you are trying to reach and the share of the market you would like to attract. Describe how you would like your customer to perceive you and how you can position your restaurant in the market to create that perception. Also, you might find it useful to contrast your restaurant with the competition and describe the ways you plan to change the way consumers perceive both. You should mention the media you intend to use to get your message out along with other promotional or public relations campaigns you may launch (print, radio, or television).

ESSENTIAL

Consider purchasing the services of a demographic research company, such as Claritas.com, for reports on your restaurant's geographic area to include in your business plan. This type of consultation adds more objectivity to your research and shows lenders and prospective investors that you went that extra mile to research the market more thoroughly.

Management Team and Personnel

This section describes your qualifications along with the qualifications of anyone else involved in restaurant operations. For a small start-up restaurant, the management team may only include you and perhaps one or two others. Describe your background, your experience, education, and anything else that might indicate skills useful in the restaurant business. Even if you have little or no experience in the restaurant industry, point out how your skills and experience in other fields can transfer to the restaurant business. You may also want to create an organizational chart and a personnel schedule describing the types of employees you'll need and the projected payroll costs.

List Your Start-Up Requirements

If you are looking for a bank loan or investors, a list of detailed start-up requirements is a must in your business plan. After all, you can't know how much money to ask for if you don't know how much you need to get started. Even if you aren't looking for outside financing, it's a good idea to itemize what you need so that you have a checklist of things to purchase and pay for once you start the building process.

There are two kinds of expenses you will have to take into account as you calculate start-up costs. The first kind consists of one-time purchases (or nonrecurring expenses), which may include deposits for rent and utilities, expenditures on fixtures and equipment, professional fees and permits, licenses, and building-improvement costs. The second kind of expense is a cash reserve for initial operating costs. A cash reserve will help you ensure payment for expenses during the restaurant's infancy, such as supplies, utilities, and other costs. You should list your start-up requirements as part of your financial projections section in your business plan. The following list shows a typical breakdown of start-up requirements.

START-UP REQUIREMENTS
- **Deposits (rent, utilities):** $7,000
- **Building Improvements:** $50,000
- **Legal and Consulting Fees:** $1,500

- **Licenses and Permits:** $1,000
- **Fixtures, (furniture, equipment, decor):** $100,000
- **Liquor License:** $25,000
- **Starting Inventory (food, beverages, supplies):** $15,000
- **Initial Marketing Expenses (business cards, menus, advertising, PR):** $3,000
- **Insurance:** $3,500
- **Preopening Employees' Payroll:** $4,000
- **Reserve Operating Capital:** $30,000
- **Total:** $240,000

Some categories, such as those including fixtures and furniture or building improvements, should be further broken down and itemized. This should be done in a separate table for each category, as appropriate.

Once you know your start-up costs, you need to determine your financial sources for the restaurant. For example, loan officers and prospective investors and partners will be interested in knowing how much of your own money you are going to put up. Be specific about how much money you want from each source. Also, although it may appear obvious to you how the funds will be used, you should show how funds will be allocated to the different expenses.

Project Your Financial Data Accurately

No matter how great your concept is, it won't mean a thing if you can't come up with the numbers to back it up. If you are seeking outside funding, investors and bankers will pay close attention to your financial data. Therefore, your business plan must show that your restaurant can generate enough sales to cover operating expenses. In addition to pleasing investors, having such information can also help you set realistic financial goals and manage your business for the long term. It is therefore important for your business plan to include some realistic financial projections, including sales and expenses projections and pro forma (meaning "as-if" in accounting terms) financial reports, such as an income statement (also called profit and loss statement), break-even analysis, cash flow, and balance sheet.

Projecting Your Sales

Projecting your financial data isn't like looking into a crystal ball. Depending on your concept, there are a number of ways you can estimate your sales. One of simplest methods is to multiply the check average (that is, the estimated average check per person) by the number of customers for a given period. The period is usually separated into lunch, dinner, and breakfast, depending on your hours of operation. You may also separate the average beverage purchase for each period as well, since people are likely to drink more at dinner. Depending on the type of restaurant, the number of customers will vary, as will your check average. You can assume in general that a high-end restaurant will have fewer customers for each meal than a quick-service or casual restaurant, but the check average will also be significantly higher.

Projecting Your Expenses

You also need to project the expenses that your restaurant will incur. Be as specific as possible on the kinds of expenses you are anticipating. Essentially, expenses can be divided into two categories—controllable and noncontrollable. Controllable expenses, as the term suggests, are the things you can affect. Controllable expenses may include costs of goods sold, payroll and benefits, direct operating expenses, administrative and general expenses, marketing, music and entertainment, repairs and maintenance, and utilities.

FACT

The industry standard for a restaurant chart of accounts is the Uniform System of Accounts for Restaurants available through the National Restaurant Association (online at *www.restaurant.org*), but you can use whatever system suits you best as long as you remain consistent throughout your system.

Noncontrollable expenses include rent, real estate taxes, insurance on building and contents, personal property and other taxes, corporate licensing fees, equipment rental, depreciation, and interest on loans and long-term debts.

To get a better idea of what expenses your restaurant may generate, take a look at a restaurant chart of accounts. A chart of accounts is a coding system used to classify types of income and expenses. Having an organized, detailed list of expenses will allow you to more accurately project other financial analyses, which you will need to include in your business plan, as the following sections will describe.

Break-Even Analysis

Next, you'll have to determine your break-even point, or the point where your revenue matches your expenses. This analysis is important because your projected sales must be equal to or higher than your break-even point. If they are not, you'll need to find ways to adjust your expenses. There are many ways you can produce this report. You can break down your expenses into different categories, such as controllable and noncontrollable expenses. You can determine your break-even point on a daily basis or from month to month. Whatever method you choose is fine as long as you know how much you need to make to cover your expenses and as long as your sales projection is above your break-even point.

Pro Forma Income Statement

This report will likely draw the most attention from investors and partners. Also called a profit and loss statement, a pro forma income statement is a detailed, projected summation of your sales and expenses. Generally, your income statement will include these items:

- **Total revenue:** Sales from food, beverage, and other items and services
- **Cost of goods sold:** Food costs and beverage costs
- **Gross profits:** The difference between total revenue and cost of goods sold
- **Expenses:** Payroll, operating expenses, administrative and general expenses, rent, and all other expenses including interest and depreciation
- **Net profit or loss:** The difference between your gross profits and expenses

Very simply, an income statement shows in detail what you're projecting to earn versus what you're going to spend. It isn't enough to simply show a profit on paper. You have to make a convincing case in projecting your sales and expenses based on your research.

Pro Forma Cash-Flow Analysis

"Cash-flow" is the term that describes the movement of cash in and out of your business. The purpose of a cash-flow analysis is to prove that your restaurant can stay operational by showing that, based on your projected sales, your restaurant can generate cash quickly enough to pay the expenses incurred during a period of time, generally over a month. Fortunately, in the restaurant business, you can turn your sales into cash almost immediately.

The Balance Sheet

Your balance sheet gives you an overview of your business at any given time. Divided into two sections or columns, it generally follows what is known as the accounting principle: Assets = Liabilities + Capital.

As the name suggests, a balance sheet must show that your assets equal your liabilities and capital. Your assets include your cash on hand, accounts receivables (any money coming to you that you haven't yet received), inventory (food and supplies), and fixed assets such as your furniture, equipment, building (if you own it), and vehicles. Your liabilities refer to money that you owe, such as accounts payable (money owed to suppliers), unpaid salaries, taxes, loans, and interests. Capital refers to the money you initially put into your restaurant and anything you've earned and reinvested.

CHAPTER 5

Location: Putting Your Plan
on Firm Ground

You are probably familiar with the conventional wisdom of real estate: location, location, location. It is no different in the restaurant business. This chapter will help you determine a location that is right for your concept. It will show you what to look for in the real estate market, how to inspect prospective locations, and how rent or occupancy costs can determine the revenue necessary to get your restaurant off the ground. You'll also get some pointers on negotiating a fair lease and suggestions on reworking your concept to suit a good location.

Space and Location: Keys to Your Success

Not every location fits every concept. Despite their quality and service, many restaurants have difficulty succeeding because of their location. However, that doesn't mean that other concepts couldn't succeed in those same locations. The right location means you can reach your targeted customers regularly. If your concept is an Italian-style restaurant targeting families with children, a self-standing building with a parking lot adjacent to a suburban shopping mall may be the right location for you. However, that same concept probably would not work in a busy, artsy urban district where a lot of young, hip singles hangout.

Even if your location is easily accessible by your target customers, it doesn't guarantee you'll draw their attention. You must also consider the visibility of your location with respect to other businesses—some of which may be other restaurants. You might have a very good concept and the ability to create a great restaurant, but if your location isn't visible and easy for your target customers to reach, you'll have a difficult time making your restaurant work.

Researching the Real Estate Market

There are a number of ways to find suitable locations for your restaurant. Start by researching the real estate market. In addition to the real estate section of your local newspaper, you can also visit neighborhoods that might fit your concept and provide the necessary traffic. Even if there aren't any locations available, you can still determine the kind of neighborhood where your concept would work well and start looking for similar areas.

Good restaurant locations can be found in established commercial districts or burgeoning neighborhoods. However, these locations may have a substantially higher price tag than other neighborhoods. There are also more people concentrated in these areas, meaning more competition as well. Nevertheless, the potential for profit in these areas is much better than so-called fringe neighborhoods.

You can also find up-and-coming neighborhoods that have not yet been developed commercially for the retail or restaurant market. Locations in these areas will likely cost less than established areas. While the rent will probably be less, these areas are also less likely to have the large customer base of established commercial areas. Though up-and-coming areas may be riskier to your restaurant's potential success, the risk might be worth taking if the real estate market shows signs of strong growth.

A commercial real estate agent will usually have some good leads on locations that aren't listed in the local paper. Agents generally charge a finder's fee, so you should ask about that. Other good sources of information include government agencies or business councils such as your local chamber of commerce and your city's business development department. These agencies can provide information concerning neighborhood developments, zoning codes, demographics, and surrounding businesses in potential locations.

ESSENTIAL

Some local civic development associations can provide excellent assistance in your search for locations in up-and-coming neighborhoods. The goal of these associations is to develop their respective neighborhoods by reaching out to viable residents and businesses. Not only can they provide information concerning demographics and locations, they can also assist in your planning and funding for your operation.

Breakdown of Occupancy Costs

Purchasing real estate may be too costly for a start-up restaurant, especially since the costs of financing the operation already add up to a considerable sum. With that in mind, you should consider the costs of leasing a space as a factor in determining your location.

Many commercial leases usually require that, in addition to the base rent, the tenant also pay at least a portion of the real estate taxes, building insurance, and maintenance. This type of lease is known as a triple net lease. If the base rent of a location is $2,000 a month, and the real estate and building insurance add up to $6,000 per year, you are looking at $2,500 in occupancy costs per month.

You should also find out if parking is a factor in your occupancy costs. The availability of parking will enhance the accessibility to the location. More than likely parking will be included as part of the package if it is available, although in some cases it might be included as part of your maintenance fee.

Always consider occupancy costs in terms of dollars per square foot. It is the easiest way to analyze the market value of potential locations and the potential costs and benefits of those locations. To calculate the cost per square foot, multiply the base rent by twelve months and add the yearly taxes and insurance. Divide by the total square footage of the space. If the monthly base rent for a 2,000-square foot location is $2,000 and yearly taxes and insurance add up to $5,000, the occupancy cost per square foot is $14.50.

How Rent Can Determine Necessary Revenue

While you may have accurately assessed your expenses to the sales projection in your business plan, calculations become a little more complicated when occupancy costs are added to the mix. Once you commit to a location, it is fixed and cannot be changed. So naturally the cost of occupying the space is also fixed. Not only does the location constrain your flexibility, so does your space. You cannot accommodate two hundred people at a time if you only have enough space for fifty. In this way, you must consider the limitations of your space when forecasting your sales.

One way to get an idea of how much revenue you would need is to base your rent as a percentage of revenue. In general, your occupancy costs should range from 5 to 9 percent of your total revenue to make a reasonable profit of 11 to 15 percent before depreciation. So if your occupancy costs are $30,000 a year for a 2,000-square foot space, you will likely need to generate at least $350,000 in revenue. Given your concept and the limitations set forth by the location and space, you can roughly estimate the number of covers (customers you'll have on a given day or meal period) and the check average you would need per day. Let's say your 2,000-square feet would account for a sixty-seat restaurant, and you figure the check average to be $10 based upon your concept. Given that you'll be open seven days a week, you will need at least ninety-six covers a day to reach $350,000.

The important question you want to ask yourself when you are considering a potential location is this: Considering all factors—the space, location, local market, and your concept—can you realistically attain the numbers necessary to reach your revenue estimate? This question is especially important if you are considering established locations that demand a high price per square foot. The following sections describe some specifics you should look for when viewing potential locations.

Inspecting the Space—Inside and Out

Regardless of whether you're looking at a space that needs to be renovated or one that is already set up for restaurant use, you should inspect the building, its history, and the surrounding neighborhood. Find out who the previous tenants were, how long they occupied the space, what business they ran, and why they vacated. Also research other businesses in the neighborhood and try to determine what succeeded and what failed, and why.

Get the Dirt on Your Potential Space

You can get information on a specific space and its location in a number of ways. Ask the owner of the building itself. If the owner is motivated to lease out the space, he should give you at least the names of tenants and the businesses they ran. Then check with the local neighborhood associations. They may provide valuable information on the neighborhood's history, real estate, businesses, and residents.

Visit the local zoning board to find information on the building's history, site plan, and structural details. (Be sure that you have either the lot number or exact address of the space.) Talk to business owners nearby and find out what they know. They may or may not have information that is helpful, but these conversations are also a way to get to know your potential neighbors and to study their operations. You can find out a lot just by inspecting the space itself. Architectural details, surfaces, and construction materials can help you figure out how the space has been used in the past and can also lend it some character, which you can use to further enhance your concept.

Consider the Convenience Factor

Consider how accessible the location is for your customers. Convenience is very often a determining factor for diners, so choose a spot where your customers can reach you without much fuss. When viewing a location, see if you can provide answers to these questions:

- Does the location come with parking?
- If the location does not come with parking, is parking readily available on the street or in lots nearby, and how much does parking cost (if anything)?
- If the location is in an urban area, how far is the location from mass transit lines that reach your target customers?
- Does the location have sufficient sidewalks and safe crosswalks for customers?

Traffic and Visibility

Traffic and visibility should also factor into your consideration of a site for your restaurant. If the location is located on a chronically congested street, people might be deterred from driving there. However, if the location is in a busy and trendy neighborhood, people will usually put up with the traffic jams. Ultimately, the way your customers feel about traffic depends on the demographic group your concept is targeting.

Watch for Traffic!

This type of traffic is not just about cars. Traffic means the flow of people passing by the potential spot for your restaurant, whether that means people walking by, driving by, riding by on a bus, or traveling by any other means. When considering a location, you should pay attention to the traffic flow and try to figure out the types of people passing. Do they fit into your targeted demographic group? Determine why these people are in the area. Are they tourists? Do they work in the area? Are they visiting some attraction or a nearby shopping mall?

Study the traffic at different times during the week to see if you can spot any patterns. For example, for a location near busy office buildings, you may have traffic around 8:00 A.M. to 5:00 P.M. Monday through Friday. However, the weekend traffic may be significantly less. By studying the traffic patterns and volume, you can determine what hours of operation work most advantageously for your plans.

Also pay attention to surrounding businesses and see how you can take advantage of the traffic that may be created by them. It is no surprise that theaters, retail stores, and other attractions all coexist and feed off each other. Restaurants are no different in that mix. However, you should consider how well your concept fits in with other restaurants in the area. If you want to open a pizza joint near two established pizza parlors, you better be able to differentiate your product significantly from the competition. If you can't, look for another location.

Visibility

Visibility can also affect the location's potential. If your location is not situated where people can easily see or notice it, you'll have a more difficult time drawing in customers. In addition, you may have to spend more on advertising to let people know where you are.

Try to find locations that stand out. Corner buildings, for example, can lend more exposure to your business because people can spot you from several different directions. Storefronts with large glass windows and interesting architectural details can also draw people's attention. Look at the site from different angles, including across the street, down the block, and so on. If your proposed location is close to a shopping mall, check out how exposed it is to those shoppers.

Also check the location at night to see if the area is well-lit. Not only is there a safety concern, dark streets are likely to have less traffic than well-lighted streets. Streetlights can enhance the location's visibility at night, especially in aiding drivers navigating the streets.

Negotiating a Fair Lease

Once you've decided on a location, don't sign a lease right away. You'll need to negotiate a deal that is fair to you and that will help keep your costs down. Some basic terms to negotiate for include rent abatement, property upgrades, lease transferability, and options to renew.

Many landlords are willing to offer some months of rent abatement, or free rent, while you are setting up your restaurant. A three- to six-month rent abatement is a reasonable request to submit to a landlord, especially if the property has been on the market for a while. Besides helping you keep your costs down, your landlord also has incentives to see you succeed. Not only does your success secure his monthly income once you open, it also increases his property value.

Negotiate for the landlord to make upgrades on the infrastructure such as HVAC (heating, ventilation, air-conditioning) and electrical systems, and plumbing. These are improvements to the building that you cannot take with you if you leave, so you shouldn't have to pay for them.

ESSENTIAL

Hire a real estate or business attorney to review the terms of the lease before you sign anything. She should be able to advise you on negotiating for terms that are most favorable to you. This advice may be costly, but at least you'll know how to protect yourself and your investments from certain situations.

Most commercial leases come with a five-year term, which means you are locked in for that period of time regardless of whether you stay in business. Include a clause in your lease that allows you to transfer your lease to another tenant just in case you want to sell your restaurant before the term is up.

The landlord might decide to sell the building before the term ends. Therefore, your lease should also include a clause that requires the landlord to transfer your current lease over to the new owner or to negotiate for a buy-out clause that compensates you for vacating the premises.

You would like your business to remain successful beyond the usual five-year lease term. You should have at least one option-to-renew clause on your lease. Try to negotiate for the amount of rent for the renewal term before signing the lease instead of waiting until the term ends.

The bottom line is that your lease is the closest thing you will have to something etched in stone. Nothing else is, not even your business plan. You can always write another plan. In fact, you should have several concepts fleshed out as alternatives in case the right location comes along. As an entrepreneur, you have to be ready to take the opportunity when the right one comes along.

Reworking Your Concept to Suit a Good Location

Ideally you want to find a location that has everything your concept needs to succeed. However, that is much easier said than done. The market for good locations and spaces is very competitive. The right location for your concept might not be available, or if it is available, it may be too expensive. There may be other locations available, but the traffic doesn't fit into the profile of your desired clientele. If locations are hard to find at a price you can afford, consider reworking your concept to suit a location.

The Two Constants: Size and Space

Once you commit to a lease, the size and space of your location are the two constants in your restaurant planning. You should stay flexible and be ready to rework your plan if difficulties in the planning process make the changes necessary, even if you have financial backers who are expecting you to execute the business plan as put forth. You must be able to make a case to your investors that it is also in their best interest to revise the concept.

Revise Without Giving Up on Your Vision

Revising your concept doesn't mean you have to start from scratch. It means retooling your package to appeal to the existing traffic at a certain location. Say your original concept is a high-end French bistro that charges top-dollar prices, and you want to feature herb-roasted guinea fowl as your specialty. After combing through established high-rent neighborhoods, you are unable to find a space that is conducive to your plans. However, you are able to find a space in an up-and-coming neighborhood where the rent is lower. The present traffic consists of young people who seek more casual fare but are still discerning enough to want quality. You might be able to revise your concept to target this group just by aiming for a lower price and making the menu simpler and atmosphere more casual. Instead of herb-roasted guinea fowl, you could feature herb-roasted chicken served with french fries.

Alternatives to Commercial Real Estate

Purchasing or building out a restaurant space is a costly and risky venture. Because availability may be limited and the cost of commercial real estate can be very high, especially in major cities, you may find the financial commitment beyond your means. There are other venues in which you may operate your restaurant that may cost less without some of the constraint, and in which you could also offer a unique alternative to the traditional brick-and-mortar eatery.

Gourmet Meals on Wheels

If you want to have something other than the "traditional" storefront restaurant, you can purchase or lease a food truck or trailer to sell your food. Gourmet food trucks have become a popular culinary trend with their owners dishing out some very creative cuisine in various cities. The advantage is you can target different locations where you can reach your customers. Choose locations that have good foot traffic, such as city colleges and business districts. Be sure to get the right permits and adhere to health and fire code requirements.

FACT

The "pop-up" restaurant is a temporary restaurant where a chef uses an existing commercial eatery as his venue—but only for a short time without regular hours. This is a creative way for fine-dining chefs to take culinary risks without taking on the huge financial risks.

Street Fairs and other Public Outdoor Venues

You can be a food vendor and rent a food booth at street fairs, conventions, and other public events. Most of these events require that you apply for a vendor license and provide a tax identification number, proof of insurance and health permits. They may also place limitations on what you may sell. Choose the type of venue and event that would attract the type of customers you are targeting.

CHAPTER 6

Financing Your Restaurant

You may have a great concept, but if you have no money, well, all you really have is just that—a great concept. To make your restaurant a reality, you need adequate funding. A restaurant requires significant capital, probably more than what most people can afford. More than likely, you will have to find ways to raise money in addition to the money you already have. You may also have to cut costs. To do that, you first have to figure out how much you need.

Calculate Start-Up and Operating Costs

The start-up costs for every restaurant are different. There is no rule of thumb that tells you how much you need. The amount of money you need depends on many factors, such as your rent, concept, choice of furniture, construction costs, and so on. It is important that you list your start-up and operating expenses in as much detail as possible so you know how much you can afford and how much you need to find elsewhere.

These costs, also called nonrecurring expenses, pertain to one-time-only purchases and payments made before the restaurant opens. Some of these costs may include deposits for leases, utilities, and other items; fees for permits and licenses; furniture, fixtures, and equipment; consulting and legal fees; construction costs (labor and material); initial marketing materials (signage, business cards, advertising, menus); and an initial inventory of food, beverage, and other supplies.

Along with the one-time start-up expenses, you also will need substantial reserve capital to cover the initial operating costs after you open your restaurant. To be safe, set aside enough cash to cover two to three months' worth of operating expenses. That way, your restaurant can stay open until it starts generating more significant cash flow.

Apply for a Bank Loan

No matter how surefire a winning concept you think you have, banks don't generally give out loans to businesses just starting out, especially those that are inherently risky, like restaurants. Banks like to know that they will get their money back—with interest. That is why most banks require a personal guarantee, making you liable to repay the loan regardless of how your restaurant does financially. The bank will ask you to put up your assets for collateral. They will also check your personal income and credit history to minimize any risk of losing their money.

When approaching a bank for a loan, you should prepare yourself as if you were giving a presentation. You must prove that you have the ability to repay the loan. Have the following information with you:

- **Your business plan:** Show them you've done your homework.
- **Your credit history:** The bank will run a credit check on you, but you should be aware of your credit history beforehand.
- **Your stake in the business:** Banks will want to know how much of an investment you will have in the restaurant.
- **Your assets:** Your house, savings accounts, and any cash value in a life insurance policy can all be used as collateral.
- **Loan amount:** Know exactly how much money to request.
- **Employment history:** Give details of your experience in the field or other businesses.

You should visit several banks to try to get as much money as you need and the best interest rate. Furthermore, different banks will have different criteria for loan approvals. Some banks may not be concerned with your lack of experience in the field as long as you have the collateral and a good credit history. Others may weigh the risk more heavily and not want to take a chance.

QUESTION

Is there any financial assistance available from the government?
Yes. The Small Business Administration (SBA) offers several loan programs for small businesses. Through the SBA, qualified applicants can get a guaranteed loan from a commercial bank. Check out the website at *www.sba .gov* for details. You may also want to research financial assistance available to small businesses through your local government agencies.

Seek Outside Investors

One way to raise additional capital is to look for outside investors. Consider carefully whom you want to approach as investors and how involved in the business you would like them to be.

Howdy, Partner!

Unlike a typical investor who does not have an active part in the restaurant's operations, a partner is usually involved in the restaurant's activities.

If you are thinking about bringing aboard one or more partners, consider what they can offer in addition to money. Partners may also provide valuable expertise to the enterprise that you lack. In fact, some partners might not invest any cash at all; instead, they contribute skills in the industry that would be helpful for your business. Whether it's skills in management, legal and financial services, culinary arts, or marketing, your partner should bring something to the table.

It is also important that the partners have common goals, at least until the restaurant has established itself. While individual partners' motivations and goals may change over time, during its infancy the parties involved in the business need to be united. That is why a business plan is crucial for spelling out the details so that partners and investors can see the overall vision of the business.

Friends and Relatives

Be careful if you are including friends and relatives among your potential investors. True, they are more easily approached than someone who has never met you or knows little about you. Your friends or relatives might even approach you to buy into the business. But you should know what you might be getting yourself into. Letting friends or relatives in on the action can potentially lead to conflicts that might jeopardize your personal relationship with them. Before you accept any money from friends or relatives, make them aware of the boundaries so that you can plan and run your restaurant comfortably and maintain control over the operation.

Approaching Other Investors

Investors may include business acquaintances you've made in another line of work. They might also be people you've met at social functions or charity events. What you are looking for here is not a working partner who will be involved with the restaurant's operations but a silent partner who only puts up the money. Some of these people may be looking to strengthen their financial position, while others may want the status of restaurant ownership. Whatever the reason, you should prepare your business plan before you start approaching other investors. Know how much money you need from them and ask for only that amount. When presenting your plan, don't just reiterate what your business plan already says. Be dynamic when you pitch your ideas. Be prepared to answer questions they might have, like how soon they might expect a return on their investment and how much.

Just as it is important that your potential investors get to know you, you should also get to know them. Different investors have different reasons for investing. Look for clues about their personalities and motivations. Pay attention to the kinds of questions they ask. For example, while questions regarding the restaurant's operations are expected, an obsession over details might raise some red flags concerning the investor's motives. You should set expectations in advance concerning the investor's role. If you don't, you may end up taking on someone who is more interested in running the restaurant's daily operations than you want.

Return on Your Partners' Investments

The way you structure the business relationship with your partners, active or silent, is important to your restaurant's overall success. Depending on whether your business is a partnership or corporation, you have several options in setting up the relationship. Some investors want a return on their investment for the short-term. They may make an initial investment and assume they'll eventually be paid back the principal with interest in a fixed amount of time. If your business is structured as a corporation, your investors may want to invest for the long haul by purchasing shares of the corporation in hopes of realizing growth and dividends. Whatever arrangements you and your investors make, work with a business attorney to draft the necessary documents stating the terms of each agreement.

ESSENTIAL

No matter how badly you need the money, consider running a background check on a potential investor, especially if you are unsure about her background. Reference search services such as PeopleData.com and USSearch.com can provide public information regarding criminal records, bankruptcies, real estate transactions, and civil litigations. These services charge a nominal fee, but in the end they may save you from a potential problem investor.

Finance the Restaurant Yourself

Suppose you want complete ownership and control of your restaurant—no partners, no outside investors. Banks will be reluctant to give you a business loan because you are just starting out—in a risky business like a restaurant, no less. What then?

You can finance it yourself. Just remember that there is no guarantee of success. If you take out a second mortgage on your home, you could be forced to sell if things don't work out. If your restaurant doesn't succeed, you could lose your savings, and it may take a long time before you're squared away again. The risks may sound frightening, but do not despair—many people have opened restaurants with their own money. And they didn't have to be millionaires to do it.

Analyzing Your Personal Assets and Equity

There are a number of ways you can fund your own restaurant. Be advised that when you're striking out on your own, there are fewer options available to you and the stakes are higher than when using investors. How much are you willing to risk as you get your business off the ground? Here are a few options you can use to personally fund your restaurant:

- **Personal savings and investments:** These can include savings accounts, stock, mutual funds, savings bonds, cash value on life insurance policies, retirement funds, and other investments.
- **Home-equity loans:** You can get a loan using the equity on your home. You will be responsible for paying back the loan even if your restaurant doesn't make a profit.
- **Personal property:** Selling cars, jewelry, furniture, stereos, and other things might bring in some significant cash.
- **Credit cards:** They should only be used for convenience and emergencies, but credit cards can be good for short-term financing. The interest rates are high, so don't get carried away, and pay them off as soon as possible.

Do It Yourself (DIY)

The DIY movement has made it much easier to open a restaurant without investors. If you're good with your hands, there's no reason why you can't shave tons of money off your start-up costs by doing certain projects yourself rather than hiring other people to do them.

Although some restaurant jobs require a professional, such as the plumbing and electricity, there are countless other items that you can do on your own. The walls need to be painted? Do it yourself. Need some shelves built into a wall? Do it yourself. The floors need sanding and refinishing? Do it yourself. The only cost is the cost of buying materials and renting any tools that you don't already have or can't borrow. You can also ask family and friends to donate some time and labor. You might be surprised how supportive they are and how willing they are to help.

Opening a restaurant can truly be a labor of love. While having a lot of money at your disposal allows for more creativity and flexibility, the lack of money forces you to be more creative and flexible. No matter how you finance your restaurant, the work you put into it and the sacrifices you make will be a worthwhile experience.

CHAPTER 7

Legal Matters, Licenses, and Insurance

To start a restaurant, you don't just pick a space and begin setting up shop. There are legal channels you have to go through and rules and regulations you must follow. You will need to choose a legal business structure that works for you, such as a corporation, a sole proprietorship, or a general partnership. You must also file the necessary paperwork and obtain the proper licenses to conduct business. And you will need to purchase insurance to protect yourself from loss and liabilities. In order to do this, you need the proper professionals to guide you through the process.

Hire the Pros

Approach the process of hiring professionals to help you with your business structure as though you were hiring personnel for your restaurant. Choose them wisely. If a professional's expertise doesn't include experience with restaurants, you may not get the proper assistance you need. You should find people with verifiable experience in setting up restaurant businesses. Check their client lists, and don't be afraid to ask for references.

Attorneys

At some point you will need to seek the services of an attorney, and those services do not come cheap. Rates fall into a fairly broad range, depending on the attorney's experience and prestige of the firm. The amount you need to spend depends on the size of your operation, your budget, and your needs. Generally, an attorney can help new businesses in the following ways:

- Advising you on selecting the appropriate business structure and filing the necessary paperwork
- Reviewing leases, contracts, and other agreements
- Drafting various agreements, such as partnerships, shareholders' agreements, and loan repayment agreements
- Advising and assisting on other legal issues, such as obtaining licenses and permits
- Representing you on any other legal issues that may arise during your start-up process

You may discover that your operation requires different attorneys to perform various services, such as a tax attorney, corporate attorney, intellectual property attorney, and liquor license attorney. It might be a good idea to look into firms that have lawyers who specialize in most, if not all, of these areas. Be aware, however, most lawyers charge by the hour. The fees will add up if they are doing work for you that you or an accountant, can easily accomplish.

Finding an attorney isn't like bobbing for apples. As in all professions, there are some good attorneys and some who are not so good. Ask established restaurateurs and other business owners in your area for recommendations. You can also check with your neighborhood's chamber of commerce.

Accountants

Your accountant is one of the most important people you'll hire, as this professional will help you handle the complex financial obligations of your restaurant. Accountants can provide numerous services, ranging from preparing tax returns and payrolls to creating a financial picture of your restaurant. When you begin the search for the right accountant, think carefully about what you can do yourself versus what services you need. If you have a small staff, you may be able to handle certain responsibilities yourself, such as payroll and bookkeeping.

ESSENTIAL

If you are taking on a partner who is an attorney, you may save money on some legal services, but you should still retain the services of an attorney who represents your interests, especially when it comes to drafting partnership agreements and establishing the roles of the partners.

In a best-case scenario, you will be in contact with your accountant more often than your attorney. A good accountant can help you avoid any number of financial and legal problems, so it is important to find a qualified professional who can advise you on various tax and financial issues. An accountant can give you solid advice on the financial aspects of your business plan. Also, your accountant will be able to help you understand complex financial lingo and keep your financial targets feasible and realistic. Once your restaurant is up and running, meet with your accountant at least once a month to prepare your monthly financial reports, file the appropriate tax returns, and prepare audits and business overviews.

Your accountant should also provide you with the following services:

- Preparing the appropriate federal, state, and local tax returns in a timely manner
- Providing monthly or quarterly financial reports, including income statements and balance sheets
- Consulting with you on the financial aspects of your restaurant, such as cutting costs and increasing sales

- Addressing any tax-related issue or discrepancy on returns filed by the accountant
- Advising you on any changes to the tax codes and any other accounting and tax issue

You should strongly consider hiring an accountant with prior restaurant experience. An accountant who has handled numerous restaurant accounts will understand the financial needs and obligations of your business, as well as the restaurant chart of accounts, which is key to organizing sales, expenses, and financial reports. Like finding a good attorney, a good way to find an accountant is to ask restaurateurs and business owners in your area for recommendations.

Decide on a Business Structure

Before you can start doing business, you and your attorney or accountant must decide on the structure that works best for your restaurant. Your choice will determine the tax structure of your business, the liabilities of the business operators, and the responsibilities of partners or officers. There are a number of structures you can choose from, ranging from simple to complex.

Sole Proprietorship

As the term suggests, a sole proprietorship means that one person (you) owns the business. This is the simplest way to start your business. You do not have to draft any partnership agreements or follow any complicated incorporation procedure. Perhaps the largest benefit of a sole proprietorship is that you are the boss and do not have to answer to anyone else regarding major business decisions. If your business does well, all profits are yours to keep. On the other hand, you also ultimately bear all accountability if your business struggles. You are also personally liable for any money you owe, even if your business folds.

Unlike partnerships and corporations, which can take time and a lot of paperwork to establish, all you need to apply for a sole proprietorship are the licenses required in your city, county, and state. While you can have your attorney take care of the licenses if you desire, it is a fairly simple process, and you can do it on your own time to save legal fees and keep start-up costs down. Some typical licenses include health permits, local business or merchant licenses, and state sales-tax licenses.

In addition to assuming all financial responsibilities, as a sole proprietor you are also personally liable for any losses or damages, such as unpaid debts, personal injury lawsuits, or any other legal actions against you or any of your employees.

Partnership

A partnership involves two or more owners. Depending on how the partnership is structured, you and your partners split the profits, but you also share all the risks. If the business has debts, all partners are personally responsible for paying off the debts, even if the restaurant folds. Like a sole proprietorship, forming a partnership is a fairly simple procedure. There are two kinds of partnerships:

- General partnership: Partners are equally responsible for the business, sharing all profits and liabilities. All partners are involved in the day-to-day operation of the business.
- Limited partnership: As opposed to general partners, limited partners take on limited risks, meaning they are only liable for their investments in the business. Limited partners are usually not involved with major decision-making or the day-to-day business operations.

ALERT

Just because your business is incorporated doesn't mean creditors can't come after your personal assets. A corporation has rules and regulations it must follow. If your creditors can prove that you are not conducting your business properly as a corporation, you can still be held personally accountable for the corporation's debts. You should discuss with your accountant or attorney how to conduct business as a corporation.

Whichever form of partnership your business takes, it is important for your attorney to draw up an agreement that spells out the details so that all partners have a clear understanding of their stakes. If the business takes the form of a general partnership, be sure that the partnership agreement spells out the role of each partner and clearly states who ultimately is the primary decision-maker. The agreement should stipulate any profit-sharing plan and salary structure as well as an exit plan should any partner bow out or die.

Corporation

A corporation is a legal business entity set up to protect you from liabilities should your restaurant fold or be subjected to a lawsuit. This type of business structure is more complicated than a partnership or sole proprietorship, and it requires close consultation with your attorney. A corporation has its own bylaws, rules, and guidelines to which it must adhere. When a restaurant is incorporated, the corporation becomes the owner, and you become merely a shareholder in the corporation. While a corporation may shelter you personally from certain liabilities, there are tax implications. The corporation may be taxed on its profits, which in turn are taxed again as your personal income. Fortunately, there are several types of corporate structures that provide some tax relief for small businesses, so you should discuss with your attorney or accountant what kind of corporation is right for you.

Obtain the Proper Permits and Licenses

Before you can legally open your doors to the public, you have to obtain certain permits issued by a government agency, either on the state or local level. In most cases, permits have to be renewed annually, so it is important that you are aware when your permits are about to expire. In the restaurant business, certain permits are necessary in all states, even if they are obtained through individual state and local governments.

Building Permit and Certificate of Occupancy

If you are constructing a new restaurant from the ground up or changing the structure of an existing restaurant, you need to obtain building permits. If you have a licensed contractor, he should file the appropriate paperwork with the municipal government to get the building permit. The building inspector may require a floor plan for reference before the building construction can take place. After you've finished construction, the building inspector will visit the premises to make sure that your building is structurally sound, all electrical and plumbing systems are up to code, your building contains no hazardous materials, all emergency exit lights and doors are properly installed, and any modifications to the existing space are appropriate.

If for some reason you do not pass the initial inspection, the building inspector will inform you of what you need to do in order to get the building up to code. Once it passes the inspection, the building inspector will issue you a certificate of occupancy, bringing you one step closer to opening your doors.

Liquor License

To serve alcoholic beverages in your restaurant, you must have a liquor license. Liquor licensing is administered on the state level, and each state has different laws. Depending on your state agency's regulations, you may need to hire an attorney specializing in liquor laws to help you obtain a license. Your state agency may offer different classes of licenses, and the availability and costs of getting a license can vary tremendously from state to state.

Health Permit

Before you can open the restaurant doors, you must apply for a health permit. Health regulations vary depending on location, but generally, the health inspector may check initial inventory, food supply, and equipment to see if they are up to standard. For specific details concerning health inspections in your area, contact your local health department.

Other Local Permits

Different municipalities have different laws regarding the types of permits businesses are required to have. Check with your local government about getting the proper permits to conduct business in your area. In many locations, you are required to have a business license that is renewable annually. Some municipalities have very specific local ordinances, such as permits for signage, live entertainment, and outdoor seating.

Local Laws and Restrictions

Aside from obtaining the proper permits to conduct business in your area, you also have to adhere to certain local laws. Among the most stringent are the laws regarding the sale of alcohol. These laws are too complex to describe here, since different states have different regulations. Consult your attorney or local liquor licensing agency to find out specifically what you can and cannot do.

You should also be aware of local zoning ordinances. Zoning ordinances are established primarily to separate commercial and residential areas. For example, some zoning ordinances may restrict the number of certain businesses, like bars and restaurants, allowed to operate in a neighborhood, or they may limit your hours of operation, specifying when you can open and when you must close. In any case, before you decide on a site, you should know the local zoning laws. If the laws for the area involve too many restrictions for your concept to be successful, consider another location.

Review Your Lease and Other Contracts

Another legal reality you need to deal with is your lease and other contracts, including equipment leases, contracts with suppliers, company cars, and so on. Your attorney should review these contractually binding documents to make you aware of your obligations and the consequences if you default. In addition, your attorney should also make you aware of what you are entitled to and the rights you may have under state law (which may or may not be written into the lease). More importantly, make sure that your landlord permits you in writing to use the premise as a restaurant. She may say it's okay to you, but unless it's in writing, she can change her mind at any time.

Aside from your lease and partnership agreements, other contracts your attorneys should look at are construction contracts. You need to make sure that all costs and estimates are spelled out in writing—what the contractors will do, what is required of them, by what date construction will be completed, and discounts or reimbursement for any delays and errors.

Insure Yourself Against Loss and Liabilities

Since the risk of damage, injury, and loss may be greater than in many other businesses, the cost of insuring a restaurant can be considerable. Although shopping for insurance can be fairly daunting, you shouldn't throw caution into the wind. Besides the insurance you are required to purchase by law, you will need to look into other kinds of coverage that are appropriate for your restaurant.

Insurance Required by Law

Although there is insurance that covers just about every kind of loss you can think of, the law essentially requires you to carry only two types: unemployment insurance and workers' compensation insurance. Unemployment insurance covers benefits for employees who are laid off. Workers' compensation insurance covers employees' medical costs, damages, and lost wages due to injuries on the job.

FACT

Unemployment insurance isn't purchased through an agency but is paid in the form of payroll taxes, such as those under the Federal Unemployment Tax Act (FUTA) and state-sponsored programs. Workers' compensation insurance, on the other hand, is purchased through a commercial provider; the premiums vary state to state and are based on industry and job categories.

Property and Liability Insurance

As a start-up, you should purchase property and liability insurance before you open. Like homeowner's and automobile insurance, insurance for restaurants essentially covers loss stemming from damage to your own property as well as liabilities due to damage or injury to another party. For restaurants, insurance carriers may include riders that cover specific types of damages and liabilities such as:

- Revenue loss due to catastrophes and theft
- Loss due to food contamination and spoilage caused by power outages

- Liabilities due to intoxicated patrons (if you serve alcohol)
- Product liabilities that cover foodborne illnesses
- Liabilities due to employment malpractices
- Loss and liabilities involving delivery services

Keep in mind that you may not need all of the coverage provided, but it is important to get the appropriate coverage for your operation. For example, you won't need liquor liability if you don't serve alcohol, but it is essential that you have product liability to cover instances of foodborne illness. Talk to a reputable agent who's experienced in selling insurance to restaurants.

Health Care and Other Insurances

The high cost of health insurance continues to be an issue for many businesses. But in a physically demanding work environment such as a restaurant, you should purchase health insurance if you don't already have it. And if you hire full-time employees, such as a chef or manager, you should provide, at the very least, partial health benefits.

As with property and liability insurance, health insurance is probably something you should have when your restaurant opens. Once you create a well-established business generating significant and steady cash flow, you might consider adding one or more of the following:

- **Life insurance:** Provides a cash benefit for your family upon your unexpected death that may help them sustain the restaurant
- **Disability insurance:** Provides a percentage of your income should you become disabled
- **Business overhead expense:** Covers operating expenses such as rent, utilities, taxes, and employees' wages should you become disabled
- **Key employee insurance:** Pays cash to your business for loss or disability of an important employee, such as your chef

Dealing with death or disability is emotionally straining, but it can also put your business in a difficult situation. Having the appropriate insurance cushions the blow to allow your business to get back on its feet.

CHAPTER 8

Menu Planning and Design

Your menu will be the heart of your operation. It influences everything that goes into planning and running your restaurant, such as your kitchen design, your choice of ingredients, the type of service, the staffing, and even the ambiance. While diners may be attracted by the decor, advertising, or prices, the main reason diners choose a restaurant is the menu it offers and the quality of food it serves. Your menu is critical to your success, so plan it well.

Design a Menu That Fits Your Concept

Your menu should be consistent with your overall concept. Remember that your concept covers how you package your restaurant as a whole, and that includes your decor, your pricing, the style of service, and so on. At the center of your concept is your menu. If you haven't thought of your menu by now, make it a priority.

Matching Your Menu with the Atmosphere

Consider the atmosphere you would like to create. Do you want the atmosphere to be hip, modern, and posh? Your menu items must reflect the atmosphere, perhaps with more creative flair in the ingredients, in the preparation, and the presentation. Fried chicken with mashed potatoes and corn may not fit with that atmosphere, but pecan crusted chicken breast with rosemary scented new potatoes and snow peas might be a good choice. On the other hand, if your restaurant has more of a down-home country feel, stick with more traditional country fare. There's no rule that says you have to have a certain style of cuisine to match your restaurant's atmosphere. The important thing is that your menu and atmosphere complement each other in a way that creates a consistent and comfortable experience for your customers.

Matching Your Menu with the Restaurant's Theme

Your theme is the common idea that runs throughout the restaurant that people can identify and associate with. Here are some ways you can match your menu with your theme:

- **A "signature" dish:** If you're planning your menu around a signature dish, you may want to choose other items that would complement it. For example, if your signature dish is gourmet brick-oven pizza, you might put some specialty salads on the menu to complement the pizza.
- **Ethnic themes:** Obviously, if the theme of your restaurant is a particular ethnic culture, then you will showcase cuisine from that culture. However, many ethnic restaurants incorporate dishes from different countries in addition to their own ethnic dishes.

- **Brew pubs, wine bars, and juice joints:** If the main feature of your restaurant is the beverages, you should have menu items that complement them. For example, a wine bar usually has a selection of cheeses and meats in the appetizer section.
- **Style of cuisine:** Fusion, Cajun, southwestern, steakhouse—the number of possibilities is limitless, and the menu can focus solely on one particular style or incorporate several. Just be sure that it is balanced and fits with the overall concept.
- **Decor and ambiance:** Your menu should complement the decor and ambiance of the restaurant. If your restaurant's decor is a fifties-style diner, you might consider a menu that features diner-style comfort food, perhaps with a creative modern twist.

FACT

A typical menu for a casual or fine-dining restaurant can be divided into four or five sections: appetizers (or first courses), salads, entrées, side dishes, and desserts. Some fine-dining restaurants even serve an amuse-bouche (French meaning, "amuse the mouth"), a small complimentary tasting of an item before the appetizer is served.

Matching Your Menu with Your Hours of Operation

You should also plan your menu around the hours your restaurant is open. If your restaurant opens at 8 A.M., customers will expect breakfast items on the menu. Breakfast hours vary from restaurant to restaurant, but in general, breakfast is normally served between the hours of 7 A.M. and 10 A.M.; certain restaurants, such as diners, may serve breakfast all day long.

Most restaurants are open for lunch and dinner. In many cases, the lunch menu is similar to the dinner menu but with smaller and less expensive versions of the entrées. Some may choose to focus on light fare, such as soups, salads, and sandwiches. Lunch is typically served from 11 A.M. to 3 P.M., with a short break to make the change to the dinner staff and menu. The way you plan to develop a menu for the hours you operate will depend largely on your customers and what they want.

You may even be open late hours and wish to have a late-night snack menu for your customers who are having drinks or coffee. Late-night hours also vary, but typically run after 10 or 11 P.M. until the restaurant bar closes, if there is one. During late-night hours, menu items are usually limited to simple appetizers and the like, but they are still consistent with the overall concept of the restaurant.

Appeal to Your Target Customers

Your menu should strive to satisfy your target customers' needs and expectations. For example, if your customers are middle-income couples in the suburbs, you should have a children's menu or some kid-friendly selections as well as items that reflect their preferences and budget. If you are located in a business district, you may want to have a menu that can accommodate office workers' limited time. Soups, sandwiches, and salads are common examples of items that are quick and have wide appeal.

If you aim to attract more affluent customers, your menu items must include some high-end ingredients prepared exquisitely to justify the high prices. You may have to be a bit more creative with your menu, but as with any art, some people like more modern approaches while others tend to be more traditional.

ALERT

If you want to create a high-end menu, be aware that your target market will shrink unless you are in a wealthy neighborhood, where competition may be tight. Research the demographics in the area to decide if there is an adequate clientele who can afford a bigger ticket.

Consider Special Diets and Lifestyles

More restaurants are creating menu items catering to consumers with special diets. Many have such diets for health reasons, others for cultural or philosophical reasons. Of course, you can't take into account every type of diet. However, you should highlight or adapt menu items to appeal to customers who adopt certain dietary lifestyles.

Vegetarians and Vegans

Since most vegetarians consume dairy products and eggs, devising a menu that suits them is relatively easy. As long as there's no meat or fish in the food you will be safe, but be sure the items do not contain any meat stock. Vegans, on the other hand, do not consume dairy products or eggs, so even items like pancakes or grilled cheese sandwiches would not work unless you're using suitable substitutes for egg and cheese. But there are numerous popular items that are vegan-friendly—pasta with marinara sauce or pesto, tofu with soy sauce and sesame, or chopped salad with balsamic vinaigrette, just to name a few.

Gluten Free Diets

In response to the growing demand from consumers with gluten sensitivity, more restaurants are developing gluten free menu options. Because wheat is a dominant ingredient in many restaurants, it is difficult for gluten sensitive consumers to eat out. Yet restaurants are addressing the need in this market—even some pizza and burger joints are making gluten free crusts and buns to meet this market demand.

ALERT

If you are advertising a menu item as gluten free, do a thorough check of ingredients. Some ingredients may be processed with wheat, rye, or barley, though it may not be apparent. Soy sauce, for example, contains wheat for fermentation, but you can use wheat free tamari.

Local and Organic Ingredients

Another hot trend in the food industry is the use of local and organically grown ingredients. Because today's consumers are more wary of their food's environmental and nutritional impact, restaurants are marketing their menus to include ingredients that are locally sourced. However, such ingredients carry a higher price tag. If your concept includes a fairly low price point, this may not be an option for you.

Factor In Your Kitchen

Your menu will also determine your kitchen needs: its size, layout, types of equipment, and storage space. When planning your menu, determine if you have the space and the money for the equipment to accommodate the preparation of your menu items. If not, then you must revise your menu.

Determining the Kitchen Space You Need

Your menu and the size of your dining room will determine the size of your kitchen and the types of equipment you need. Different preparation methods call for different equipment, and in turn, determine your kitchen size and layout. For example, if you have char-grilled burgers and fries on the menu, you will need a gas grill and a deep fryer. If the prep methods for your menu require equipment that your space cannot efficiently accommodate, revise the menu.

Mixing the Menu: Station to Station

A station is an area of the kitchen where the food is prepared in a particular way. The basic stations include the grill, fryer, sauté station, broiler, and oven. You should create a mix of menu items based on cooking methods so that you are less likely to have one station backed up while another station is idle. For example, if you want grilled rib eye steak on your menu, you might include poached salmon, fried chicken, and baked lasagna to distribute the kitchen duties more evenly.

Using Your Inventory Efficiently

Determine if your menu allows your inventory to be used efficiently. Can an ingredient for one particular item be used in another item? While you probably want a menu that is diverse in terms of preparation methods and ingredients, you want your food supply to move quickly, especially the perishables. When planning your menu, include items that have common or versatile ingredients. Potatoes, for example, can be baked or mashed, but they can also be made into french fries or hash browns or diced and put into soups. This way, you can manage inventory more efficiently and save on storage space as well.

Calculate the Cost of Food

Once you have your menu items, you must calculate the cost of the ingredients for a single serving of each item. This is the first step in determining each item's price. It is important that you standardize the recipes so that each serving uses the same amount of raw materials. Let's say you want to figure out the food cost for an eight-ounce New York strip steak with a baked potato and bread. To calculate the food cost, follow these steps:

1. Calculate the cost of the steak: Eight ounces (half a pound) at $7.00 per pound equals $3.50.
2. Add the cost of the baked potato: Four ounces at $0.60 a pound equals $0.15.
3. Add the cost of any garnish and condiment: Two ounces of onion ($0.05) plus half an ounce of sour cream ($0.10) equals $0.15.
4. Add the cost of bread and butter: $0.50.

ALERT

Test all your recipes. If you don't yet have a kitchen in place in your restaurant, do it at home. Invite some friends and family for the taste test and get some honest opinions. During your testing, time how long it takes to make a dish and how it tastes and smells, and develop standards for your recipe.

The total food cost for this menu item is $4.30. Remember, you are only calculating the cost based on a standardized recipe. This process will not be exact because you're not taking into consideration other factors that affect food cost. In the real world, prices for raw ingredients fluctuate, food becomes wasted or spoiled, and errors occur that will require food to be prepared again. You can help minimize such losses by maintaining effective inventory control.

Price Your Items Strategically

Once you've determined the food cost, you'll need to figure out the price. A number of factors affect the pricing of your menu items. Among them are the following:

- What your customers are willing to pay?
- Your total costs in doing business.
- Your desired profit margin.
- What your competitors are charging for similar items?

There are numerous ways to figure out how to price your items. No matter what method you use, you'll ultimately have to choose prices that will cover all your costs and generate a profit. However, if your customers aren't willing to pay what you charge, you'll need to do some adjustments. The best way to make these adjustments is to come up with a menu-pricing strategy.

ESSENTIAL

In general, food costs for restaurants range somewhere between 20 to 35 percent. The point at which you set your food-cost percentage depends on a number of other factors including all your operating costs (rent, utilities, labor, and so on), the pricing standards for your type of restaurant, and your desired profit.

We have already calculated the food cost of a New York strip steak dinner. The total for that example was $4.30. Normally you would convert the food cost into a desired percentage of the price of your item. Remember, however, that the food cost is only part of your total cost. You also need to consider the labor, supplies, utilities, rent, and other expenses you incur in the course of doing business, not to mention your desired profit margin. If you set your desired food cost percentage to be 25 percent, then the price of your item will be $17.20. (You'll want to round up the price to $17.25 so that the price doesn't look strange on the menu.) You need to determine if the price set can recover some of the other costs and bring in a reasonable profit. For example, if it costs $6.00 in labor to prepare the dish, you must add that to your total cost. If all the costs incurred don't bring your desired profit, you may need to increase your price, or adjust the portion size to bring down the food cost percentage. Let's say you pay a lot for your busy waterfront location. A low menu price would recoup the cost of raw food materials, but you would still need to recover the high cost of rent by charging more for your food. In that case, your food cost would represent a lower percentage of the total menu price of a food item. If you want your food cost percentage to be 20 percent for that strip steak dinner, you'll have to charge $21.50 to reach that goal. However, be careful not to set a price that your customers aren't willing to pay.

Price Points

Figuring out how much your customers are willing to pay can be difficult. If you are in a competitive market and you want to charge a higher price because you are serving a higher quality product, it is essential to have a firm foundation for your pricing points. Pricing points are the price limits your customers are willing to pay for your product. Several factors can influence the pricing points of your menu, including these:

- **Your target customers' demographics:** If your desired clientele is affluent, the willingness to pay a higher price for quality is greater than a college student with a limited budget. Your competitors: If you plan to charge higher prices than your competitors, you'd better be able to differentiate yourself from them in terms of quality, service, and so on.
- **Your concept:** The appropriate pricing points take the whole restaurant into consideration—the atmosphere, the service, the decor, and so on.
- **Your location:** If you are in a high rent neighborhood, that difference may have an effect on your pricing strategy.

Take the example of the New York strip steak earlier. If you go by your desired food cost percentage of 25 percent and price the item at $17.25, you might be within the limits of your pricing point if your target customer considers quality steak worth that kind of money. However, if you provide paper napkins instead cloth, placemats instead of a tablecloth, or a less-than-impressive wine list to complement the dinner, your customer may not feel the atmosphere is worth the price you charge. But if you upgrade your tableware and add a better wine list, your customer may even be willing to pay more. In essence, there's no scientific method to help you determine your pricing points. The best thing you can do is to find out as much as you can about the market you're in and test it.

Maintaining Your Food-Cost Goals

You must calculate the plate cost of every item you sell. Depending on your other expenses, aim for your final food cost percentage to be between 20 and 35 percent. Not all items on your menu will hit your desired percentage perfectly. The key is to price your items so that the final menu mix achieves your percentage goal. Take a look at the following table to see a menu mix with the desired food cost percentage of 26 percent overall.

▼ **SAMPLE MENU MIX**

Item	Food Cost %	Menu Price	Total Sold	Total Revenue
New York Strip Steak	25% ($4.30)	$17.25	30	$517.50
Jumbo Shrimp	36% ($7.00)	$19.50	20	$390.00
Chicken	20% ($3.00)	$15.00	40	$600.00
Pork Chop	25% ($3.50)	$14.00	40	$560.00
Overall Food Cost =	26% ($529.00)			$2,067.50

In order to achieve the goal of 26 percent, the example priced the items fairly closely to achieve a balanced pricing strategy. The key is not to price the items out of the range that customers are willing to pay. For this particular menu mix, $20.00 is the pricing point. If you set the price of shrimp at 26 percent food cost, the price would be $27.00, well above the pricing point. Therefore, you price it lower, but you still make $12.50 on each order, and that's significant revenue per order sold. On the other hand, you priced chicken higher to lower the food cost percentage to 20 percent. The number of chicken dishes sold helps to balance out the higher food cost percentage of the shrimp, partly because chicken is less expensive and partly because people generally eat more chicken than steak or shrimp.

Decide How Your Menu Should Look

The look of your menu should also complement the feel of your restaurant. Designing a menu can be fun, and you can use your creativity to produce a menu that makes an impression on your customers. Be as creative as you want to be in your design, but don't lose focus on what you're really presenting—your delicious food. Great menu design doesn't have to be complex. You can do a fine job with subtle, simple menu presentation. Your customers will remember your restaurant for what your menu offers, not how it looks. However, there are some practical aspects of menu design you should be aware of that will make it more appealing to your customers and, therefore, better for your business.

Perhaps the best place to start is to select the right format for your menu. Choose the format that best presents your menu items, serves your customers' needs, and complements your restaurant's atmosphere. Although menus can come in many shapes and sizes, the menu format can be summarized in three basic ways: the centralized-menu board, single-page format, and the multiple-page format.

ESSENTIAL

If you are just starting out and don't have a huge budget to work with, don't focus on designing an elaborate menu. Menu production can be costly, especially if it involves materials other than paper, like wood or metal. Don't bear that cost when you're still testing the waters. Keep your menu design simple and flexible. When you've established yourself, you can make changes to the menu design if you want.

The Centralized-Menu Board

Centralized-menu boards are most commonly found in fast-food restaurants and delicatessens although some casual and even high-end restaurants have adopted this format. This menu style promotes quick and efficient service—people read the menu while they wait in line and order quickly when it's their turn. The centralized-menu board works well if you are opening a quick-service restaurant and your customers are familiar with your menu items. But if your menu needs to be more descriptive to help your customers understand their options, this format can be very limiting.

If you are using the centralized-menu board in part to help shape the atmosphere, make sure that it fits your concept and that it won't put your customers off. Gimmicks may have a place in the restaurant business, but they shouldn't be at the expense of practicality. Your customers should be able to read your menu with ease and comfort.

Single-Page Format

The single-page format is common in many casual and fine-dining restaurants. It can come in different sizes and shapes, single- or double-sided, but essentially the advantage of the single-page format is its simplicity and flexibility. It doesn't require as much paper as a multiple-page menu, so revisions are less costly. The single-page format works well if your menu has a moderate number of items that don't require a lot of explanation. Some restaurants use a bigger paper size to accommodate descriptions.

Multiple-Page Format

If your menu has a large number of items that require detailed descriptions, the multiple-page format might be your best bet. The main advantage of a multiple-page menu is that it can individually showcase each course on each page, allowing the detailed description to sell the item. Typically, these menus include a page for appetizers and salads, a page for main courses, and perhaps one for dessert and one for beverages. One drawback, of course, to having a menu with a lot of choices and descriptions is the anxiety that it may cause. Your customers may take longer to peruse the menu and decide what they want, and that may lengthen your turnover (that is, the time it takes for the table to clear).

ESSENTIAL

A multiple-page format can come in a variety of forms. You can fold one sheet into three sections. Or you can fold the pages into a booklet. Your menu might be spiral bound, like a notebook. You can even have a menu that unfolds like a road map. There are many possibilities—just be sure the design serves your customers well and gets your message out.

Spice Up Your Descriptions!

If you read, "Roast chicken with mashed potatoes and mixed vegetables" on the menu at a nice casual restaurant, you probably wouldn't pay much more than $10 for it, would you? However, if that same dish were described as "Herbes de Provence roast chicken with garlic whipped potatoes and spring vegetables julienne," you might be willing to pay more than $20 for it. The use of descriptive language to spice up your menu can dramatically influence your customers' perceived value of your product. Such specific details in the menu description draw your customers' attention, but they also affect their willingness to pay a higher price. When you're developing your menu, don't leave out these details if you think they can up your price. To get you started, here are some ways to make your menu descriptions more appealing:

- **Method of preparation:** Cooking methods add perceived sophistication to the dish. Pan-seared, flash-fried, poached, steamed, and blanched are just some of the ways to describe some cooking techniques.
- **Special or seasonal ingredients:** Describing these ingredients makes the menu item sound tantalizing and exotic. For example, Thai chicken curry can be "Thai chicken curry with lime leaves and lemongrass."
- **Unique characteristics:** Is there something characteristically unique about the item? For example, you might use descriptive terms like "free-range" chicken, "fresh-baked" corn bread, and "organic" vegetables.
- **Origin of ingredients:** Where the ingredients come from can also increase their appeal. Examples include Tahitian vanilla beans, French feta cheese, and Prince Edward Island clams.
- **Style of cuisine:** Does the dish come from another culture or region? Is it influenced by a recipe from a specific region or country? Moroccan lamb couscous, Cajun-spiced catfish, and Creole-style gumbo are some good examples.

Again, your menu description should match your overall concept. Consider who your customers are and how much they know. If they don't know the terms you use to describe the food, they may not feel comfortable with your menu.

ALERT

Be creative, but be truthful. Never mislead your customers with your menu descriptions. If you mention organic vegetables on a menu item, the vegetables you use had better be from an organic farm. Your customers will know, and even if they don't complain, they won't return. Not only that, you might even get sued for misrepresentation.

Update Your Menu Periodically

Because market conditions change with increasing competition and increasingly discerning consumers, you should update your menu to stay competitive. There are a number of ways you can update your menu:

- **Run specials:** You can do this either on a daily or weekly basis, or "while supplies last." Most often, specials are run because items are in season or there is a price reduction in supply.
- **New food trend:** Whether its upscale burgers, fancy pizzas, locally grown produce, you may want to capitalize on a hot new item, even if the trend is short-lived.
- **Revising existing menu items:** Reworking less popular menu items that seem dated may boost interest in them. For example, instead of iceberg lettuce, switch to mixed greens for salads.
- **Adjust to the seasons:** Many high-end restaurants change their menus according to the seasons. They may feature more grilled items and seasonal greens in the summer, and stews and roasted vegetables in winter.

Be judicious when updating your menu. Make small changes, unless conditions call for drastic measures. A change in chefs may be one of those times, but in general, you want to keep doing what you do well for your customers, while tweaking a few things to give the menu a fresh look.

CHAPTER 9

Choosing to Serve Alcohol

Selling alcoholic beverages can provide a tremendous source of income for your restaurant, but there is an enormous responsibility that goes with it. You must adhere very closely to the state laws that govern the sale of alcohol, or you risk losing your license and, worse yet, being confronted with legal action. But if you set up and manage your bar properly and efficiently, the return on your investment can be extremely rewarding.

The Pros and Cons of Selling Alcohol

Choosing to serve alcohol for many restaurant owners is a virtual no-brainer. The high-profit margins from alcohol sales and the hefty overhead of restaurants almost make it necessary for many restaurants to sell alcoholic beverages. However, considerable responsibility goes with selling alcoholic beverages to the public. There are laws you must follow, some of which you are probably already aware of and some that may leave you scratching your head. That being said, you do not have to serve alcohol to be successful in this business. Like every other aspect of your operation, the answer to the question "To serve or not to serve?" depends on your concept, your desired clientele, and their needs. So before you start designing your bar, think about how the sale of alcohol serves your operation.

The Advantages

There is one enormous advantage to selling alcohol: the high-profit margin. The more booze you sell, the more money you make. But there are more advantages to serving alcohol than just the money alone. The high-profit margins can allow more financial flexibility, such as paying your employees a better wage, providing them benefits, and so on. Alcohol service may also be central to your concept. If your restaurant has great food and you offer twenty imported beers on tap, that service could be a huge draw for consumers.

Your restaurant's image may depend on a beverage service to complement your menu. A French bistro seems a little less French if it doesn't have a good wine list. Additionally, in some states, the liquor license itself is a commodity. Depending on the demand, it may increase in value.

The Disadvantages

There are always two sides of every coin. For all the advantages to serving alcohol in your restaurant, the choice does have a few downsides. Your liability increases dramatically when you sell alcohol. Mishaps resulting from intoxication can result in legal actions against your establishment, the revocation of your license, and the closing of your operation. There are strict laws that you must obey, and they vary by location. You must make sure that your staff knows these laws and, more importantly, that they abide by them.

Making the decision to serve alcohol should come very early during your start-up process. The application process for a liquor license can take a long time, depending on where you are located. Start that process as soon as possible.

Theft and nuisance become larger issues. Whether it's your employees pilfering bottles, siphoning cash paid at the bar, or over-portioning drinks for bigger tips, you run a bigger risk of theft when you serve alcohol. And every restaurant has dealt with nuisance customers every once in a while. Dealing with a nuisance customer who is intoxicated is even worse. If you have a bar, you're always running the risk of attracting the wrong elements at times.

Finally, acquiring a liquor license is not an easy process, and in some cases, can be extremely expensive. Depending on where your restaurant is located, a license to serve alcohol can cost as much as $100,000.

Acquiring the Liquor License

You need to be licensed if you want to serve alcohol, no matter where you are in the country. Liquor licenses are administered on the state and local levels and will require an application process. Most likely, there will be an initial licensing fee, and your license will need to be renewed every year afterward (for a fee, of course).

The first thing to do is to find out which agency administers the licensing in your area. Go to your state government's website and do a keyword search, or do a keyword search on a search engine, such as "restaurant liquor license" plus your state's name. You'll probably need an attorney who specializes in liquor laws to help with the application process at some point, but to start out, you can check with the agency that issues the licenses and see what needs to be done.

Classification of Liquor Licenses

Liquor licenses have different classifications according to the types of establishments that sell alcohol. The class of license you need will depend on your concept. Different states have different names and licenses with varied provisions, but in general, the licenses can be categorized in the following manner:

- **On-premises liquor:** This is considered the standard bar license, which allows an establishment to serve beer, wine, and spirits. Many states require that you serve food such as soups and sandwiches to some minimum degree.
- **Restaurant:** In most cases, to be issued a restaurant license, your establishment must have at least a certain percentage of sales from food. A restaurant that sells beer, wine, and liquor is considered to be fully licensed.
- **Hotel:** This license allows alcohol to be served in restaurants that are on a hotel's premises and also allows off-premise or carryout sales. Independently owned restaurants in the hotel may need separate licensing.
- **Beer and wine:** This license allows only for the sale of beer and wine. Some states may have different definitions for "beer" and "wine," depending on the alcohol content.
- **Retail:** This designation refers to places that retail liquor to the public—that is, by the bottle, rather than by the drink. These could include grocery stores, convenience stores, drug stores, and liquor stores.
- **Tavern:** This means a place that sells wine and beer on the premises. Some states require food to be served, others don't.
- **Club:** A club license allows private clubs, such as country clubs and fraternal organizations, to serve alcohol to their members.
- **Caterer:** Some states have licenses available to caterers who provide food-and-beverage services for private functions, such as weddings, graduations, and retirement parties.
- **Restaurant/brewer:** Commonly known as a "brewpub" license, this type allows a bona fide restaurant to brew beer on the premises. However, in some states, you may need a separate license to serve the alcohol to the public.

The above list describes only those licenses that pertain to the food-service industry. Many other kinds of licenses serve different functions. Be sure to check with your state agency concerning the classifications. Each state has a different system and different provisions for each class.

The Application Process

After you've checked with your state's agency to find out about licenses, fees, and the application process, and after you've researched the different classes of licenses, you must figure out the type of license that is most suitable for your business. The cost of acquiring a liquor license varies from state to state. Many states have quotas on liquor licenses (that is, they offer only a fixed number in any given area). If your area has no licenses available because the quota has been reached, you'll have to buy one from another business, probably at a premium.

Designing Your Bar

If you are going to have a bar, you must decide how to feature it in your restaurant. If you expect the bar to generate the majority of your sales, you should allocate significant space for it, perhaps creating a lounge area if the space allows. However, if you feel that your sales will mostly come from customers sitting at tables and ordering drinks and food, then your bar should not take up significant space. You should ask yourself whether your bar will be doing business on its own besides servicing diners in the restaurant. Your answer to that question depends on your target market and on your concept. Are you trying to achieve a pub atmosphere? If so, your bar will probably generate solid sales on its own, so you should allocate enough space to accommodate the people who want to mingle at the bar. However, if you have a French bistro catering to an older clientele, you may want to set up just a service bar that's only accessible to the waitstaff and thus allow more space for table seating.

If your bar is going to generate significant business on its own, then consider setting it apart from the rest of the dining room, either by setting up some kind of barrier or wall to provide privacy for those in the dining area.

Where should the bar be located? In many restaurants, the bar is located closest to the entrance. Having the bar close to the entrance and away from the main dining area helps the overall traffic flow of the restaurant. When customers enter and no table is available immediately, they can go directly to the bar without navigating through the dining room.

Essentially, you want your bar to be functional and efficient, but its functionality and efficiency depend on the degree you want your bar to be part of your overall operation.

Basic Bar Equipment

Once you've determined the function and position of your bar, you'll need to purchase the necessary equipment and lay it out properly. The number of bar customers you anticipate will determine the quantity and size of the equipment, the amount of bar supplies, and the number of stations—the areas where bartenders mix their drinks. While equipment differs from bar to bar, there are basic requirements you'll need to get started.

Large Equipment

Some pieces of large equipment are part of the permanent layout. Once in place, these things shouldn't be moved. Your aim should be to produce an efficient system for your bartender when you lay out the following items:

- **Three-bowl sink with drain board for the purpose of washing glasses:** The first bowl contains detergent and self-standing brushes to clean the glasses, the second contains hot water to rinse, and the third has sanitizer to sanitize the glasses.
- **Coolers:** You'll need a large cooler to store your inventory of alcohol that needs to be chilled as well as smaller coolers, or "reach-in coolers," at the bar for quick service.
- **Bottle wells:** These hold your well-brand (cheap) liquors. Each bar station should have its own bottle well.
- **Soda system:** A typical soda system has guns that dispense different kinds of soft drinks, including tonic water and grapefruit mixers.

- **Beer taps:** The beer kegs usually go under the counter or in a separate cooler, to which you'll need to run lines.
- **Ice bins:** These stainless-steel containers resemble sinks, but they're meant for holding ice at the bar.
- **Overhead glass racks:** Having them installed above the bar counter saves space.
- **Cash register/point-of-sale (POS) system:** Your bar should have its own cash drawer and payment system.
- **Blenders:** You need these for frozen drinks such as margaritas, piña coladas, and daiquiris.

You can purchase other pieces of specialty equipment, such as a frozen margarita or daiquiri dispenser or an ice crusher, depending on how useful these expensive items will be to you.

ESSENTIAL

Keep a drink-recipe file system near your bar area for quick reference. You can do this with index cards, a binder, or a computer database. The number of drinks to put in it is totally up to you, and you can even invent your own! Just keep the recipes a secret.

Small Equipment and Utensils

Some utensils and small pieces of equipment are necessary for a full-service bar. You can set the following items up in any way you want and move them around as needed:

- **Cocktail shakers and strainers:** Use these for mixing drinks with or without ice.
- **Corkscrews:** Industrial wine openers are great, but they're expensive. A small waiter's corkscrew works very well.
- **Bottle openers:** If you sell a lot of bottled beer, get an opener that screws into a sturdy surface with a bottle cap bin underneath.
- **Garnish holder:** This is usually a four- or six-compartment bin that holds lime and lemon wedges, maraschino cherries, olives, and other garnishes.

- **Knives and cutting boards:** Use for cutting limes, lemon wedges and twists, and any other drink garnishes.
- **Ice buckets and ice scoops:** You need the ice bucket to fill the ice bin in the bar. You need the ice scoop to scoop the ice from the ice machine to the ice bucket.
- **Cocktail mix/juice containers:** Color-coded spouts distinguish different kinds of drink mixes, such as orange juice, Bloody Mary mix, and so on. Keep these chilled by putting them in wells in the ice bin or in the cooler.
- **Small mortar and pestle:** This will be handy for crushing mint leaves, cherries, and sugar mixtures.

Basic Bar Supplies

Anything that you have to restock on a regular basis is considered a supply. Here's a list of basic bar supplies you should have on hand:

- **Paper products:** This category includes cocktail toothpicks, beverage napkins, straws, cocktail stirrers, and coasters.
- **Cleaning products:** Be sure you always have basics like glass cleaner, detergent, hand soap, and spray cleaners on hand.
- **Glassware:** Depending on what you serve, you need an assortment of glassware, such as highball glasses, martini glasses, and wine glasses.
- **Garnishes:** A full-service bar must have a full array of drink garnishes, including lemon and lime wedges and twists, olives, mint leaves, celery, maraschino cherries, and others.
- **Rags and sponges:** These are necessary for wiping up the counter, beer taps, shelves, and sink area. Remember to soak them in a bucket of sterilized water when not in use.

Preparing to Sell Beer and Wine

The choice to serve only beer and wine can be much more manageable than providing a full bar, as you don't have to stock liquors and the many garnishes that come with mixed drinks. You may not need as much equipment or space to store your inventory. There may not be a need for a bartender, but depending on your concept, such as a wine bar or a gourmet beer hall, a beverage manager who has knowledge of beer or wine may be necessary.

ALERT

When you first open, avoid offering a large selection of beer and wine. Start with a modest selection, and then add to your list as you become more familiar with your customers' preferences. Beer and wine can be a huge expense, so it's best to avoid investing in a large inventory until you are sure that the product will sell.

Building Your Beer Repertoire

As with just about everything in your restaurant, the size of your beer menu depends on your concept. Many restaurants have limited beer selections, serving perhaps a few popular domestics and an import or two. However, today's beer drinkers may demand a little more than the usual selections from the largest domestic breweries. Imports, microbrews, and gourmet beers have become more popular with diners, and restaurants have responded to this demand. Even if you don't intend your restaurant to be known for its beer selection, a little knowledge about beer won't hurt. Many Internet sources can provide even the non-beer drinker with plenty of information about beer.

Working the Wine List

The selection of wine you offer your customers will depend largely on your concept. Some restaurants choose to serve only a house wine by the glass or carafe, but you should take advantage of wine's rising popularity (and its price) to elevate your customers' experience and increase your revenue. Find a good wine salesperson from a reputable wholesaler to guide you on wines that match your concept and give you tips on great values.

Consider your customers. Don't stock overly familiar and inexpensive wine if your customers think that's too low end. Start with good, recognizable labels and then expand the list with less familiar wines as you get to know your customers better.

Have a few selections available by the glass, but avoid putting high-end wines in that group. Offer a good balance between moderate and expensive wines, familiar and not-so-familiar ones. Additionally, your wine selections should pair well with your menu. Chardonnays shouldn't dominate the wine list if you're selling a lot of steak and rack of lamb.

Don't be intimated by the vast world of wine even if you don't know much about it. You can ask for help from your wine representatives. They want your business, so they'll be willing to help you in any way they can.

Stocking the Liquor Shelves

One common mistake among new restaurant owners is to overstock the bar. As a result, they get stuck with inventory that doesn't move and which costs money in the long run. As with every facet of your operation, knowing what brands of liquor to stock and how much to stock depends on your concept and your clientele. Older clientele tend toward the dark spirits such as scotch, bourbon, and whiskey. Younger clientele mostly prefer clearer spirits such as vodka, gin, tequila, and rum. Choose brands based on the atmosphere you want to create and the type of customers you'll likely have. You can check on the Internet to see what kinds of cocktails are currently popular. The website *www.bartv.com* is a good place to do cocktail research.

Brands of the same kinds of liquor can be divided into categories based on their prices: well brands, call, and premium. Some brands may even be described as super-premium, ultra-premium, or top shelf. Well brands, which you use if the customer doesn't specify a brand, are the cheapest. The table below illustrates the categories of sample brands of vodka, currently the dominant liquor on the market.

Category	Sample Brands
Well Brands	Nicholai, Odesse
Call	Stolichnaya, Smirnoff, Finlandia
Premium	Ketel One, Absolut, Turi
Ultra-Premium/Top Shelf	Ultimat, Grey Goose, Chopin, Belvedere

Remember, when you're just starting out, begin with a moderate inventory of liquors. Monitor your sales for a time, and adjust your purchases accordingly.

Maintaining Control of Your Bar

One of the harsh realities of having a bar is that you run more risk of theft and other losses. If you do not run a tight ship, you may find your profits slipping, and you may become subject to legal penalties. Furthermore, the safety of your staff and clientele may become an issue if you do not take the proper steps to maintain control of your bar. Therefore, it's a good idea to develop a system that can minimize such situations.

Protecting Your Bar from Theft and Other Losses

Pilfering by employees is an unfortunate but frequent occurrence in the restaurant business. Many restaurants install video cameras to record bar activities and thus prevent theft. However, the process of "skimming off" is not limited to stealing inventory and pocketing cash. Unscrupulous employees can drain your profits in many other ways, some difficult to detect even with cameras. Here are a few of the most common:

- Giving out "complimentary" drinks to customers for the purpose of increasing tips.
- Over pouring liquor for stiffer drinks, again to get better tips.
- Giving free drinks to employees, even managers.
- Pocketing cash from sales of certain liquors, then replacing the liquors later to avoid suspicion.
- Failing to empty a bottle completely before throwing it away.

Waste, spillage, and errors are expected losses that occur in running a bar. However, there are steps you can take to minimize losses that aren't accidents. Here are a few tips on how to accomplish that:

- Establish good hiring practices.
- Store your inventory under lock and key and allow only certain personnel access.

- Keep regular track of your inventory. Some restaurants even go so far as to chart the level of liquor in each bottle every night to compare against sales.
- Avoid overstocking. It will be easier to keep track of inventory and reduce the chance of theft.
- Establish good rapport with employees and treat them fairly. Sometimes employees act out on their discontent by stealing.

Protecting Yourself, Your Staff, and Your Clientele

There are many risks involved in serving alcohol to the public. If you don't take the proper measures, you could be risking the safety of your staff and clientele, not to mention subjecting your business to fines, lawsuits, and possible loss of your liquor license. Here are some important steps you can take to minimize your risks:

- Know and abide by the laws pertaining to alcohol service in your state. Train your staff to obey these laws.
- Have a consistent system for checking customers' ID to prevent underage drinking.
- Require your bartenders to attend responsible alcohol service training.
- Have phone numbers for taxi services readily available.
- Deal with intoxicated customers in a calm, diplomatic manner. Never force them out of your restaurant without making sure they're in the care of others, even if you have to call the police.
- Train your staff to recognize potential problem situations.

Problem situations get even trickier when alcohol is added to the mix, which is why it is such a good idea to hire experienced bartenders. They should be able to take control of a situation before it becomes a problem and tactfully refuse service to anyone who has had too much, even if that person is a steady customer.

Charging the Right Prices

Beverage prices can be determined in the same way you price your menu items. It is easier to price bottled and canned beverages like beer because you can calculate cost per bottle simply by dividing the cost per case by number of bottles. Bottles of wine can be priced in the same way. Pricing becomes a little more complicated when you're selling cocktails, wines by the glass, and draft beer. Then you'll need to figure out how many drinks you can get out of a single container, whether it's a keg, a bottle of wine, or a bottle of liquor, and how much it costs per "pour." Obviously, the number of drinks you get depends on the size of your drinks.

Pricing Beer

How much above cost you price your beer depends on your concept and your clientele. Some restaurants may be able to negotiate better prices through volume purchases and special promotional deals, but in general, the cost of beer is the same for all restaurants. However, different restaurants charge different prices for the same brand of beer. The difference in price can be attributed to the difference in concepts. For example, a pizza parlor that caters to families may charge less than a high-end restaurant whose customers are willing to pay more for the atmosphere, the service, and the status.

ESSENTIAL

Use the same strategy to price your beer selections that you do your menu items. Many restaurants have a set price for domestic beers, another for microbrews, and another for all imports. This strategy assumes that the profit percentage on less expensive beers will balance out the more expensive brands, as long as the cost per bottle stays in a certain range.

Pricing draft beer is much more complicated. It is difficult to determine how many servings you can get from a keg of beer. Draft systems sustain multiple spills and waste, but the profit margins are much higher than bottles and cans. If you serve draft beers along with bottles and cans, the price of your draft beer should be lower per ounce than comparable beer brands in bottles and cans.

Pricing Wine

Determining your price for wines by the bottle is simple. Most restaurants multiply the cost of a bottle by two or three. If a bottle of wine costs you $10, you might charge $30. However, for more expensive wines, you may want to use a lower factor so you don't price a bottle so high no one will buy it. For example, you may charge $80 for a bottle of wine that costs you $40.

To determine what to charge by the glass, you'll have to decide on your pour size (the amount of wine you pour per glass). Say you want your pour to be 6 ounces, and your wine costs $12. A standard bottle of wine is 750 millimeters (or approximately 25 ounces). So you'll get about four pours per bottle, at a cost to you of $3 per glass. If you choose to multiply that number by three, you would charge $9 per glass. If you decide to charge triple for the whole bottle, you can bump the price per glass to $10 or $11.

Pricing Liquors

Determining a pricing system for cocktails is the most complicated of all. The price you charge for cocktails depends heavily on your concept and clientele. One restaurant might charge $4.50 for a cocktail, while another charges $9.00 for the same drink. Many things can account for the price difference, including atmosphere, service, marketing costs, and so on. But another thing to consider is the quality of the cocktail. If you use freshly squeezed orange juice in your screwdriver, you should take that into consideration when pricing.

A typical pour of liquor in a cocktail is about 1.5 ounces. A 750 ml bottle yields about sixteen drinks, minus an ounce or so for spillage. If a bottle of premium vodka costs you $20.00, then one pour would cost $1.25. Add another $0.25 for garnish, ice, and mixers, and your cost increases to $1.50. If you have determined that you want your cost percentage on liquor to be 25 percent, you'll have to charge $6.00 for that cocktail. If the cost of a well-brand vodka is $8.00 per bottle, then your cost per pour for the same cocktail is only $0.75, and by percentage you would only charge $3.00. Even though the cost percentage is the same for premium drinks, you make more in terms of dollars selling premium drinks than well brands.

CHAPTER 10

The Front of the House

In the restaurant industry, the term "front of the house" refers to the areas the customer can enter, such as the dining room, bar, restrooms, lounge, and waiting area. These are the areas that you will use to create the atmosphere you want to win over your customers. Your primary focus in these areas should be your customers' satisfaction, in both the interior of your restaurant and the exterior.

Communicate Your Message in the Design

The design of the front of the house should communicate your concept to your customers. Everything your customers experience in the restaurant is part of your message. The decor, the furniture, and even simple details such as silverware and tablecloths will define their initial expectations about your concept and the experience they want. It is therefore important that you determine your target customer before you design the front of the house. With your market in mind, you should develop a design plan that is consistent with your overall concept.

Thinking about Design

Spending a lot of money on design won't make your restaurant successful. In fact, many restaurants have failed because the owners spent too much time and money on the design and not enough in other areas. Whether they fail to match their design with their concept or fail to assess their target market correctly, those restaurants rely on design to draw their customers in and then don't meet the expectations that the concept creates. When thinking about design, keep these issues in mind:

- Make sure the design is compatible with your overall concept. That includes your menu, the atmosphere, style of service, tableware, and linen.
- Consider the wants and needs of your target customers. Design the space with their expectations in mind.
- Be sure your design is practical. Maintaining a good "flow" in this area is important for efficient service.
- Keep the design flexible. Consider removable walls and shelves rather than spending money on built-outs (permanent fixtures on the premises) as long it works with the concept.
- Coordinate your furniture, flooring, ceiling, lighting fixtures, and other decorative features with your design. Think of the design as a whole, not just as individual parts.

Hiring Professionals to Help

Many restaurateurs seek out help from design firms in planning their restaurants. If you want to achieve a certain look, and it is within your budget, you might consider hiring an architect or interior designer to implement your vision. You might also be able to do a lot of the designing on your own. The help of a good designer makes things a little easier, but it does come at a price.

ESSENTIAL

As with any other consultant or contractor, have the specific terms of your agreement with your designer laid out in writing. That includes cost estimates, a schedule of work to be completed, a timeline, and penalties for delays. Delays and complications can occur due to various circumstances, but they shouldn't happen because of the consultant's lack of preparation and organization.

One type of designer you may need, especially if you are renovating a raw commercial space for restaurant use, is an architect. An architect can envision the space configuration and draw up the floor plans to make sure that the layout is safe and allows easy traffic flow as well as conveys the right atmosphere. The architect doesn't necessarily deal with decorative features like color scheme or the type of flooring. (That's what an interior designer does.) Rather, an architect suggests where to build a wall, put in a staircase, and how to construct other design elements related to the structure.

You may also need a general contractor with experience in restaurants to supervise the construction. A good contractor can implement the design and suggest alternative ways to work around parts of the plan that might not be practical or structurally sound. He should also know all building codes and requirements related to plumbing and electricity for restaurant use. It is important that the designer and the contractor coordinate with each other to get the construction right. At times, however, you as the client will have to step in and mediate between the parties.

Construct an Efficient Floor Plan

Your floor plan should focus on the comfort and enjoyment of your customers while maintaining an efficient traffic flow. Traffic flow refers to the movement of service and guests throughout the front of the house, which includes the waiting and dining areas, the restrooms, and the bar if you have one. The floor plan must allow servers to move easily to deliver food and beverages as well as guests to move in and out of the restaurant. You have to allot adequate space for movement and seating, but you also have to consider guiding the direction of movements for efficient flow. Cost per square footage is also a concern, so you should maximize your seating capacity without disturbing your customers' expected level of comfort.

Allocating Adequate Space for Flow

The amount of space needed for adequate flow depends largely on your concept. A fine-dining restaurant may require more space per seating than a quick-service restaurant. Fine-dining restaurants tend to have bulkier furniture and require more space around a table for servers. Furthermore, fine-dining customers definitely prefer more space for comfort. Quick-service restaurants, on the other hand, may have booths and tables closer together because there is no table service. However, the area in front of the order counter and the aisles in the dining area may need to be wider because customers move about the dining room more frequently. If your concept calls for any of the following, keep these considerations in mind:

- Self-service counters such as salad bars, buffet stations, desserts, and beverages
- Space for moving carts for food prepared tableside, such as Caesar salad, fajitas, or bananas Foster
- Large decorative items, such as fountains, potted plants, and hearths
- Coolers, microwave ovens, trash bins, and condiment stands for quick-service establishments

Your architect can help you determine the layout of your restaurant, but you must communicate your needs clearly so that he's able to incorporate them into the design.

Some Guidelines for Your Layout

Although it is important that your layout for the front of the house promotes good traffic flow, you must also consider working with the limitations of your existing space. If you are taking over an existing restaurant, changing the structural layout will be difficult and costly. You may have to accept that the plumbing connections in the restrooms and wait stations, for instance, will stay where they are. Even if you are working with totally raw space, you still might have some structural limitations. Nevertheless, you can work around any limitations and design a layout that helps with traffic flow. Consider these guidelines:

- If you have a bar, it should be located along a wall and near the entrance, but customers should not have to walk through the bar to enter the dining area.
- Avoid placing tables in busy paths such as near the entrance, kitchen doors, bar and wait stations, and restrooms.
- Restrooms should be located as far away from the dining area as possible, in a rear corner or in a separate corridor.
- Locate the kitchen convenient to the service entrance to avoid having deliveries made through the dining area.
- If you anticipate a heavy bar business, consider putting up a barrier between the bar and the dining area to avoid having the bar crowd spill over into the dining area, where it will cause congestion.

The Dining Area

Your customers will be spending more of their time in your dining room than anywhere else (unless your restaurant is very busy, and your customers have to wait a long time for a table!). It is therefore essential that your dining tables and their surroundings are comfortable and pleasant. Choosing how to decorate your dining room is a lot of fun, but you still have to consider your concept. Your decor should immediately impress your customers with what your restaurant is about. If you have a flair for design, this is your moment to shine. You also have to consider other logistics, such as the number of seats and tables you'll need and appropriate table layouts, including table sizes.

Choose the Appropriate Decor

Your decor should fit in with your overall concept. For example, a fifties-style diner might have a jukebox playing oldies, some photographs of 1950s icons, and black-and-white checkered-tile flooring. When it comes to the decor, the possibilities are limitless. The best way to start thinking about it is to eat out often and see how other restaurants are designed. Look for ideas in magazines, including food, interior design, and restaurant trade publications. The more you see, the more you'll get the creative juices flowing. If you are hiring a designer, be sure that you communicate what you want, but allow the designer to use her professional skills, too. Just be sure you stay within your defined budget. Spending a lot of money on the decor can set you back in other areas, and that can make your business suffer.

ESSENTIAL

Lay out tables so that they can be easily put together into larger tables. You might also consider purchasing square tabletops with built-in extensions that fold out to make a large round tabletop. That way, you can expand the table when needed and conserve space when the situation doesn't call for it.

Select the Appropriate Table Sizes

As with every aspect in the restaurant business, selecting the appropriate table layouts depends largely on your concept. Consider your clientele and their needs. If a couple has to be seated at a table for four because there are not enough smaller tables, then you are not fully utilizing your space. On the other hand, if a party of six has to wait a long time because there is no larger table on hand, and you have no adjacent smaller tables that you can put together, then you are not fully utilizing your layout. Therefore, you should have a variety of table sizes to accommodate your customers. If your concept involves an intimate bistro setting targeting couples, you should consider a significant number of small tables built for two. However, if your concept is for a family restaurant, then you should consider having more tables built for four and six.

The Wait Station

The wait station is the area that holds supplies for your servers. Here, your servers may dispense and prepare nonalcoholic beverages, store items for cleaning and resetting dining tables, and essentially anything else your servers need to perform their work. You should try to locate the wait station away from the paths customers use frequently or block it from customer view. Position the station so it is easy to reach from all the tables, perhaps against a side wall, but not in the actual dining area. Some items that may be part of the wait station include reach-in coolers for milk, juice, cream, butter and desserts; a beverage station, including coffeemaker and accessories; iced-tea dispenser, soda gun, cold-water faucet, hot-water dispenser for tea, ice bin, scoop, and glassware; paper and linen supplies, such as tablecloths, napkins, bar towels, straws, toothpicks, and carryout containers; condiments that aren't already at the guests' tables, such as pepper mills, ketchup, steak sauce, and oil and vinegar; trash receptacles and cleaning supplies, such as window cleaner, spray disinfectant, and a bucket filled with sanitizing water; service tools such as trays and tray stands; and clean tableware, such as silverware, glasses, cups, plates, and bread baskets.

The list is by no means comprehensive. Depending on your concept, you can store various other items at the wait station. Your servers should have the supplies available for them to do their jobs efficiently, and that also means they should be responsible for keeping the station clean, organized, and well stocked.

Don't cram your wait station so full it makes it difficult for your servers to do their work. However, you also don't want to allocate unnecessary space that could serve a better purpose. The key to an efficient wait station is to organize items so that tasks can be done with relative ease. For example, keep water glasses within reach of the ice bin and faucet, coffee cups near the coffeemaker, and napkins, tablecloths, and silverware together in one area. Shelves or hutches that hold items like glasses and cups should be within easy reach.

You may also consider setting up a few mini-stations in other parts of the restaurant to keep a few important items handy. A mini-station may hold some condiments, tray stands, and maybe a few pitchers of water to make things more convenient for servers.

The Cashier Counter

The cashier counter is essentially where all checks are paid. It is where the cash register, sales receipts, credit card terminals, checks, check holders, and tip trays are kept. This is the station the manager probably monitors frequently, so there is likely a phone as well. In quick-service restaurants, the cashier counter is also the point where customer orders are taken. In some casual family-style restaurants and diners, the cashier counter is situated in the front of the entrance and sometimes also serves as the host stand. Customers take their checks and pay at the counter before leaving. In most casual and all fine-dining restaurants, however, customers pay at the table. Depending on the size of the operation, there may be one or more cashier counters in various sections of the dining room.

Point-of-Sale (POS) Systems

Many restaurants now have turned to point-of-sale, or POS systems. A POS system is a computerized system for ordering food and beverages. Depending on the size of the restaurant, there may be more than one. The system can perform many restaurant administrative functions, such as scheduling and monitoring sales, but for daily use by your servers, here's how it works. The server punches the food order into the computer. The order is automatically printed in the kitchen, and the server then also uses this system to prepare the check for the customers.

The Old-Fashioned Way

POS systems are great tools for your business, but they do come at a price. If you choose not to have a POS system, be sure that you set up some kind of system that keeps track of the check numbers and inventory to minimize theft from "missing" checks (servers discarding checks and keeping the cash). You'll also need checks that you can order from a restaurant or office supplier, check holders, tip trays, a cash register or cash drawer, and a business calculator. If you choose to accept credit cards, you should have a separate phone line for the credit card terminal. Your cashier station should be in an area where only you and your staff have access, and that is monitored frequently.

The Restrooms

One of the areas many restaurant owners overlook is the restroom. Restrooms are part of the front of the house, and their appearance affects the way your customers perceive your restaurant. Make sure that your restrooms are properly designed, with handicapped accessibility, and follow the health codes in your area.

ESSENTIAL

Many local health departments stipulate the number of toilets and urinals an establishment must provide based on its seating capacity. Furthermore, there must also be at least one handicapped-accessible stall in each restroom. Be sure to check with your local agencies to find out the requirements.

The design of your restrooms should fall in line with your overall concept. In a fine-dining restaurant, your customers will expect no less from your bathroom facilities than they would other areas. Your selection of fixtures and decor does create an impression. Consider your concept, your clientele, and your budget. Bathroom fixtures come in a wide range of styles and prices. In a casual diner, an ordinary functional restroom will be sufficient, as long as it is well maintained. You do not have to spend a lot of money on fixtures to have a nicely designed restroom. There are ways you can spruce up your restrooms to make your guests feel more comfortable using them. Paint the walls with interesting colors, hang a framed poster or two that matches your overall decor, or place a bowl of dried-flower potpourri on a corner stand.

Regardless of how you choose to decorate them, you have to conduct regular maintenance on your restrooms to make sure that they are clean and in working order. Maintain a schedule, and assign an employee or two to check on them. Make sure that the facilities are functioning properly and that they have an adequate supply of toilet paper, soap, and paper towels. The trash bins should be emptied daily. For a fine-dining establishment, you may consider hiring an attendant to facilitate guests' needs, if the space allows. Use your discretion. Having an attendant in the restroom may seem appropriate in some places. In others, it might just be totally out of place.

The Waiting Area

Most casual and fine-dining restaurants have a waiting area for customers needing a table. This can be the bar or lounge area or a foyer in front of the host stand. Some restaurants offer very little space for a waiting area, mainly because their total space is limited and maximizing seating capacity is a priority. However, other restaurants devote generous space to the waiting area, especially if they have a bar or lounge area.

Creating Space to Wait

When deciding on your waiting area, you have to consider two things: where your customers are going to wait and what they will be doing while they're waiting. As with every aspect of your restaurant, think about your concept and your customers. Does your concept offer a hip, trendy atmosphere catering to young professionals going out for a night on the town? Then consider allocating enough space for a comfortable bar or lounge to serve as a waiting area. However, if your target customers are families or an older clientele, you might consider a smaller waiting area to create dining space for more tables. Parents dining with their children want to avoid a long wait, as do older clientele. Larger restaurants that try to appeal to a wider demographic often have both a sizeable bar and waiting area so customers can choose where they'd like to wait. Of course, smaller restaurants don't have the space to do that. That's why you need to configure your space to what works best for your concept and your customers.

Deciding on a Host Station

The host station is where the host greets the customers when they first arrive. Depending on the size of the restaurant, the host station may simply be a podium or a counter that is manned by two, or sometimes three, people. The host station may hold menus, a reservation book or computer, a telephone, and other items the host uses.

Some restaurants, such as family diners, have a cashier counter that serves as the host station as well. Some don't even have host stations, merely a sign that says "Please wait to be seated" so customers don't assume they seat themselves.

Having a host station visible lets your customers know that they should wait to be seated. If your concept necessitates a host station, be sure that it fits the ambiance. At a fine-dining restaurant, your customers will certainly expect to see a host behind a podium or counter to greet them when they enter the restaurant. However, in a small, casual bistro that seats fewer than thirty people, having a host station might seem a bit out of place and might even take away some of the restaurant's homey charm. Customers who walk in might just assume they have to wait to be seated, as long as they are greeted promptly.

The Exterior and Signage

The exterior is just as important a feature of your restaurant as your interior. The exterior of your restaurant can impress your customers even before they walk in the door. There is more to opening a restaurant for business than putting up any old sign and unlocking the door. Just as you spend time and energy on your interior, you should give some serious consideration to your exterior as well. Your exterior might even be part of your dining area, as with outdoor seating, including patio and sidewalk.

Blending In with the Surroundings

When designing your exterior, consider your surroundings. Many areas, especially historic neighborhoods, have zoning ordinances that stipulate what is an acceptable exterior for a business. Others may not have such restrictions, but you should still consider the neighborhood. A flashy, bright exterior may work very well in areas brimming with nightlife, but not in a quaint neighborhood of brick town houses. Of course, you want to draw attention to your restaurant, but be sure it's the right kind of attention.

Choosing the Appropriate Signage

Signage makes more of a public statement than just your existence. As with everything else, consider what signage will work best for your concept. Consider your location and your target customer. If you are located near shopping centers on a busy main road in the suburbs, consider putting a large, lighted sign high enough that your customers can see it from afar as they are driving. However, if you are located on a small street with plenty of foot traffic, a subtle sign at eye level might be more effective. Make your sign easily readable, and make certain your logo and lettering clearly state the name of your establishment.

The type of signage, of course, has to match your concept. A small, intimate bistro should not have a large, flashing neon sign, just as a large, casual restaurant wishing to draw crowds should not have a small unassuming sign. If your restaurant's atmosphere is festive, your signage should suggest it. If you are trying to create a subtle, elegant atmosphere, then your signage should have that same understated intonation.

Dining Outdoors

Dining outdoors, or alfresco, has become a popular draw for many diners. Many restaurants have designed their exteriors to provide outdoor seating in the form of patios, courtyards, and sidewalks. Some commercial spaces may already have a layout that can be easily converted to outdoor dining, while others may require significant remodeling. If you are planning to offer outdoor seating, consider how you will arrange it. Will it be on a patio, a courtyard, or sidewalk, or a combination? How open will the interior be to the outdoors? Many restaurants have folding French doors that can expose the dining interior to the street. Some restaurants have garage doors that serve the same function. If your restaurant's surroundings provide the right atmosphere, having outdoor seating would be definitely advantageous to your business.

CHAPTER 11

The Back of the House

The term "back of the house" refers to all the areas that are related to food production and storage. It also includes sanitation stations such as the dishwasher and mop sinks, locker rooms, administrative office, and other areas customers don't normally enter. Setting up the back of the house efficiently is more important than any other part of your restaurant. If it isn't running smoothly, your whole operation suffers.

Determine the Equipment You Need

Your menu will determine the kitchen equipment you'll need. If you're designing a kitchen from scratch, you'll have more flexibility than working with an existing one. To begin, you must go through your menu items one by one to determine what equipment you'll need to store and prepare each dish from start to finish. You'll also have to figure out the size of equipment needed to accommodate the desired output at a given time. It's not an exact science, but you'll need to have some idea of the volume you'll be anticipating.

Create a list of equipment you'll need by going through the preparation and storage of each menu item. Take a look at the following table for an example of how to list your equipment need based on your menu items and their methods of preparation.

▼ **LIST OF EQUIPMENT NEEDED**

Menu Item	Storage	Preparation Method	Equipment Required
Hamburger	Cooling	Grilled and garnished	Walk-in freezer, grill, sandwich prep cooler
French Fries	Freezing	Deep-fried	Freezer, gas, deep fryer
Garden Salad	Cooling	Tossed and chopped	Walk-in, sandwich prep cooler
Fried Chicken	Cooling	Deep-fried	Reach-in cooler, deep fryer
Broiled Haddock	Cooling	Broiled	Reach-in cooler, oven/broiler
Fettuccine Alfredo	Cooling	Boiled and sautéed	Cooler, multiburner range

Keep your list simple initially. List only the large equipment you'll need, like coolers, grills, and deep fryers, for the time being. Determining the larger items first will help you start designing a good kitchen layout. Once these items are in, they'll be difficult to move. Smaller items such as blenders, mixers, and even microwaves can be moved around to suit your needs, so decide where the large equipment goes before anything else.

There are numerous kinds of restaurant equipment available, too many to describe in this book. You can get a good idea of what's out there by looking through a restaurant equipment catalog. Simply do a search on the Internet for restaurant equipment suppliers and request that a catalog be sent to you.

Once you have your list, you'll have to determine the capacity of each piece of equipment and the quantities it has to put out in a given period. For example, if your menu is made up of 50 percent grilled items and 15 percent sautéed, and the rest of the items are either deep-fried or require no cooking, you might consider acquiring a medium or large grill, a six-burner range, and a small deep fryer. On the other hand, if your menu has a majority of sautéed items (cooking done on a range), you might go with two six-burners or one twelve-burner and a small grill. Of course, you'll have to take into account the size of your restaurant and your expected output at a given time. It is also important that your menu is composed of a good balance of different preparation methods so the various areas of the kitchen are equally busy.

FACT

"Cooler" is restaurant-speak for a refrigerator. A walk-in cooler is basically a refrigerated room. Reach-in coolers are upright commercial refrigerators of various sizes. Worktops are small reach-ins that have flat stainless-steel tops that you can use for counter space. Sandwich or salad prep coolers have flip-up hoods that allow easy access to condiments, fresh garnishes, and deli meats.

Leasing Equipment

Leasing some of your equipment can be a good way to free up some initial capital you would have used up front by purchasing. The decision to lease equipment depends on your business arrangements and the type of equipment you'll be leasing. Don't lease all of your equipment. As a restaurant operator, you have to assess your situation and take the most appropriate course of action. In some cases it may be better to lease, while in others it will clearly be better to buy. The decision can be made a little easier if you understand what's involved in leasing equipment.

The Advantages of Leasing Equipment

Aside from saving some money up-front, there are other advantages of leasing your equipment. Here are some of the pros:

- Lease payments are tax deductible as a business operating expense.
- You are not responsible for repair costs when the equipment breaks down.
- At the end of your lease, you can sign a new lease and switch to an updated model.
- You don't have to worry about selling off your equipment, which may not bring very much in return.
- Lease payments are fixed, so you'll know how much to account for in your operating expenses.

Remember that a lease for equipment is like any other contract. Verbal arrangements you made with a salesperson don't mean a whole lot if they're not in writing. Get all financial details in writing, and make sure you understand all the terms and conditions of the lease.

The Disadvantages of Leasing Equipment

As with virtually every financial decision you have to make, there are disadvantages to leasing equipment. Here are some of the cons:

- Leasing companies will require that you personally guarantee the lease. You are financially liable for the terms of the lease even if your restaurant closes down before the term ends.
- At the end of the lease, you might have paid as much as double what you would have paid had you bought the equipment.
- You don't get to write off the equipment as depreciation in your tax return.
- You need to prove you have adequate property insurance and list your leasing company as an insured.
- The leasing company may not pay for repairs and replacements if any damage to equipment is proven to be from negligence or ill-treatment.

The one glaring disadvantage in this list is the requirement of a personal guarantee. That means the leasing company will also be checking your personal credit history, like any financial creditor. Should your restaurant close, you still will be personally responsible for the terms of the lease. If you have some uncertainty, but would still like to lease some equipment, try a short-term lease, perhaps a three-year instead of a five-year term. You will most likely pay more per month, but you might get out with minimal losses if your restaurant closes its doors.

ESSENTIAL

There is some equipment you might be better off leasing than buying. Buying these pieces of equipment not only incurs a high up-front cost, but you run the risk of the equipment breaking down after the warranty expires. Dishwashers, coolers, ice machines, espresso machines, and freezers are all good items to lease.

Used Equipment

Buying used equipment can cost 40, 50, even 60 percent less than buying new equipment. If there's a little dent here and there, a knob missing, or maybe some scratches, so what? The thing you have to worry about is whether or not the equipment is reliable. Used equipment does not have the warranties and support that come with new equipment. When shopping around for used equipment, don't settle on the price listed. Always negotiate for a better deal. If the salesperson won't budge, go somewhere else. If you see two or three items you want, offer a package price. Most likely you won't be able to test the item right in the store, so get a written guarantee of some sort.

Coolers, freezers, dishwashers, and other heavily used motor-driven equipment may not be good items to purchase used. They generally don't last long and cost a lot to maintain without a warranty. Plus, you don't know how hard the equipment was worked. You are better off leasing new equipment than buying used.

There are, however, many pieces of used equipment that should work well, such as gas ranges, gas ovens and broilers, deep fryers, and wood or gas grills. As with all equipment, inspect the items carefully before purchasing. For ovens and deep fryers, be sure you get a written guarantee that the thermostats work and are calibrated to read the temperature correctly. For grills, make sure that the flame tubes aren't rusted away and burned out and that the grates are all in one piece.

Most major cities have a section of town that is concentrated with restaurant supply places. You'll likely find what you need there, new or used. If you're not in a major city, it might be worthwhile to travel to one. You will find a greater selection to choose from, and with all the nearby competition, you can probably negotiate some good deals. If you are purchasing large equipment, most suppliers can make shipping arrangements, depending on your location.

You can also look in the newspaper for restaurant auctions and in classified ads. Used equipment vendors usually advertise in the "Business Opportunities" section of the classifieds. Of course, you should also check the Internet to see if there are any vendors of used restaurant equipment in your area.

The Kitchen

Once you've decided on the kinds of major equipment you'll need, it's time to start thinking about the kitchen's design. The most important aspect of kitchen design is creating good flow. Your products should move in a steady direction from the point at which the order is received to its delivery to the customer as a finished product. Your kitchen can run much more smoothly and efficiently when you have good flow, and that keeps the business thriving.

Sizing Up Your Kitchen

The amount of space you need for your kitchen depends on three factors: the size of your equipment, the amount of work space needed to perform tasks, and the kinds of food you will be storing. There's no single formula that tells you what percentage of your total space your kitchen should occupy. Some restaurant experts believe that your kitchen should be no less than 30 percent of your total space, excluding storerooms, locker rooms, and other back of the house facilities. However, your menu ultimately dictates the needs of your kitchen and the amount of space required to accomplish the various tasks.

Typical Kitchen Stations Defined

An area of the kitchen that facilitates a particular cooking technique is known as a station. Usually, a station is designated by the main piece of equipment used for cooking, such as the fryer or the grill, and the supporting products and supplies that the cook uses to prepare a dish. For example, Chinese egg rolls and fried chicken may be prepared in the fryer station while hamburgers, grilled tuna steaks, and shish kebabs may be done at the grill station. The basic kitchen stations are the following:

- **Sauté:** The sauté station refers to anything that is cooked in a sauté or sauce pan using a multiburner range, from pan-searing to poaching. It is usually manned by highly skilled cooks because items cooked here require consistency and speed.
- **Grill:** There are two basic kinds of grills, the charbroiler and the griddle. The charbroiler has metal gratings over an open fire that make the grill marks on foods like steaks and burgers. The griddle, or a flat-top grill, has a flat, level surface that cooks more evenly, like a large frying pan.
- **Deep fryer:** Deep fryers cook by immersing food completely in a vat of heated oil. They are needed for foods like french fries and onion rings, and they are also good for supplying other stations with partially cooked products to speed up the cooking process.
- **Broiler:** Sometimes confused with grilling, in which heat comes from below, broiling is cooking by intense heat from above. Broiling is usually good for items that cook easily, such as fish and shrimp.
- **Oven:** Used for baked menu items like roasts and lasagnas, the oven also serves other roles, like warming precooked foods and holding hot foods. This station might also be responsible for finishing the sauté process for foods like rack of lamb or duck breast.
- **Cold station:** This is where all food that is served cold is assembled. This station may be a stainless-steel well filled with ice that holds containers (like a salad bar). Salads, cold-cured meats like ham and prosciutto, smoked salmon, and fresh fruits all can be found here.

There are also other stations you might find in some kitchens, such as pastry and dessert stations, which may use a convection oven, or holding stations that use steam tables to keep cooked food warm. You may or may not need all these stations. You might even need some kind of specialized equipment that isn't mentioned here. For example, a Chinese restaurant needs ranges with high heat output specially designed for use with woks. Determine your stations based on your menu.

Laying It on the Line

The line encompasses all the kitchen stations. The people who work on the line are known as line cooks. Each line cook may have a specialized job, whether it's working the grill, the fryer, or the broiler, but if you have a small staff, your line cooks may work in a variety of stations. You need to lay out the individual stations properly so that the line flows efficiently with no one bumping into each other or crisscrossing paths. Furthermore, servers, prep cooks, and dishwashers must also be able to move through the kitchen without getting in the way of the line. Consider some of these ideas to help you design a good kitchen layout:

- Put the busiest station nearest to the point where food is picked up and the least busy off to the side.
- If your staff is going to juggle a couple of stations, put the stations that require less food handling together (for example, the fryer and the grill, broiler and the oven).
- Put enough reach-in coolers close to specific stations to keep refrigerated items at arm's reach when an order comes in.
- Locate the dishwasher and trash can at the entrance of the kitchen so servers can drop off dirty dishes before coming near the line.
- Pastry and dessert stations should have their own reach-in coolers.

- The stations should be configured so that the preparation of menu items can move in one direction, from the time the order is in, to the garnishing, to the point of customer delivery.
- Food pickup for delivery to customers should always be done on the opposite side of the stations, facing the equipment, never in the path of the line.

The Prep Area

"Prep" is short for preparation. The shortening of the word is actually quite appropriate considering what prepping does—it shortens the time that it takes to prepare and plate a dish when the order comes in. It means getting the ingredients ready for cooking so that the finished product can be served efficiently. Some examples of prep work include peeling and cubing raw potatoes for home fries, trimming fat off a roast, or scraping the dirt off mushrooms (yes, you scrape the dirt off with a knife, instead of washing them).

The prep area should be located near refrigerators or walk-in coolers but close to the line (the main kitchen stations) so long as it doesn't disrupt the flow. Even though most prep work is done during off-peak hours, such as in the hours before the noon lunch rush, very often the food supply for the stations needs to be replenished. The prep cooks must be able to move around the prep area without hindering the other stations, the dishwasher, or servers.

Prep work needs to be done comfortably, efficiently, and safely. To accomplish that, you need the proper equipment:

- **Walk-in/reach-in coolers and freezers:** Your coolers need to be close to the prep area. Prep cooks need to move items in and out efficiently without dodging other workers.
- **Work tables:** Depending on your volume of business, you will need several well-placed stainless-steel work tables for accomplishing various tasks.
- **Large-bowl sinks:** Have a two- or three-bowl sink for washing vegetables, thawing meats and seafood, and draining noncoagulating liquids.

- **Rolling trash cans:** Prep work results in trash. Make sure there's enough room around the work tables for a few rolling trash cans.
- **Proper prepping tools:** Mixers, food processors, meat slicers, knives in racks, and cutting boards—all the things your prep cooks need to do their work should be within reach.

Refrigeration Requirements

Proper refrigeration is essential to the quality and safety of your food supply and products. Your menu and the amount of fresh ingredients you will store at a time will determine the amount of refrigeration you need. Most health agencies have some kind of refrigeration requirement, based on the type of food you serve and the seating capacity of your restaurant. Very often, however, you need more than what the agencies require or recommend.

Coolers

Anything that's perishable should go into the cooler, including raw meats, vegetables, fish, prepared foods, and dairy products. Your coolers should be appropriate for commercial use and bear the NSF (National Sanitation Foundation) approval seals. Most restaurants that do a moderate volume of business have a combination of walk-in and reach-in coolers. If you're dealing with a lot of prepackaged and canned goods, then you probably don't need more than a walk-in or two double-door reach-ins. However, if you plan to store many perishables, you'll need at least one good size walk-in and a couple of reach-ins or worktops. Just be sure you rotate your stock, meaning that you put the most recently delivered products to the back of the refrigerator so you use up the earlier items first. If you're going to have daily deliveries of fresh ingredients, then you're probably okay with a small walk-in or a couple of large reach-ins. The bottom line is that you must analyze your needs and acquire the equipment accordingly. Sure, too much might be better than not enough, but refrigeration costs a lot of money to acquire and maintain, and it takes up space. So do your homework and invest wisely.

Freezers

Freezers, like coolers, vary in sizes and styles. Many restaurants have walk-in freezers as well as walk-in coolers. You may not have the space to accommodate a walk-in freezer. Sometimes one or two upright or chest freezers are sufficient. You can be a bit more economical with space in a freezer than you can in a cooler. You can stack certain items in freezers, like meats and seafood, without worrying about smashing them. Large chest freezers are good for storing large bulky items like turkeys and sides of beef. Upright reach-in freezers are great to keep prepackaged frozen vegetables and seafood organized and stacked neatly on the shelves. You might also consider a small chest freezer to keep frozen desserts, like ice cream and prepackaged cheesecakes, and backup bags of ice for beverage service.

Ice Machines

Some restaurants install ice machines in the front of the house near the bar or wait stations. Others keep them in the back of the house. If you are going to have your ice machine in the back of the house, be sure that your bartenders and servers have a clear path so they can refill the ice bins when necessary. Ice machines come in a wide range of production capabilities, from eighty pounds of ice a day to more than a thousand. Smaller under-the-counter versions usually come with built-in storage bins, but larger ice machines have separate storage bins and machines so you can mix and match according to your needs

The Dry Storage Area

Dry storage is the place where you store, well, your dry goods. You can store all your canned items, dried foods, and other nonperishables in this area. Other supplies such as paper products, takeout containers, and canned and bottled beverages can be stored here as well.

Devote adequate space for your dry goods, but organize your storage area to be efficient and easily manageable for doing inventory. One approach is to imagine the room set up like a small grocery store. Consider the following tips for organizing your dry storage area:

- Locate your dry storage area as close to the delivery door as possible. It cuts down on the traffic in the kitchen and saves a lot of energy moving and unloading supplies.
- Set up adequate shelving in the storage area. Make sure the shelves are strong enough to hold heavy items like large cans and bottles.
- Lighter items should go on the higher shelves; large cans and jars should go at about chest level; and heavy bins and sacks like sugar and flour should be laid standing up on the shelves near the floor.
- Group items together so they are easy to find. For example, grain products like rice, flour, and pasta might be grouped near each other, and so could mustard, ketchup, and relishes.
- Store expensive nonperishables like gourmet olive oils, spices, and dried exotic mushrooms in locked security units or cages.
- Never allow your employees to change clothes in the storage area. Also, do not allow them to keep their personal belongings there, especially knapsacks and duffel bags.

What If You Already Have a Kitchen?

You may have found a space in a good location already equipped with a kitchen. In that case, you get to avoid a lot of the start-up cost associated with building a new kitchen. However, plans to modify or reconfigure the space can be even costlier than building from scratch. Whether you're purchasing the restaurant from someone else and taking over the lease or leasing the space directly with the equipment included, give the place a thorough inspection before signing any agreement. Make sure that the equipment is in good working order and that the price is right. Don't pay a lot of money for used equipment simply because it's already there.

Inspecting the Kitchen

Approach purchasing an existing kitchen the same way you would a used car. Obviously, it is not going to be in pristine condition, but you must be able to work with the equipment. Don't turn away simply because the kitchen floor is dirty or the equipment is grimy. The kitchen can be cleaned up. Instead, look at the plumbing and electrical fixtures and other equipment that can't be moved easily, like ranges and walk-in coolers. Consider hiring a contractor to inspect the plumbing, the electrical, and HVAC (heating, ventilation, air-conditioning) systems to make sure that they are working and up to building-code standards.

Dealing with the Existing Layout

You will have to deal with structural issues when you take over an existing kitchen. You'll need to be creative and resourceful to work around obstacles large and small along the way. Equipment such as reach-in coolers and freezers can probably be moved around, but walk-in coolers are best left where they are. Cooking equipment like ranges, grills, and fryers can also be moved along the gas line, but it would be difficult and costly to move the gas line to another area of the kitchen. If the existing layout has good flow, you can probably move a few pieces of equipment here and there to accommodate your concept. However, if you want to make major changes to the structure, consult a professional. Making changes to the structure may not be as easy as it seems at first glance.

ESSENTIAL

Stay flexible, and don't hold too firmly to your ideas and designs. Most of the time, structural features such as load-bearing walls and columns are too costly to remove or reconfigure, so you must accept these features as they are. With a little creativity, you might even be able to incorporate these architectural elements into your concept.

Fitting the Kitchen for Your Concept

Sometimes your concept calls for changes to be made in the kitchen. For example, if you're going to open a Chinese restaurant, your kitchen must accommodate a range designed specifically for woks. That might mean removing some other piece of equipment or modifying the gas line. The same goes for any concept that calls for specialty equipment.

Your existing space must be able to accommodate features that are necessary for your concept. If it can't, you have to rework your concept. If you want to stick with your concept as is, then you should find another location.

But before you make that decision, consider other issues at hand: the location, the occupancy costs, and the space itself. You might have done a lot of work preparing your business plan around your concept, but you should ask yourself whether you are passing up a good opportunity. Good concepts can be retooled many ways to suit a space and still be successful, but it's not so easy to find an affordable space in a good location.

CHAPTER 12

Buying and Managing Supplies

In the restaurant business, you are a buyer as well as a seller. Making the right purchasing decisions and managing your supplies effectively will ultimately save you a lot of money, which in turn means higher profits and more cash in your pocket. You must know the types of supplies that work best for your concept; research your suppliers to get the best prices and terms of service; and create effective inventory control to avoid theft and waste.

Create Your List of Supplies

The types of supplies you purchase will depend on several factors, including your concept, your menu, the kitchen staff, and the time it takes to prepare menu items. First, you will need to draw up a list of your supplies. Initially, this list will not be very specific. You might not care about the brand of sugar or flour you buy, but there might be products that you need to research for quality and suitability, like extra-virgin olive oil or soy sauce. You'll also need to decide on the convenience factor when it comes to your supplies. For example, will you be making soup from scratch, or will you be heating up frozen prepackaged soup?

Categorizing Your List

After you generate a list of supplies based on your menu, categorize them according to certain food groups, such as meats, seafood, baked goods, dairy, and so on. Take a look at the following table for a sample supplies list.

▼ **SAMPLE SUPPLY LIST**

Item	Category	Unit
Chicken Breast, Boneless and Skinless	Meat	Case, 40 lbs.
Leg of Lamb, Boneless and Tied	Meat	Case, 20 lbs.
French Feta Cheese	Dairy	Tub, 10 lbs.
Iceberg Lettuce, Wrapped in Plastic	Produce	Case, 20 heads
Carrots, Whole	Produce	Bag, 25 lbs.
French Fries, Frozen, Shoestring Cut	Frozen foods	Case, 50 lbs.
Tiger Shrimp, 21–25 Count	Seafood	Case, 40 lbs.
Beef Tenderloin, Prime, Block Ready	Meat	Whole, 10-13 lbs.
Bread, French Baguette	Baked goods	Bag, 12 loaves

Your list may not be as specific as the one above until you've met with potential suppliers. After you meet with them, you'll have a better idea about the unit quantities and forms your supplies are sold in to create your final list. Use a spreadsheet on your computer to easily arrange an organized list that can be grouped and sorted by category.

ESSENTIAL

Because food is what you're mostly going to buy, this chapter focuses mainly on how to make good food purchases. The same purchasing principles can also be applied to other supplies, such as beverages, paper products, linens, glasses, silverware, and everything else.

The Convenience Factor

When going through your list of supplies, consider the time and money you want to allot for prep work. For example, say that whole bone-in, skin-on chicken breasts cost $24 per 40 pound case (or $0.60 per pound), and boneless, skinless chicken breasts cost $64 per case ($1.60 per pound). It might take a prep cook a couple of hours, at $9 an hour, to skin and bone 40 pounds of chicken breast. The total cost (labor and supply) of those breasts would rise from $24 to $42, still less than the $64 you'd pay for the boneless breasts. Sounds like a no-brainer, right? It would be, except that the $42 includes the waste skin and bone, leaving you with only about 25 pounds of breast meat. Now the actual cost of labor and supply involved in getting the same 40 pounds of skinless, boneless breast meat is more like $60. The cost is now just slightly lower. And consider this: Wouldn't you rather pay the extra $4 (or $0.10 a pound) to have this relatively menial task already done, especially when it makes little difference to food quality? Instead, you could have your prep cook use that time to do something requiring more care. Time that would have been spent skinning and boning chicken breasts could be used on prepping your famous homemade barbecue sauce.

Another factor to consider when thinking about supplies is convenience foods. These are prepackaged, commercially prepared foods that come in a variety of ways—already cut, cooked, portioned, washed, or frozen, fresh, or canned—and they cut down on prep time. Convenience foods tend to cost a bit more than made-from-scratch ingredients but can make good economic sense, especially if you don't have the staff to prep items from scratch.

Research the Purveyors

Purveyors are what restaurateurs call suppliers. Ideally, purveyors will be willing to work with you to win your business. Instead of settling on the first purveyor you talk to, scope out different purveyors and choose the one who can best meet your needs and advise you on your purchases. Purveyors are trying to make a sale, but they also want to keep your business, so they will work to give you fair prices and see that you are stocked properly. Most purveyors specialize in a certain kind of product. Here is how some purveyors are classified:

- Meat and poultry
- Fruits and vegetables
- Fish and seafood
- Dairy products
- Bakery items
- Convenience foods (canned goods, frozen foods, packaged products)
- Ethnic products

QUESTION

How do you find potential purveyors?
You can get names of potential purveyors from the yellow pages, an Internet search, or food-service industry trade shows. But the best way to get names is to find out who supplies other restaurants, particularly those using items you need for your menu. You can do this the hard way by spying out supply trucks on delivery days, or you can do it the easy way, by simply asking the manager or owner.

Many purveyors sell more than the products they specialize in. For example, a seafood distributor may also sell frozen vegetables, and a meat and poultry company may stock some frozen seafood. If you're looking for specialty items, such as fish, however, you should definitely buy from a specialty purveyor.

Contact at least three purveyors for every product category you need. Set up a meeting with a sales rep or the owner/manager, and have them come to your restaurant so they can see your operation. Give them a categorized list of your entire supply needs. Remember, purveyors are in the business to sell, so they may try to entice you with volume discounts, but beware—the quantity may be too much for your operation. If you clearly communicate to them the kind of relationship you would like to establish, and if they want your business, they'll work with you to help you meet your goals.

Compare Services and Negotiate Better Pricing

Once you've met with your purveyors and let them know what you need, give them a chance to respond with their price quotes and terms of service. Be sure they know you are considering other purveyors as well. When reviewing purveyors' bids, consider factors other than prices, such as payment terms, delivery schedule, minimum order requirements, and anything else you requested.

Many restaurants make contractual agreements with their purveyors in order to receive consistent quality and the best possible pricing. In exchange for these terms, the restaurants agree to purchase selected items from an individual purveyor on a relatively consistent basis for a contracted time period. This may or may not be a viable choice for you. Larger operations with a greater supply volume benefit from entering into a contract with a purveyor because they get competitive prices and more consistent product quality and services. However, high delivery costs and stringent minimum order requirements make this strategy a poor choice for smaller operations.

ESSENTIAL

Be sure that you have adequate storage space if you make volume purchases. A crowded storage area can lead to disorganization, and it makes maintaining an efficient inventory system difficult. Your employees will be less efficient if they have to waste time searching a cluttered storage room.

Purveyors are often willing to drop prices on items you purchase in large quantities. For example, say a case of tomato sauce cost $10. You may be able to get your purveyor to drop the price to $7 a case if you buy five or more cases. Tomato sauce has a long shelf life, and it's a fairly versatile ingredient, so you should be able to use it all over time. However, avoid buying large quantities of fresh ingredients with a short shelf life, such as avocados or lettuce, simply to get the lower price per case.

It is important that you keep some sort of written record of supplies ordered from your purveyors. When you place a call to your purveyor, your order goes through several channels, from the sales rep to the warehouse, to the delivery person, and finally to the restaurant. If you do a lot of ordering, you will inevitably end up getting the wrong item sometimes. A written purchase order allows the receiver to compare the items ordered to the items shipped.

Inspect Products When They Arrive

Before signing for any order, not only should you make sure that the purveyor got the order right, but you or your chef should also make sure that the quality of the goods is acceptable upon arrival. If the quality is not acceptable, either reject the items delivered or negotiate for credit or reduced price.

You should be ready to refuse products that don't measure up to your standards, especially if the products have a direct effect on the quality of your food. If your 20 pounds of frozen cod fillets arrive already thawed, you can't accept the shipment without causing a food-safety issue. Reject the shipment, and call your sales rep or his manager to rectify the situation immediately. If the sales rep wants to keep your business, he should resolve the matter for you, even if it means delivering the frozen cod fillets himself.

While it is sometimes necessary to reject an entire order, you might be able to accept certain products that fall short in quantity or quality. Most likely, these items will not have a direct effect on the quality of your food and will present, at most, an inconvenience to you. If two bottles were broken out of a sixteen-bottle case of ketchup, the other bottles will be covered in ketchup. Because it will be difficult for the purveyor to sell that case to anyone else, you might get it for half price.

Establish Efficient Inventory Control

Your inventory represents the amount of supplies you have at any point in time. These are the materials that you've invested in to create your product in order to sell it for a profit. Food and beverages obviously constitute a part of your inventory, but so do consumables like paper towels and napkins, bathroom tissue, placemats, and takeout containers. You may not be selling these products directly, but these items do figure into the cost of serving your customers. In order for you to establish efficient inventory control, you must first stock a manageable supply based on your needs and make a habit of routinely tracking your inventory.

Avoiding Excess Inventory

You need to have adequate supplies on hand with some extra for emergency backup. However, you should avoid tying up cash on excess inventory that may not generate a return for a long time. Say you have one dish on your menu that requires rice, and your sales rep tells you that he'll give you a 10 percent discount on instant rice if you purchase fifty 25-pound sacks at $20 per sack. Sure, you're saving $100, but you've also spent $900 for an inexpensive item with only one use! Furthermore, you'll be stuck for a long time with stock that takes a lot of your storage area. Don't buy in volume simply for the reduced price. Plan your inventory adequately to meet your needs.

Keeping Adequate Supply on Hand

Knowing how much of what to stock seems a little complicated when you're planning your initial inventory. But you can build something to work with by looking at your menu, ingredients, and the projected sales of an item. As you begin to develop a sales history of a menu item, you can adjust your inventory accordingly. Most restaurants keep track of supplies using some kind of system. Before or after a shift, the manager assesses supply levels and determines what needs to be purchased, prepped, or supplied. This assessment is based on established par levels, or the amount of an item that will carry you over until the next preparation or stock period. For example, a delicatessen near office buildings might set the par levels for macaroni salad at 15 pounds for busy lunches Monday to Thursday, while the par levels Friday to Sunday are only 5 pounds because the lunch business is so much lighter.

ESSENTIAL

You don't need to count and establish par levels for nonperishable items that you purchase in bulk, such as sugar and flour. Items such as these are economical, so it's not worth the time to count or weigh the item to see how much was used. Because the supply will last for a while, you don't need to worry about when it's time to order more until you're nearly out.

Your staff should keep some kind of written food count, of food items used during a particular shift, so the next shift knows how much of each item is available and how much needs to be prepped. Par levels apply to kitchen staff, waiters, and bartenders, who should also pay attention to the levels for items such as napkins, fruit garnishes for beverages, glasses, and silverware. The following table shows an example of daily food count.

▼ **DAILY FOOD COUNT AND PAR LEVELS**

Product	Amount Available	Par Levels	Amount Needed	Shelf Life
Burgers	50 patties (8 oz.)	70 patties	20 patties	3 days
French Fries	10 lbs.	10 lbs.	0	frozen
Chicken Wings	10 lbs.	15 lbs.	5 lbs.	4 days
Turkey Breast (sliced)	7 lbs.	10 lbs.	3 lbs.	3 days
Clam Chowder	2 quarts	2 gallons	1.5 gallons	4 days
Cole Slaw	1 gallon	2 gallons	1 gallon	5 days
Swiss Cheese (sliced)	2 lbs.	5 lbs.	3 lbs.	5 days

Doing Monthly Inventory

Taking monthly inventory will help you keep track of your stock and help your accountant see that your assets (your inventory) balance out your liabilities (bills outstanding or paid out). Make this task a monthly routine. You'll find that maintaining control of your inventory is worth the effort in the message it sends to your staff, that you are keeping a close eye on things.

Even though the actual task seems a bit tedious, the procedure is actually quite simple. Sometimes all you have to do is make a good estimate.

When possible, count the number of each item you have in stock and multiply that number by the item's price. Add up the values, and there you have it. Using spreadsheet software makes this process a little easier to manage. The following table shows a sample monthly meat inventory.

▼ **SAMPLE MONTHLY INVENTORY OF MEAT**

Product	Unit Size	Unit Price	Total Units	Total Value
Ground Beef	case 40 lbs.	$80.00	0.50 case	$40.00
Pork Butt	case, 40 lbs.	$1.25	10 lbs.	$12.50
Beef Tenderloin	10 lbs.	$8.00	0.5 lbs.	$40.00
Leg of Lamb	whole leg	$2.50/lb.	5 lbs.	$12.50
Flank Steak	case 40 lbs.	$60.00	0.25 case	$15.00
Total cost:				$130.00

Control Losses with Proper Handling and Storage

Losses due to breakage, unnecessary waste, and spoilage can put a real dent in your cash flow. Improper handling and improper storage are the root causes for this type of loss. Of course, accidents do happen, and sometimes waste and spoilage are beyond anyone's control. Power outages can wreak havoc on your fresh food supply. Hot weather will make your cooler work harder, and your food might end up with a short shelf life. Yet when breakage is occurring frequently, and you keep reordering glasses and silverware, or food gets thrown away often, you have a problem. In order to minimize the losses, you need to take the proper steps.

Breaking the Habit of Breakage

Although you can't totally prevent breakage, you can minimize its risk. Breakage of "hard" supplies (such as glasses, bowls, and plates) is often the result of a disorganized and inefficient set-up. If your restaurant has easy flow of traffic in both front and back of the house, you have a good start. Here are some steps you can take:

- Stack clean plates neatly on shelves within arm's reach. Depending on the size and shape, dishes should be no higher than one foot per stack on an overhead shelf.
- Your dirty dish area should be organized. More fragile items such as glasses, ceramic teapots, and cups should be separated from dinner platters, pasta bowls, and other heavy items.
- Make sure that dishes and glassware are being washed in their appropriate racks in the dishwasher.
- Provide adequate work space so that dishes and other breakables don't get knocked off accidentally.
- Install a magnetic flatware retriever on the trash can where employees scrape dirty dishes to prevent silverware from ending up in the trash.
- Place rubber mats in dish and storage areas that hold breakable items. This will reduce the chance of an item breaking when something does fall to the ground.
- Purchase sturdier dishes and glassware.

Cutting Down on Waste

When you are running a high volume, fast-paced business like a restaurant, your assets won't always be used as efficiently as possible. Waste can occur in virtually all areas of the business—supplies, labor, utilities—you name it. Here are some ways your supplies can be wasted:

- **Inefficient use of supply:** If your pastry chef puts more flour on the floor than in his cake, it's waste, but it might not seem like a big deal. However, if a prep cook tosses out a $10 bottle of olive oil when it is still a quarter full, that's a significant loss.
- **Underutilized products:** Say you have a 40-pound case of bananas for making bananas Foster, but you only need 20 pounds. Unless you find something else to do with the remaining bananas, they'll go rotten.
- **Over-portioning:** If you set one serving of filet mignon at 6 ounces, but your prep chef portions out 8 ounces, he's giving away a free dinner for every three you sell!

Training and managing your staff to be aware is the best way to reduce waste. You must be organized and communicate to your staff about proper handling of supplies. More importantly, you have to practice what you preach.

Preventing Spoilage

Spoilage of perishable items is preventable if you're organized and you plan your purchases well. To start, buy only the amount of fresh items you need, and use them before they spoil. Prepare your items according to the par levels you've set, and check the items during every shift. When you replenish your items, rotate your stock to use up the old items before starting on new ones. You should have the proper equipment to store and preserve the shelf life of foods. You should also check the thermometers in your coolers to make sure that they are between 34° and 38° Fahrenheit (F).

Be thorough with the handling of food by making sure items are labeled, dated, and held at the right temperature. Train and encourage your employees to practice safe food-handling procedures.

Protect Your Supplies from Theft

It's not pleasant to think about, but theft in the restaurant business is quite common—from skimming off supplies, to shorting the register, to giving away items for better tips. But it's not just employees you have to worry about. Customers, delivery personnel, and anyone else coming in contact with the restaurant are potential culprits. While you won't be able to eliminate theft altogether, you can take steps to deter it or limit theft to items with little significance. Here are a few tips:

- Lock up valuable items, not just your cash registers, office equipment, and safes, but any expensive items you may hold, including seafood, meats, wine, and liquor.
- Do not allow employees to change clothing or place personal belongings in storage areas.

- Limit keys to a few trusted personnel to lessen the chances of theft. It will also encourage the "key" employees to be more vigilant against theft because they do not want to be held accountable.
- Install a security system, including security cameras, alarms, and emergency response communication.
- Check references of potential employees. Even if they received good references from former employers, it doesn't mean they've never stolen—just that they've never been caught.
- Be present, and be fair. Theft often occurs because employees feel they've been treated unfairly. Establish good relationships with your staff, and compensate them fairly for the job they're doing.

CHAPTER 13

Promoting a Safe and Eco-Friendly Restaurant

As a restaurant owner, you are ultimately responsible for maintaining safety for everyone on the premises. Implementing proper safety measures is no easy task. It requires consistency, organization, and constant attention. Proper safety means knowing your local agencies' rules and procedures and training your staff to adhere to them. Safety measures not only protect the people in the restaurant, they also protect you from fines, lawsuits, and even criminal charges.

Food-Safety Concerns

You've probably heard news stories about foodborne illnesses acquired from restaurants. E. coli bacteria, salmonella, and hepatitis are a few pathogens that have made headlines and caused the public to be uneasy about eating out. But many cases of foodborne illnesses go unreported each year because people do not seek medical attention. Foodborne illness is preventable, but it takes more than just keeping your restaurant clean and organized. You must also know the cause of food contamination and what measures you must take to prevent it.

Your local health agency has specific health codes that apply to the type of establishment you run. Know these codes. Make sure that your staff is trained to follow these codes and to handle and store food safely. A few times a year, you can expect health inspectors to drop in unannounced to check out your operation, and if a customer files a complaint against you, it is certain they will pay you a visit.

ALERT

Take health department guidelines seriously. Not only do you want to avoid the fines that come with health code violations, but a clean, safe environment benefits your customers and your business. Your customers put their trust in you and your staff, so it is your responsibility to take the necessary precautions to protect the food you serve.

Many local health departments require some or all employees to be licensed in food protection or food handling. If you're going to be involved in the daily running of your restaurant, you should be one of the licensed staff. You'll probably need to attend a short course on food microbiology and proper food-handling techniques and pass a test in order to receive a license. Your manager, chef, and anyone else who supervises food preparation and handling should have a license. Food-protection licensing programs are usually available through your local health department. Many states and cities accept certificates such as those from programs sponsored by the National Restaurant Association, but you should check with your local department to make sure.

The Causes of Foodborne Illness

The cause of most foodborne illnesses can be traced to one source: bacteria. Not all bacteria cause disease, but those that do are known as pathogens. The symptoms of the illnesses caused by pathogens usually include fever, nausea, headache, vomiting, abdominal cramps, and diarrhea. What people may often refer to as a stomach flu or virus may actually be a foodborne illness, and most people do not seek medical attention. However, some forms of bacteria, such as E. coli, can be life threatening if symptoms are left untreated.

FACT

Refrigeration does not kill bacteria, it just slows their growth. Freezing stops their growth but does not kill them. Once the food is thawed, the bacteria will continue to grow. Thaw perishable items in the refrigerator or under running cold water in the proper sink. Never thaw at room temperature.

Bacteria may already be present in your food supply by the time you get it. They may be present in raw meat and are almost always in poultry, but they can also be found in produce such as lettuce, potatoes, and melons. While the foods that arrive at your restaurant may not contain enough bacteria to cause illness, if not properly handled and stored, the foods may become contaminated. Cooking certain foods such as meat and poultry to the proper temperature will kill most bacteria, but cooking does not destroy the disease-causing toxins that some bacteria produce.

Bacteria also get into food by cross-contamination. Safely cooked food can become cross-contaminated if it touches surfaces that have been touched by raw, contaminated food, such as poultry. Always guard against cooked food coming into contact with raw meats and poultry.

Cooking, for the most part, does destroy most bacteria. However, some bacteria may survive, and they will multiply quickly if the cooked food is not held at a safe temperature. Furthermore, given the right conditions, some pathogens can produce spores and toxins that cannot be destroyed even with cooking. It is important to handle and store your food properly to control bacteria growth.

Practice Proper Food Handling and Storage

Proper food handling and storage maintains food safety. This practice applies to everyone working at your restaurant, from the chef and manager down to the dishwashers and busboys. Your staff must practice proper hygiene and food handling to avoid cross-contamination. They must also understand the critical elements of time and temperature when preparing and keeping foods. Ultimately, you and your managers are responsible for implementing and monitoring these practices.

FACT

Hazard Analysis and Critical Control Point, or HACCP (pronounced "hassip"), is a food-safety program originally developed for astronauts. It is now designed to help many food-related industries develop systems to identify, monitor, prevent, and remove potential hazards in their operation. This system was adopted by the Food and Drug Administration (FDA) and still presents the model of food safety for most local health departments.

Crossing Out Cross-Contamination

Cross-contamination is a common food-safety problem because it can happen in so many ways: employees handling cooked food after touching raw meat without washing their hands, raw meat juices dripping on ready-to-eat items, waiters touching food after handling dirty rags, and so on. Regardless of how many ways cross-contamination can occur, the problem can always be traced to a common cause: improper handling and storage. Here are some steps you can take to prevent cross-contamination:

- Inspect your product purchases to ensure quality and freshness with no signs of spoilage or pests.
- Always store raw products below 40°F in ice or in coolers until ready to use.
- Store raw meat and poultry in a separate cooler from fresh produce and fruits.

- Separate meats in reach-in coolers according to proper cooking temperature, with poultry on the bottom, pork on the next shelf up, then beef, then fish and seafood on top.
- Provide sufficient work space for your employees so that foods do not cross paths.
- Use different colored NSF-approved cutting boards for raw meats, prepared foods, and foods served raw, like lettuce and fruits.
- Wash and sanitize equipment such as meat slicers and grinders, knives, and cutting boards after every use.
- Keep towels soaked in buckets of water with the right amount of sanitizing solution for wiping down countertops.

Check with your local health department for detailed information on proper food handling and storage. Many health departments hold certification classes on food safety for people in the industry. You should require that some or all of your kitchen staff be certified. There may be a nominal fee for taking the course, which you should consider paying.

Cooking, Holding, and Cooling Foods Properly

One of the most critical aspects of food safety involves the cooking, holding, and cooling of foods. Raw meats and seafood vary in cooking temperatures; cooked foods must hold at a proper temperature and cool to a safe temperature within a certain time period. Below are some essential tips on handling cooking time and temperature:

- Cook raw meat and seafood to proper temperature as required. For example, poultry must be cooked to an internal temperature of 160°F, pork to 155°F.
- If you want to precook foods such as soups, stews, meat sauces, and roast, to be chilled for later use, you must cool them from 140°F to 70°F in two hours, then refrigerate to 40°F in another two hours.
- Check the temperature every hour with a sanitized thermometer after the cooked food reaches 140°F. Be sure to check the surface, where it can cool to 140°F more quickly, not just the interior.
- Stir or turn food for more even cooling.

- Reheat cold premade foods to 165°F and hold in a heating element at 140°F.

One note about reheating cooked foods—the more you reheat food, the more likely it is that bacteria will develop heat resistant spores and contaminate your food. Reheat only the amount you think you need for a given period. You can always reheat more if needed.

ESSENTIAL

There are several ways to cool your foods down quickly. Transfer the items into smaller stainless-steel containers or a long shallow rectangular pan no higher than 3 inches. Avoid using plastic or foam containers that insulate heat. You can also use NSF-approved ice wands or ice baths to accelerate the cooling process.

Instilling Proper Hygiene

It is essential that you demand good hygiene from your employees as part of their work habits. Along with bathing and proper grooming, you should also have your staff do the following:

- Practice proper hand washing procedures after using the restroom and doing other activities that may increase risk of transferring bacteria to food.
- Tie long hair back to avoid getting into food and groom hair only in locker rooms and restrooms.
- Wear hats if doing prep or line work in the back of the house. Handle food with latex gloves whenever possible.
- Waiters and bussers should touch only dishware and glassware with hands (not food or drinks).
- Inform the manager of any flu-like symptoms, including diarrhea, nausea, and fever, and be sent home immediately.

It is especially essential that your staff practice proper hand washing using hot water, antibacterial hand soap, and an approved drying device.

Your local health department should provide guidelines illustrating proper hand washing techniques.

Encourage Good Cleaning Procedures

A clean restaurant helps your image and business, and it also helps control problems such as pests, safety hazards, and wear and tear on equipment. Maintaining a high standard in cleaning should be just as important as your standard in food quality and preparation. Your staff must uphold the standard and practice proper cleaning procedures, but the responsibility for scheduling the tasks and implementing the procedures falls to you or your managers. It is up to the managers to monitor cleaning duties to make sure they are done correctly.

Cleaning Duties for Kitchen Staff

Cleaning should be as routine as food preparation. Based on your type of operation, you should first determine what needs to be cleaned and how often. For example, if you prepare mostly fried foods, you probably need to clean your fryer and change the oil two or three times a week. Divide the cleaning duties by specific job titles so that grill cooks are responsible for cleaning the grill, fry cooks the deep fryer, and so on. Most restaurants divide cleaning duties into schedules by shift, as well as on a weekly, monthly, semiannual, and annual basis. Here is how you may set your cleaning schedule, along with some examples of chores:

- **Duties performed as needed during shift:** Clean cutting boards, clean and sanitize meat slicer and grinders after use, sweep the prep areas, empty trash, change sanitizing buckets.
- **Duties performed before shift ends:** Sweep kitchen floors, clean and filter oil in the fryer, brush off grill, clean all prep tables and surfaces with sanitizer, wipe down equipment on the line, replace old rags with new in sanitizing buckets.
- **Duties performed before restaurant closes:** Wash floor mats, clean off the range, sweep and mop kitchen floors, drain and clean the dish

machine, clear out grease traps, clean out residue pans in ranges and grills.

- **Duties performed once a week:** Sweep and clean underneath range, grill, and other cooking equipment on the line, clean ovens and broilers according to manufacturers' instructions, empty reach-in coolers, clean walls and shelves.
- **Duties performed monthly:** Defrost, if necessary, and clean freezers, change air filter in furnace, empty and sanitize ice machine, clean dirt off cooler fans, wipe down shelves in storage area, prepare surfaces for exterminator's visit.
- **Duties performed annually or semiannually:** Call for maintenance on refrigeration equipment and dish machines, deep clean the exhaust fan and hood, deep clean dining room carpet, replace older and worn plumbing fixtures.

Keep in mind that duties performed weekly and monthly require more time and effort, so schedule and rotate these duties during slower days, not Fridays or Saturdays. Prepare a checklist of duties so your staff can check off and date when a particular cleaning job is done, and that way no job will get repeated unless it is necessary.

ESSENTIAL

It is important that you have an employee handbook or operating manual that includes a detailed cleaning schedule. The cleaning schedule should clearly state what needs cleaning, who should clean, how to clean, and how often. List every piece of equipment and area of the restaurant and give specific instructions.

Cleaning Duties for Waitstaff, Bussers, Bartenders

Just as the kitchen staff has duties maintaining the cleanliness of the kitchen, so too the employees who work the front of the house have their own tasks. Although the cleaning chores may not be as rigorous as the ones in the kitchen, they are no less important. As with the kitchen, you should determine what needs cleaning and how to divide the duties among your staff. Bartenders may have duties specific to the bar area and beverage coolers, but dining room and wait station duties may be divided among servers and bussers. You should schedule cleaning in the same way you would for your kitchen staff with duties set on a daily, weekly, and monthly basis. Here are a few examples of daily cleaning duties:

- Wipe down wait station with damp towel from sanitizing bucket. Clear glassware off shelves and wipe them clean.
- Sweep crumbs off chairs and wipe off each dining table. Use spray cleaner if necessary.
- Wipe down bar counters and bar stools. Clear out, clean, and sanitize ice bin.
- Sweep or vacuum the dining room. Mop certain areas in the front of the house such as the wait station and customer waiting area.
- Soak soda gun in a glass of clean soda water to dissolve syrup and stains.
- Empty out sanitizing bucket and replace with clean water and solution. Replace old bar towels with clean ones.
- Empty trash near wait station, if there is one. If full, tie up dirty tablecloth and napkin bags for linen supplier to pick up.

The types of cleaning duties will vary according to your concept. Essentially, your servers and bartenders should maintain their stations just as your kitchen staff maintains the kitchen. You'll also have to schedule more rigorous cleaning on a weekly or monthly basis, ranging from cleaning the dairy cooler and the coffeemaker to cleaning windows and restrooms. Just remember to pick slower days for these tasks.

ALERT

You will need to purchase industrial-strength cleaning products, such as degreasers and sanitizing formulas. These products can be very harmful if they are accidentally ingested or come into contact with skin and eyes. If you put these chemicals in a spray bottle for convenience, label it and add "Danger!" as a warning. Always wear proper protective equipment when using such products, like rubber gloves and aprons.

Pest Control

Pest control is a problem that many restaurants face. Some owners who keep very clean establishments still face a serious challenge from pests. Insects and rodents from neighboring buildings can enter through cracks in doors, walls, and windows. They can also be brought in with incoming supplies. Hiring a professional exterminator is an effective way to handle the problem. In fact, many local health departments require that restaurants contract with a pest-control company for routine service. The exterminator should let you know what needs to be done to deal with the problem, but you should make an extra effort to keep pests out by implementing some measures of your own. Keeping the restaurant clean, of course, is most important, but you should also consider these ideas:

- Fill in holes and cracks in basement walls, floors, and ceilings. You may not be able to block every crack and crevice, but at least you're giving pests fewer options.
- Unpack incoming supplies as soon as possible. Break down boxes and trash them. Roaches can sometimes be brought into the restaurant with supplies.
- Don't let boxes, old books, or any items you don't need pile up in your basement. Pests often use these areas to hide and nest.
- Monitor areas that have a lot of activity and notify your exterminator. Clean and sanitize areas that have pest wastes.
- Coordinate with adjacent businesses to have extermination services on the same day. This will keep pests from moving easily from building to building.

Safety Measures to Prevent Accidents

Just as you are responsible for ensuring food safety for your customers, you should take the necessary precautions to protect your customers, employees, and anyone else on your premises. You can avoid most accidents by taking the proper safety measures. For one, an efficient restaurant layout that allows good flow of traffic can reduce the chances of people running into each other. Before you open your building, fire and health inspectors will make sure that your premises are structurally sound and that proper safety equipment is installed. Nevertheless, it is your responsibility to check continually and maintain safety levels as you operate your business.

Checklist of Safety Measures

Occasionally check to make sure that all safety equipment and fixtures are working properly and safely. Here are some items you may want to check:

- Inspect fire-suppression system and fire extinguishers every year. Some fire departments and insurance companies may require this to be done by a certified fire-safety inspector every six months.
- Test all emergency lights and exit signs to make sure they are working properly.
- Whenever necessary, change furnace and air-conditioning filters for equipment efficiency.
- Check wires, plugs, and outlets for wear and potential hazards.
- Test all alarm systems (burglar, smoke) to make sure they are working properly.
- Check for any kind of leak in the plumbing, gas lines, or any equipment.
- Replenish any first-aid supplies if needed. Be sure to include bandages, gauze, first-aid tape, ointment for burns, antibiotic ointments, and anti-septic wipes.

You and your staff should always keep an eye for potentially hazardous situations. The best mode of prevention is to stay on top of things so they don't become a problem. Much of the time, the problem can be easily solved, but the longer it goes unchecked, the more complicated the problem becomes and the more risk of danger is presented.

In Case of Emergency

Include procedures and instructions regarding emergency situations in your operating manual. Your local building and fire codes will already have determined specific requirements, such as the number of emergency exits and the kinds of door hardware you need to have. In your operating manual, instruct your staff on what to do during an emergency and how to help customers to safety. Fire and medical emergencies are situations that every restaurant must be prepared to face. Depending on your geographical location, you might also have instructions on what to do in case of other emergency situations, such as tornadoes or earthquakes. In general, the following are your basic requirements:

- You must have clearly marked exits. Exit signs must be lighted and have sufficient backup power supply in case of a power outage.
- Emergency exits must be able to unlock from the inside and must never be blocked by any objects.
- If you have doors in your dining area that lead to closets or other dead-end rooms that are not restrooms, mark these doors "Employees only" or "Not an exit."
- Train your staff in cardiopulmonary resuscitation (CPR) in case someone goes into cardiac arrest or stops breathing; include the Heimlich maneuver in case of choking.
- Post a layout or diagram of the restaurant showing the escape routes and emergency exits where your employees can see it.
- Instruct your employees on how to organize and guide guests to safety if they need to evacuate the premises.

The most important thing your staff should do in an emergency is to stay calm. Panic can lead to chaos. Chaos leads to danger. You and your staff must know the procedures and respond with immediacy, but you must all do so in a way that is calm and organized.

Run an Environmentally Friendly Restaurant

Just as consumers are keen on the ecological impact of the food they eat, they may also wonder how environmentally friendly the restaurants they go to are run. Making your restaurant more eco-friendly doesn't take a lot of time or money, but it does take a concerted effort as a whole from the owners down to the dishwasher. Not only will such efforts help make the world a better place for the future, but you will also save money with waste reduction, energy efficiency, and reduced water usage.

FACT

Some restaurants claim that by recycling and composting, they are reducing their waste by as much as 70 percent, thus, lowering their waste removal costs. These savings can be especially significant in larger cities, where waste removal may be more costly.

Here are some ways on how to make your restaurant more eco-friendly:

- **Recycling:** Set up an organized system such as labeled blue bins in the kitchen and dining room to separate recyclable materials: metals, plastics, paper, and glass.
- **Composting:** Save vegetables scraps, teabags, coffee grounds, and so on. Don't include meat or dairy products, or chemically laden products. You can donate the scraps to local gardeners (or set up your own garden!).
- **Grease recycling:** Many companies send old grease to refineries where it is converted to biodiesel, soaps, or animal feed.
- **Energy efficient lighting:** Switch to fluorescent or light-emitting diode (LED) bulbs, or lower lighting earlier in the day and light candles for ambiance.
- **Forgo Styrofoam and plastic takeout containers:** Replace with more eco-friendly containers made with potato starch, corn, or recycled paper.
- **Limit water usage:** Install low-flow aerators on all sink faucets.

CHAPTER 14

Hiring the Right People

No matter how unique the concept, a restaurant is only as good as the people working in it. It is essential that you develop a staff that is right for your restaurant. It isn't as simple as looking over résumés and interviewing the candidates who seem most qualified. A restaurant, like so many businesses, requires a diversity of skills and personalities. You must decide on the type of applicant you're looking for to match the types of job.

Staff Turnover

High staff turnover has always been a problem in the restaurant business. The cost of training employees who are likely to be replaced in a short time is a serious concern for restaurant managers. Some of the reasons for high turnover involve the nature of the business itself. For many people, restaurant positions such as servers, bussers, and dishwashers are temporary or provide supplemental income in addition to another line of work. Restaurant hours are usually long, and the work can be physically demanding. Restaurant jobs usually require employees to be available to work on short notice, as well as weekends and holidays. Additionally, in general, the pay scale in restaurants is lower than other businesses (overhead is very high, while prices must be kept competitive). Many people who think that working in a restaurant might be "fun" soon discover that it is hard, fast-paced work where personalities often clash.

Of course, poor management and insufficient training of employees also contribute to the problem. While you can never eliminate employee turnover in a fast-paced business such as a restaurant, you can minimize the problem by establishing a proper management program. Proper training and management are important factors in retaining productive employees, but the process begins with implementing good hiring practices.

Identify the Positions to Fill

Before you can determine whom to hire, you need to figure out the job positions you need to fill. In the very least, you'll need someone to take and deliver customers' orders, someone to prepare the food, and perhaps someone to supervise the process. However, the other types of jobs will largely be determined by your menu and concept. If you're operating a bar and grill, you'll be in the market for a bartender or two, but if you're operating a fine-dining restaurant with a superb wine list, you may also want to consider hiring a sommelier (or wine specialist). In general, you can divide the positions into three categories: management, kitchen staff, and front-of-the-house staff.

Defining Your Managers

As the owner of the restaurant, you will most likely take on the responsibilities of a general manager even if you don't take on that title. The general manager must have a handle on all areas of operation, including the hiring and supervision of all restaurant personnel, customer relations, marketing, and the financial activities of the restaurant. General managers must also be able to delegate responsibilities to their support staff, including assistant general managers, assistant managers, shift managers, or floor managers, though title, rank, and job description vary from business to business. Here is a list of managerial positions you might consider:

- **Assistant manager:** Generally carries out the duties delegated by the general manager. Should have a strong grasp of the operation (same as the general manager) and should report directly to the general manager regarding the overall picture.
- **Chef:** In general, is responsible for supervising and training kitchen staff, creating a menu, and running the kitchen efficiently. Many restaurants call this position executive chef or chef de cuisine.
- **Bar/beverage manager:** Supervises the bar and beverage program. Among some of the bar manager's duties are hiring and training bartenders and bar backs, overseeing beverage purchases, and reconciling bar sales and inventory.
- **Floor/shift manager:** Reports to the general manager or assistant general manager, but is usually not involved in the overall financial picture of the restaurant. A floor manager supervises front-of-the-house employees, makes schedules, and generally tries to ensure customer satisfaction during his shift.

- **Kitchen manager:** Usually manages a staff and does the purchase ordering, but doesn't have the creative and menu control a chef has. A kitchen manager is useful if your restaurant has a simple menu that depends more on consistency than creativity.

Before you decide to hire a manager, determine whether you even need someone to work in that position. Use the financial projections in your business plan to figure out what you can afford in a managerial team.

The Kitchen Staff

Your menu and the size of your operation will largely determine the kitchen staff you need. Kitchen work can be grueling, and it requires a high level of physical stamina. Look for candidates who have a real desire to be in the business and who can literally "take the heat." Beyond culinary skills, look for dependability, punctuality, organizational skills, and basic math and reading skills. A good kitchen employee doesn't need to be a people person, but she should have a positive attitude and a willingness to learn. Some basic kitchen positions include the following:

- **Sous chef:** Second to the executive chef. Sometimes runs the kitchen, other times assists the chef. Sous chefs may have professional culinary training, but actual restaurant experience is a must.
- **Line cook:** Finishes and cooks food to order at a particular station on the line, such as grill, sauté, or fryer. Requires previous experience on the line or doing prep work. Sauté station usually requires the most experienced cooks.
- **Prep cook:** Prepares all ingredients for the line. May involve a lot of grunt work, but is involved in many parts of the menu. A good candidate should be able to follow directions, complete repetitive tasks, and have basic kitchen skills.
- **Dishwasher:** Considered the lowest rung on the restaurant ladder, but also an indispensable part of the restaurant. Usually good for people with few culinary skills who may pick up some experience and move up. Many chefs start out this way.

The most essential position in the kitchen is also the most underappreciated and underpaid—the dishwasher. A restaurant can usually get by if it is short a line cook or a prep cook for a day, but if it has no dishwasher, the restaurant can easily become chaotic. So treat the position and the person in it with the respect they deserve.

You might also consider hiring an expediter, who works at the end of the line to make sure that all the stations are working together and that the food is going out in a timely and organized manner. A round cook, or swing cook, can serve as relief for any station on the line that needs help or be ready to step in when one of the other line cooks is absent.

Remember, though, you should also budget your expenses and come up with adequate revenue projections to meet your actual needs. You may find that you don't need an expediter or a round cook if your staff is coordinated and versatile enough to adapt to changes. The bottom line, as always, is budget. If you can't make the money to pay for these positions, you can't hire the people to fill them, regardless how necessary you consider them to be.

The Front-of-the-House Staff

The front-of-the-house staff are the employees who work in the dining area. They have regular contact with customers so they should be outgoing, friendly, and adept at handling people in good situations and bad. In many ways, your front-of-the-house staff reflect the attitude and image of the restaurant, so when staffing the front of the house, take your concept into consideration. A fast-food restaurant doesn't need hosts or a waitstaff, but it does need cashiers working the POS (point-of-sale) counter. A small family-run bistro probably doesn't need a food runner, but it could use a good host to greet customers. Write down job descriptions for the front of the house just as you would for the kitchen staff. In general, look for employees who are punctual, organized, and well-groomed, with good communication and customer service skills. The front-of-the-house positions you might find in a typical casual restaurant include the following:

- **Host:** Greets and shows customers to their table, maintains waiting list, estimates waiting time, answers phone, and takes reservations. A good host often creates the customer's first impression, so look for polite and organized individuals who can stay calm and friendly even when the restaurant is hectic.
- **Waiter:** More than just taking down orders and serving dishes. A good waiter relates to your customers, suggests dishes, and "up sells" in an appropriate manner. He should know how to react to different kinds of clientele, when to be funny, and when to tone it down. And, yes, he should know your menu well.
- **Busser:** Sets and clears tables, brings water and bread, and may perform other services as needed by the waitstaff. Many bussers gain experience and eventually become waiters. Experience isn't really necessary, but bussers should be dependable, fast learners who respond courteously to customer needs.
- **Food runner:** Takes food from the kitchen to the customer. Not every restaurant has or needs food runners, but many find them useful for busy periods. Food runners may be waiters in training needing to learn about the food, the service aspect, and the restaurant itself.
- **Bartender:** Mixes and pours alcoholic beverages. A bartender should be skilled in making popular cocktails and specialty drinks associated with your concept. Like all front-of-the-house employees, a bartender should be friendly with guests but also organized, attentive to detail, and able to maintain the bar area. It's also imperative that a bartender is exceptionally responsible and practices sound judgment at even the busiest times due to his or her direct involvement with guests consuming alcohol.

Get Good Candidates for Interviews

A good candidate doesn't necessarily need extensive experience in restaurants. Someone with good communication and organizational skills from another line of work can probably perform in a host or server position. Positions such as bussers and dishwashers are good entry-level positions for someone with little or no work experience who has the right attitude, so long as they have the necessary physical abilities. With the proper training, someone without restaurant experience may also do very well as a prep cook.

Placing a Newspaper Ad

Placing a help wanted ad is the most effective way of getting the word out. You can place one in the classified section, but don't limit yourself to a small three-line ad that tells little about your restaurant. Spend a little more money, and run an ad that catches applicants' attention. Let them know the positions you're hiring for, the kind of restaurant, the location, and the type of people you want.

Recruiting Through Schools

If there is a culinary school nearby, you can also find some good job candidates there. Post an ad on a bulletin board or contact the school's career center to include your restaurant on their job listings. Not only will potential graduates be interested, you might also attract current students looking for some part-time prep work. High schools and nearby colleges are also good places to find candidates for part-time bussers, servers, and dishwashers. Connect with the school's career center, run ads in the school newspaper, or post flyers on available bulletin boards.

The Application Process

The application process varies from restaurant to restaurant, position by position. Some restaurants review applications before calling candidates back for interviews. Others conduct initial interviews as they take applications and then call qualified applicants back for second interviews. You'll get many more applications for server positions than you will for sous chefs and line cooks, so the process of finding servers will be a little easier.

The Application Form

Applicants should first fill out an application form, even if the applicant submits a résumé. An application form helps you keep track of applicants for your records, and it can tell you if the applicant can follow simple written instructions. You can request certain information such as previous experience and education, but you can never ask an applicant's gender, race, religion, sexual orientation, political affiliation, national origin, disability, age, marital status, or number of children.

ALERT

Although you shouldn't request an applicant's age, it is perfectly legal and necessary to ask if an applicant is over the age of eighteen and has proof of age. Labor laws regarding minors vary from state to state. If you are serving alcohol, the person serving must be over the age set by your state. Furthermore, you need to know the hours in which minors can work since most restaurants run later hours.

In general, you may request the applicant's name and address, social security number, telephone number, education, previous work history, position desired, hours and schedule desired, and salary required. Make your application form as detailed as you think necessary. There are many sample job application forms on the Internet that you can use as a reference to create your own. Just make sure the information you are requesting does not violate any antidiscrimination laws or privacy laws. Check out the EEOC (Equal Employment Opportunity Commission) website for information, at *www.eeoc.gov.*

Reviewing Applications

Use applications as a means to screen applicants you want to interview, not to hire. Look for errors, vague or inconsistent information, and other suspect information as a way of narrowing the prospects. For example, if an applicant puts down a supermarket as the last place of employment, but fails to specify what his job was, that's a "no." Also look at work history. If an applicant has had ten different jobs in the last two years, that's a bad sign. Don't make experience in restaurants a requirement for an applicant to be interviewed. If someone lacking experience in restaurants has a completed application with good work history and seems to have good skills and attributes, get to know that person more to see if he fits in.

Conducting the Interviews

After deciding whom you want to interview, arrange times with your prospective employees to meet. It is normal for businesses to interview prospective employees at least a couple of times before making a decision to hire. Use the first interview to rule out applicants you don't want to hire. Ask fairly basic questions to get a feel for how the applicants answer. During the interview, pay attention to their appearance and mannerisms. At this stage, you want to see who fits in and who doesn't. Is the person neatly dressed and groomed? Does he seem attentive and willing to learn? If the person is applying for a host position, is she friendly, outgoing, and well-spoken? If time allows, let the applicant talk and ask questions about the position and the restaurant. Does the person seem interested about your restaurant? This kind of dialogue is a good way to see what motivates a person.

Communicate Your Needs to Your Applicants

After you finish your first round of interviews, you should separate the best prospects for a second interview. List the number of slots available for a position, and line up the candidates to their positions desired. This stage of the interview is where you find out which applicants fit in best for your restaurant. Here, you might ask more specific questions related to work experience, the position being applied for, the applicant's knowledge of the restaurant or about the industry in general. You can quiz applicants on how they would resolve certain situations. You might try out their skills. Try to find out as much as you can about a candidate's abilities, attitude, and motivations.

Tell candidates what you're looking for and what you need and expect from your employees. Show them your employee manual, and go through some policies concerning various issues and job specifics. Find out if they have what it takes before you move any further. Here are a few things you might consider bringing up to your applicants:

- **Availability:** Must be able to work the hours you need them and possibly more hours if circumstances call for it, including weekends and holidays.

- **Positive attitude:** Must have a positive attitude, a willingness to learn, and the ability to work well with others.
- **Dependability:** Must be dependable, meaning they should be at work on time when expected.
- **Productivity:** Must learn skills relatively easily and improve productivity in due time.
- **Responsibility:** Must be responsible for their own actions. If they can't come in to work, they must phone in and find a substitute.

Answer any questions from your applicants as honestly as you can. You might want to rule out more applicants as you go further along with the interviews. If you feel good about a particular candidate, you can ask about the pay requirement, if appropriate for the position. If you're still not sure you're ready to offer the job, let applicants know that you'll be in touch and thank them for their time.

Size Up the Prospects

Once you've finished with all your interviews, it's time to decide whom to hire by sizing up your final prospects. Assess the applicants' qualities, work experiences, and personalities, and determine how they will fit in with the restaurant and with other employees. Rank your prospects with respect to the number of openings in each position, including perhaps an alternate or two in case someone turns down your offer.

Get applicants' permission to contact previous employers for references and background check. Let the applicant know when you will be contacting their references. Ask the former employers about the applicant's job title and description, length of service, performance, dependability, and reason for leaving. If the factual information given by the former employer doesn't match what's on the application form, don't jump to the conclusion that the applicant has given you false information. The employer could have given you the wrong information. If an applicant left her previous job on less than amicable terms, she should let you know why. You should call the previous employer and hear the other side of the story, if they are willing to talk about it. When situations like the ones above arise, you might have to go with your gut feeling. If you feel a particular applicant will fit in well with your restaurant despite inconsistent background information, then give her the benefit of the doubt.

ESSENTIAL

Once you hire your staff, they will need to complete some government forms. These forms include Form I-9, to show proof of eligibility to work in the United States, and Form W-4, for declaring income tax withholding from their pay. Create a file for each employee to hold these forms along with the employee's application, emergency contact information, attendance record, and other pertinent information.

Before you make the decision to hire someone, consider some of the following questions:

- Did the applicant show enthusiasm for your restaurant and a desire to learn?
- Is the applicant able to work the needed hours?
- Does the applicant have good work history, if any?
- Did the applicant demonstrate enough ability and skill for the position?
- Did the applicant receive positive references from previous employers?
- Does the applicant fit the concept and the work environment you're trying to create?

Make sure that your decision is based on some concrete information along with the overall impression you had of the applicant during the interview. But if it doesn't work out the way you'd hope, don't sweat it. In this business, there are no guarantees when it comes to hiring employees, even when interviews go well and backgrounds check out. The only way to find out if someone can do the job well is to let him learn and do the job. By implementing good hiring practices, you can maximize your chances of hiring the right people.

Consider a Probationary Period

Hiring prospective employees on a probationary basis can be a good way to test out new employees. During the probationary period, you monitor and assess employees' progress to determine whether or not you will continue their employment. The length of the probation period is up to you, but generally it may take two to three months for new employees to learn the ropes and be productive. If after two or three months the employee still hasn't performed satisfactorily, you can terminate the employment in writing.

You can also set up different probationary periods for different positions based on the level of difficulty and skill required. Some kitchen workers, such as line cooks and prep cooks, might be better off with a longer probationary period than servers and bussers. There are two reasons for this. It may take cooks more time to adapt to the menu and the kitchen and be productive due to the level of expertise needed to do their jobs. Also, good cooks are more difficult to find than good waiters. A new prep cook might be working very slowly during the first month, but given adequate time to learn the menu, organize, and manage different tasks, she could make progress and improve her skills. Your kitchen needs some level of consistency, so it's best not to keep training new cooks because the last one didn't learn within a certain time frame. Yet if a waiter is slow, forgets customers' orders, and is just not performing satisfactorily after a month, he's probably not cut out for the job.

CHAPTER 15

Training and Managing Your Staff

Finding the right people for your staff is only the beginning of a well-run operation. You also have to train and manage them properly. Poorly trained employees can easily become unmotivated, uncaring, and unproductive. Provide them with the proper instructions and tools, and let them learn by doing. Manage them efficiently, keep them motivated, and compensate them adequately for their work. You will have a more productive staff, more return customers, and more room for success.

Company Policies

Before your new employees begin their training, they need to understand what your operation is all about. They should know what is expected from them and what they should expect from you. You need to address your restaurant's policies and issues consistently—which is why you need a written employee manual.

Your employee manual spells out everything about your operation and policies in detail. Although specific policies differ from business to business, the general topics you might cover in your employee manual include these:

- Company history
- Company mission
- Orientation period
- Training period
- Menu
- Management/employee relations
- Smoking and coffee breaks
- Scheduling and attendance policies
- Vacation policies
- Leave of absence (maternity leaves, military service, etc.)
- Customer service procedures
- Pay periods and advances
- Dress code, grooming, and general appearance
- Job performance standards
- Safety standards and precautions
- Emergency situations
- Ongoing training
- Disciplinary measures
- Fringe benefits (insurance, sick days, employee meals, etc.)
- Performance appraisals and advancements
- General employee conduct
- Drugs, alcohol, and illegal substances
- Policies concerning harassment

There may be other topics you'd like to cover in your employee manual. Attach a signature page at the end of the manual with a statement that essentially says the employee has read, understood, and agreed to follow the policies set forth. Make sure that everyone receives a copy of the manual, including managers and chefs. After reading the manual, have the employee sign and date the statement and return it to you. Keep the signed statement in the employee's file that includes the required government forms (Forms I-9 and W-4), the employee's application or résumé, and other pertinent information. Remember also to give the employee a copy of the manual for reference.

ESSENTIAL

The orientation period is the time during which new employees become familiar with the company and receive training. It's basically a probationary period, usually thirty days to several months, aimed at determining whether new employees can handle the responsibilities of their positions.

Your employee manual provides written documentation of your policies. A signed statement from your employee acknowledging the manual gives you some protection from wrongful termination lawsuits in case you have to let someone go for violating company policies.

Before you open, plan a welcome session for your new employees and let them get to know you, your managers, and each other. Explain your company's mission and the importance of your staff's contribution to reaching that goal. Go over the employee manual—not every detail—but important topics such as calling in sick, requesting schedule changes, and anything that might be of immediate concern. Answer any questions your newly hired staff may have as honestly as you can.

Learn-by-Doing Training Program

Training can be a fairly simple task if you approach it as an ongoing learn-by-doing program. First, the new employees need to know the what, where, when, and how of their specific duties. You can do that by going over in detail their job duties and the standards you expect from their performance. These details should all be written in your operating manuals. Each position should have its own manual that explains the purpose, duties, and standards expected, ranging from dishwasher to executive chef and beyond. Furthermore, train by demonstrating how to perform specific duties and then allow employees to do the job under close supervision until they can hold their own.

The Operating Manuals

Every restaurant should have operating manuals for each job function, whether you have five employees or five hundred. Be specific about the responsibilities of each position and the standards to which they are to be performed. While the job descriptions and their duties will vary, you can categorize their responsibilities in the following manner:

- **Opening duties:** These refer to tasks performed before opening for the day, or at the start of a shift to prepare the restaurant for business. A bartender might fill the ice bin at the bar as part of his opening duties.
- **Main duties:** These refer to the duties that are central to the position. For example, a fry cook prepares food in the deep fryer; a dishwasher washes dishes, pots, and pans.
- **Side duties:** These are responsibilities allocated to various positions for general maintenance of their areas. Waiters, for example, may fold napkins and fill salt and pepper shakers as needed as part of their side duties.
- **Closing duties:** These refer to tasks done toward the end of the shift to prepare for the next shift or closing. For example, the dishwasher may mop the kitchen floor as his last task.
- **Periodic duties:** These are jobs performed weekly, monthly, or beyond. A sous chef, for example, may take monthly inventory of food supplies to report to the general manager.

ESSENTIAL

Once your employees become familiar with their job duties and can hold their own, you should consider training a few of them in other areas as a way to develop staff backup. For example, a waiter can train as a bartender so you'll have backup in case the bartender calls in sick. In the same way, a grill cook should be able to work the fryer, and vice versa.

Train by Showing, Learn by Doing

Restaurant work involves a lot of physical activity. It requires coordination, manual dexterity, strength, and stamina. Your operation manuals should specify employees' duties, including where, how, and when jobs should be done. Effective training usually has four stages:

1. **Preparation for training:** Create a dialogue with your new employees to get them feeling confident. Ask something about their experiences and share yours. Let them know why it is important they do their jobs correctly.
2. **The tell-and-show:** Don't just tell your employees how to do something. Tell them how, and then show them how in step-by-step procedures. Don't move to something new until they do the procedure correctly.
3. **The trial run:** Let the employees perform their duties under close supervision. Give them feedback on what's done well and what needs improving. Work on their shortcomings before moving on.
4. **Gradual independence:** Let employees work independently, but check on their work several times a day for a few days, giving them feedback every time. Then gradually reduce checkups.

Continuing the Training Process

Never assume that once your employees are working independently, their training is complete. Training is a continual process. Your staff always has something new to try, and some things they've learned to do, they can do better. If your staff feels they are doing the same things day in and day out, they can become disinterested, and their work may decline as a result. Present them with new challenges to add something different to their routine work. If your menu includes some daily or seasonal specials, diversify the cooking methods so each line cook has something new to learn. And don't forget about your front-of-the-house staff. Your servers will need to learn what the new dishes are and how they're prepared. Let them taste menu items so they can describe them to your customers. If your restaurant serves alcohol, add new wines every now and then to the wine list, or come up with some funky new cocktails, and have your wine rep give your staff some tips on pairing wine with food. Introducing new products not only helps your staff stay on the ball, it also keeps your restaurant fresh and innovative.

Scheduling Staff Efficiently

Restaurant employees usually work in shifts with hours and days that may change throughout the week. Post a clearly written schedule detailing who works when in a place where all employees can see it. Your schedule must be done efficiently so you'll avoid under- or overstaffing. You can create an efficient scheduling system in two steps. First, chart out your staffing needs by position and anticipated business for every shift, and second, schedule employees for specific time slots.

Determining Your Staffing Needs

Adequately staff your restaurant for each shift to accommodate the anticipated business, but be careful not to overstaff. Create a chart of your schedule by determining the number of people needed at each position and the anticipated number of covers (the restaurant term for customers) for each meal period. The following table illustrates a sample charting of kitchen staffing needs for Monday through Thursday lunch shifts.

▼ **LUNCH SHIFT KITCHEN STAFFING NEEDS: WEEKDAYS**

Position	Monday	Tuesday	Wednesday	Thursday
No. of Covers	50	50	50	80
Dishwasher	1	1	1	1
Grill	Split	Split	Split	1
Fryer	Split	Split	Split	1
Cold Station	1	1	1	1
Sauté	1	1	1	1
Prep Cook	2	2	1	1

The "split" for the grill and fryer position simply indicates that one or more cooks are splitting the grill and fryer work. Notice that there are more prep cooks scheduled on Monday and Tuesday. Schedule your prep work during slower periods at the beginning of the week to replenish the supply sold over the weekend and get ready for the busy periods later in the week. For most restaurants, weekdays are less busy than weekends (Friday is considered part of the weekend in the restaurant business), although Thursday is usually busier than other weekdays. If your restaurant is open on Sunday, you may have a very busy brunch, but dinner may draw business more like a weekday. The following table shows how the weekend schedule for the kitchen staff during the lunch shift might look.

▼ **LUNCH SHIFT KITCHEN STAFFING NEEDS: WEEKEND**

Position	Friday	Saturday	Sunday
No. of Covers	**90**	**110**	**110**
Dishwasher	1	2	2
Grill	1	1	Split
Fryer	1	1	Split
Cold Station	1	1	1
Sauté	1	1	2
Prep Cook	1	1	1

Determine your needs, and make adjustments once you figure out how much your staff can handle. For example, you probably don't need a bartender during weekday lunches because people generally don't order cocktails then, but you will likely need one during dinner and maybe even two on weekends. You'll also need to figure out how many servers, bussers, and hosts to work the room.

FACT

Some restaurants schedule some employees, mostly servers, to be on call in case someone calls in sick or the restaurant unexpectedly becomes very busy. On-call employees phone the restaurant an hour before a scheduled shift to see if they have to work. Rotate on-call duties among your employees. Don't have the same people on call all the time.

Filling the Shifts

Because many restaurant employees, especially the waitstaff, are part-time workers who may be students or have other jobs, you may have a real challenge accommodating their schedules and meeting your needs. Other employees, such as some of your kitchen staff, will have a more consistent schedule. Check your employees' availability so your scheduling won't conflict with school, other jobs, or any other commitments they may have. Create a weekly schedule sheet that shows the days of the week, the meal period, the times of the shift, and spots to put in employees' names. The following table shows a partial-sample work schedule for the week. The person who shows up earlier during a lunch or dinner shift performs the opening duties, and the person who stays later performs the closing duties.

▼ **PARTIAL WORK SCHEDULE FOR WAITSTAFF**

Employee Name	Thursday	Friday	Saturday	Sunday
John	10 to 3	Off	10 to 3	10 to 3
Tony	Off	10 to 3	Off	Off
Jim	4 to 10	4 to 10	4 to 10	3 to 9
Wendy	3 to 9	3 to 9	3 to 9	4 to 10
Lillian	Off	4 to 10	4 to 10	4 to 10

Employees may sometimes need a day off for personal reasons. Your employee manual should have policies regarding requests for time off. The best way to handle requests for time off is to allow the employees to resolve the issue among themselves and get the manager's approval for shift changes. If a waiter wants a day off, he should ask another waiter to work his scheduled shift and then have the change approved by management. You (or the manager who approves it) must make sure that the substitute can fill in adequately. You may not want a newly hired waiter working a weekend dinner shift.

Motivating Your Staff

Motivating your staff effectively in positive ways is crucial toward instilling good work habits and production from your staff. Employees want to feel appreciated and respected for their involvement in the company. Proper motivation achieves two things: cooperation from your employees and good employee morale. Cooperation as a result of good employee morale is the best response your motivation can receive.

Getting Cooperation from Your Employees

Cooperation should be won and not gained through instilling fear. You must motivate your employees to want to cooperate with you and with each other. Even generally agreeable people can become uncooperative if they don't feel they are being treated with fairness and respect. Consider the following ways to make getting cooperation from your staff easier:

- Inform your employees up-front about your policies and expectations.
- Set realistic expectations and offer constructive feedback concerning their performance and ways they can improve.
- Provide your staff with the proper tools and safety equipment.
- Be receptive to their ideas and opinions. When you use someone's idea, give credit and kudos.
- Praise them for doing a job well, especially those doing a lot of grunt work like dishwashers, prep cooks, and bussers.
- Be responsive to their needs, and help them resolve issues if possible.
- Don't be afraid to admit a mistake to let your staff know that you are a person who wants to do the right thing, not a person who just wants to be right.
- Be firm, but be polite when you want something done in a certain way, and let your staff know why it must be done that way.

Cooperation is a two-way street. You can't expect cooperation if you aren't cooperative yourself. If you want your staff to perform their jobs well, you must make yourself available for them and respond to their needs as best you can.

Building Employee Morale

When an employee feels good about herself and the company she works for, she will have an easier time working with others, be more comfortable with the surroundings, and produce better work. The most effective way to build employee morale is to create a working environment that inspires your staff to do their best day in and day out. Here are several strategies to build morale in your staff:

- **Appreciate your staff.** Don't just say it, show it. Give them a small bonus or gift, throw them a party, or give them a day off.
- **Show pride in their work.** Put up positive restaurant reviews from newspaper and magazines in the dining room and kitchen.
- **Promote a support system.** Support your staff, and encourage them to help each other during work and offer support during times of personal stress.
- **Offer assistance when needed.** Sometimes employees may have difficulty performing a task and need assistance. Give them help, and show them how to improve.
- **Show genuine interest in their lives.** Ask them about their interests, their studies, their families, etc. But don't get too personal unless they bring it up first.
- **Recognize their contributions as individuals.** They work as part of a whole team, but you must value each person's contributions individually, from the head chef to the dishwasher.

People by nature seek approval and recognition. They become more motivated when they receive appreciation for their work. Of course, money is also a big motivator. Your employees want to be compensated fairly for their work. But they must also understand their role in the business is to help create a quality product that sells, and if customers aren't buying, no one makes money. You can do your part by fostering an environment that helps employees thrive.

Disciplinary Actions

You have spelled out all the policies in your employee manual, gone over them during training, and had your employees sign off saying that they've read the contents. Yet, despite these efforts, sometimes rules still get broken. Most established restaurants use a discipline system in stages, with penalties getting harsher with each offense: verbal warning, written warning, suspension or cut in shifts, and finally termination.

ESSENTIAL

"Texting" has become one of the main forms of communication, especially among the younger generation. As restaurant owner, you are likely to hire younger employees who text frequently. It is important that you firmly establish a texting policy from the get-go. How strict a policy is up to you, but in general, under no circumstance should an employee be texting while performing a task. Employees should never be seen texting in front of diners. And as the employer, you should adhere to your own rules.

Take rule infractions seriously, but be fair on disciplinary measures as written in the employee manual. Allow your employees to make their case. When you issue a written warning, date it and detail the specifics of the infraction as well as the consequence of another infraction. Keep all written warnings in the employee's file. This will help you evaluate your staff and provide written proof in case an employee sues you for wrongful termination.

Some offenses are grounds for immediate termination. Here are some instances that may call for such action:

- Gross insubordination
- Falsifying personnel records, such as time cards and social security numbers
- Theft
- Possession of a weapon on the premises
- Endangering the life, safety, or health of others
- Use of alcohol or unlawful drugs while on-duty
- Failure to report to work without notifying manager

- Using abusive language or threatening others
- Unlawful activities on the premises

No matter how selective you are in hiring your staff and how well you train them, there's no guarantee that everyone will work out. As a restaurant owner, you have to be fair but firm.

Performance Appraisals

Yearly appraisals are a good way of reviewing employees' performances when it comes time for issuing raises or promotions. You should have a file on each employee that has the original application and/or résumé and other pertinent documents. In this file you should also keep notes on the employee's performance, attendance record, and general conduct in the workplace. You will need to maintain this file for personnel records in case your employee needs a reference in the future.

ALERT

Never comment on a person's race, gender, sexual orientation, religion, national origin, or handicap. Keep your commentary job related, and address the employee's conduct, not personality characteristics. Be sure that the manager doing the appraisal has had sufficient contact with the employee to make valid judgments.

Designing the Appraisal Form

Create a standard evaluation form with space to fill in the following information:

- Name of employee
- Period in which the employee is being evaluated
- Date of the appraisal
- Job description and duties
- Commentary on specific job duties
- Overall commentary on job performance

- Plan of action on making improvements
- Line for signature of manager performing the evaluation
- Line for signature indicating employee accepts or has read the appraisal

There are a number of formats you can use for evaluating an employee. If you have managers making evaluations, you can implement a standardized system that rates the employee's specific area of performance (excellent, good, needs improvement). Or you can simply write essay form, but be clear and concise with your comments. Research a few books on performance appraisals or look for tips on the Internet.

Meeting with Employees

In general, the first appraisal of an employee is done after the first six months of employment beyond the training and orientation period. Every appraisal after that is usually done on a yearly basis. Some operations do appraisals throughout the year based on the employee's anniversary date. Others choose to do them all around the same time, either toward the end or beginning of the year. Give your employees two weeks' notice of these meetings so they can prepare. While the meeting is a time for you to discuss your employees' performance, it is also a time for your employees to provide feedback concerning their jobs and the restaurant. Hold the meeting in private. Go over the appraisal point by point and give the employee a chance to respond. Praise him on his strengths, and give specific details on what needs improvement and why. Discuss areas of disagreement constructively. Then come up with some plan of action for improvement, both on the employee's part and yours. Update the appraisal with points brought up during the meeting, and have the employee sign and date the form.

Fringe Benefits

When people think about fringe benefits from employers, health insurance and pension plans usually come to mind. However, the cost of running a restaurant is very high, especially for start-ups and small operations. Furthermore, the rising costs of health insurance make it even tougher for small businesses to offer benefits for their employees. Before offering a health or retirement plan to your employees, determine if you can realistically afford it for an extended period of time. Consult a reputable insurance agent or financial consultant to discuss your options.

ESSENTIAL

The length of the appraisal meeting depends on the employee's job description and responsibilities. Chefs and managers have more responsibilities and more at stake in terms of promotions, raises, and benefits. Bussers and dishwashers will probably have short meetings. Waitstaff and bartenders should be given adequate time to discuss performance because they have the most contact with the customers.

There are some perks you can offer your employees that may not cost you much money. Free or discounted meals are perhaps the most common benefit restaurants offer. Many fast-food operations offer free meals to on-duty employees. Some casual restaurants offer half-price discounts, but they may restrict the times and menu offerings to which the discount applies. Others offer discounts across the board with no restrictions, but the discount might be lower. Consider your food and labor costs before deciding on a meal discount program.

CHAPTER 16

Marketing Your Restaurant

Developing a great concept and hiring the best staff may result in a great restaurant, but if people aren't aware of your existence, you'll have a great but empty restaurant. In a competitive market like the restaurant industry, you need to get your message out to your desired customers and draw them into your restaurant. There are numerous ways to attract attention, including advertising, public relations, promotions, and the Internet. You need to create a marketing plan.

Reach Your Target Market

During the initial stages of your restaurant planning, you need to determine your target market. You make that determination based on various demographics, including age range, income bracket, preferences, and education. Now, how do you reach those people, and what is your message? What do you want your target customer to know about you? Successful marketing of your restaurant means effectively getting your message across to your target customer.

To market effectively, shape your message in a way that speaks to your target audience. The easiest way to market your restaurant is to throw all your ideas out there and see what sticks, like passing out flyers to people walking by on a crowded street. But most likely, people will refuse the flyer or toss it in the garbage can. Consumers are hardly a homogenized group. You may categorize them according to their age range, gender, education, residence, and income, but they also may vary in terms of their interests, attitudes, cultural identities, and tastes. Your efforts will be most effective if you think carefully about your target audience and act accordingly.

Communicate your concept—that is, how your restaurant is packaged—including the type of service, your menu, atmosphere, price, and decor. But do it succinctly, or your audience won't care.

A simple yet effective message is the most difficult part of marketing. Companies pay millions of dollars to advertising agencies to come up with slogans such as "We do chicken right" and "Think outside the bun." You can tailor your message by focusing on a specific aspect of your restaurant. For example, a casual restaurant featuring creative dishes with fresh ingredients can target budget minded but health-conscious professionals with a slogan like, "Freshness shouldn't have to cost a fortune."

ESSENTIAL

Your target audience may be categorized into different groups as well. Focus on a category by coming up with a specific message to address those shared characteristics. For example, if your target audience is young, working professionals with a median income of $50,000, you can create two messages—one that targets the women in this category, and one that targets the men.

Meet and Beat the Competition

Your message should convey to your target audience the reasons they should prefer you to the competition. You need a marketing strategy that drives that message home.

Differentiating Your Restaurant

You can shape your message explicitly to focus on your competition's perceived weaknesses. How aggressively you want to pursue that course is up to you, but remember that negative advertising that doesn't also emphasize your own strengths doesn't always translate into more customers. You can point out that your competition fries their burgers, but if you don't emphasize that flame-broiling is better and tastier, consumers may not care enough to switch to your restaurant.

A subtler message can emphasize how you are different from your competitors without mentioning your competition by name. For example, if you're the new Italian restaurant on the block competing against old-time favorites, your message can convey freshness and innovation with a home-style flavor—for example, "Old-World Flavors, New World Attitude." Here, you're not saying explicitly that the older established places produce an inferior product, but you are emphasizing that you have a bit more flair and creativity that lets your food break from tradition but still retain its flavor.

ALERT

Be aware that the competition will also be trying to exploit your perceived weaknesses, so always try to improve on your weaknesses while reinforcing your strengths. Keep the competitive edge by never resting on your success—continue to reshape your message for the purpose of attracting new customers.

Going Head-to-Head

As a new restaurant, you can also try to penetrate the market by simply going head-to-head with the competition. Rather than differentiating yourself from the competition, you simply convey to your target audience that your product is better, less expensive, delivered faster, and more convenient. For example, if your competitor claims that it can prepare its customer's lunch in ten minutes or it's free, you can respond by doing it in nine minutes. Or if your competitor's meat loaf dinner is $7.99, you can match that price and include a free beverage.

Head-to-head competition is an often used strategy, but it can be a difficult battle to fight. If a southern rib joint with an award-winning secret sauce has been in the area for twenty years, it may be very difficult for you to compete with your own secret sauce. Instead, you might want to try that sauce on chicken and see how the new twist works in the market.

ALERT

Never start a price war with a larger, more established operation. Larger establishments can control their costs much better with volume purchasing and higher volume sales. Instead, play on their weaknesses, and work on increasing your product quality, whether it's service, food, or decor. Cheaper and bigger doesn't mean better. That's the way to set your restaurant apart.

Focusing on a Niche

One way to gain a competitive advantage is to direct your message to a select group within your target market that your competitors either don't know or don't care about. Here are places to look for niche markets:

- **Your restaurant's neighborhood:** Get to know the people in your neighborhood and find out some specific needs and wants.
- **Specialized interests or lifestyles:** For example, if your café is located near a gym, offer nutritional information such as calories and fat content for items on your menu.
- **Taste and preferences:** If you are targeting foodies who prefer eco-friendly food products, state the source of your meat and produce.
- **Cultural and religious groups:** Offer a specialized menu (kosher, for example), or include a biblical passage in your ads. Also, some

restaurants in culturally diverse neighborhoods often have multilingual menus.

- **Special diets:** Offer gluten free, vegan and vegetarian, low fat, low salt, etc. Denoting such items on your menu with a symbol often avoids the hassle of customers asking if an item conforms to their diet.

Before directing your attention to a niche market, do some research to see if the market is worth exploring. Don't limit your effort to niche markets alone. You still have to look at the bigger picture and focus on your target audience. Be sure that your marketing efforts are focusing on media that can reach these smaller, specialized groups, such as neighborhood newsletters, special interest magazines, and websites.

Advertise Effectively

An ad campaign is a plan that involves different media outlets, from print to radio to television to the Internet, but it can also include flyers, direct mail, and even someone walking around the neighborhood with a sandwich board. Hiring an ad agency may be too costly, but there's no reason that you can't do your own ad campaign. After all, you know your concept the best, and whom you want to reach. You just need to figure out where and how to "hook" them.

Choosing the Right Medium

The key to successful advertising is choosing the right medium to reach your target customer. The effectiveness of each medium may depend on the demographic group you're targeting and the strategy you plan to use. Below are some forms of media to consider and strategies to employ:

- **Newspapers:** Good for attracting a clientele over sixty-five. Local entertainment weeklies are also good for attracting tourists. All work effectively to advertise promotions and special events.
- **Internet:** Good for targeting people under forty, tourists, and business travelers.

- **Billboards:** Ideal if you're located near a highway and want to attract out-of-towners and commuters.
- **Local magazines:** Good for attracting older, local residents and regional tourists. Create brand awareness with well-placed logo, graphics, and succinct copy.
- **Radio:** Good for hooking commuters. Choose stations that target your customer base. For example, if you're opening a bar and grill, try a sports talk or a rock station.
- **Television:** Time slot and channel determine demographic group.

Which medium you should use depends on your budget, your concept, and your target customer. Independent restaurants do not usually advertise on television because it's expensive and difficult to determine if the ad is reaching the target customer. But many do place ads in local newspapers and magazines because the target area is more focused—the dining or food sections, for example.

ESSENTIAL

Unless you are offering a special promotion, or there's a special event or holiday, advertising is more effective when it is delivered consistently over time. You should consider having an ad placed regularly in at least one form of media. To save money, try to negotiate a package with the advertising sales rep to run a smaller ad regularly and upgrade to a bigger ad during holidays or for special promotions.

Conveying Your Message

Communicate to your target audience what you have to offer and why they should be your customers, but do it concisely and economically. Your ad space may be limited, and you'll lose your audience's interest if you use too many words. This can be a very challenging task for a new restaurant owner. Not only do you have to make your existence known, you have to be informative and persuasive with limited words. Therefore, emphasize the kind of information that will mostly likely attract your target audience's attention. Here are a few pieces of information that should stand out in the ad:

- **Your name and logo:** These shouldn't be in your heading, but they should be prominent, in the middle or bottom of the ad.
- **Location:** Be sure to include your neighborhood or part of town, especially if it's near other attractions, like shopping or the theater, even if you don't include the exact address.
- **Your "newness":** The phrases "Grand Opening," "Coming Soon," and "Now Open" indicate you're the new and exciting thing happening in town.
- **Your concept:** Emphasize the aspects that appeal to your target audience the most.
- **Your point of difference:** Mention what sets you apart from the competition.

Because you have to be succinct, write your copy in a way that expresses all these ideas in one or two sentences. For example, if you have the first New Orleans-style restaurant in your neighborhood, your headline might read, "Cajun has finally come to East Hills!" This wording conveys the concept, the location, and the newness, and since it's the first restaurant of its kind in East Hills, you also have a point of difference.

Create an Appealing and Informative Website

To create a website for your restaurant, you'll need to decide on a variety of issues, from choosing a host, a domain name, and a web designer. You might also choose to design your site yourself. It is imperative that your website be easy to use and informative. You may have the most beautifully designed site in the world, but if it doesn't produce results—getting your target audience's attention and communicating your message—it might as well be lost in cyberspace. Here are some factors that may determine how well your website is working for you:

- **Ease of search:** Make it easy for people to find your site. Use an easy-to-remember web address, and include it on business cards, menus, etc. Get other sites, like restaurant guides and entertainment websites, to link to your restaurant.

- **Design and layout:** Your website should be aesthetically pleasing, as well as easy to read and navigate. Text and graphics such as photographs should be sharp and laid out strategically.
- **Usefulness of content:** Include your menu, wine list, mission, history, philosophy, profiles of you and/or your chef, recipes, and anything else to make your site interesting to your visitor.
- **Tracking system:** It's useful to be able to track the activity on your website, including how many hits you get and how long visitors stay.
- **Maintenance:** Update your website promptly with promotions, menu changes, and events. Answer e-mails as soon as possible. Update mailing list information regularly.

Having a website on the Internet can make information about your restaurant much more accessible to your customers. It can be enormously beneficial to your business if you design it well and commit to maintaining it routinely.

Market Through Social Media

In its short time of existence, social media has become a powerful marketing tool for businesses. While there's a plethora of social media sites, two are most commonly used: Facebook and Twitter. They provide platforms for restaurants to communicate with and relate to their customers, who in turn can link their networks of friends, creating an ever-expanding customer-networking base.

Advantages of Social Networking

One of the main advantages of social networking over other media advertising is that it usually costs little or no money. Setting up a Facebook or Twitter profile for your business is free, and it enables you to deliver your message to whomever you connect. Secondly, your message, whether it's a promotional discount, new menu item, or announcement, is disseminated immediately. Unlike media outlets, social-networking users are there because they want to engage. You can easily track your page activity and monitor customers' impression of your restaurant. Also, you can create brand awareness more easily and inexpensively by uploading images of your restaurant and dishes as well as links to your website.

ALERT

Don't use the same strategy for Facebook as you would for Twitter. While you might "tweet" several times a day, your Facebook fans may find that annoying and hide your posts. Also, Facebook posts have more characters to work with, so you should use the space to craft a better message.

Creating and Managing Your Social-Networking Page

Set up your Facebook and Twitter pages before your restaurant opens to create anticipation, just like a preview to an upcoming movie. Below are a few tips to help you achieve what you want in a social network:

- **Create goals:** What would you like your page to accomplish? Promote specials? Build brand? Share knowledge?
- **Organize a schedule of items:** Select deals, events, or photos to post a few times a week.
- **Invite your friends and family:** Get them to join your page, which will get the networking ball rolling.
- **Upload photos:** Include pictures of your restaurant, dishes, events, and logo. Describe the photos with captions.
- **Link to your restaurant's website:** Add a Facebook Badge or Fan Box. Mention your pages on promotional materials like business cards, flyers, and ads.
- **Give your page personality:** Craft a consistent voice that speaks to the type of customers you want.

Run Promotions

Promotions are a good way to draw customers in, and they can also be used as a way to differentiate you from the competition. Be creative with your efforts. Don't just rely on the old standards of coupons and free food or prizes as incentives.

The following ideas work particularly well for casual-dining restaurants—it's important to choose promotions that mesh with your concept and draw the customers you're trying to attract. See how you might spin these into something creative:

FACT

Birthday promotions can be a huge draw to your business. According to a National Restaurant Association study, more than half of all Americans dine out on their birthdays. People from two-person households with income of $35,000 or more and college graduates dine out on their birthdays more often than other groups.

- **Business social events:** Contact local business organizations and industry groups and let them know you'd be interested in hosting an event or social hour.
- **Birthday discounts and specials:** You could offer a percentage discount based on the customer's age (for instance, 65 percent off for 65-year-olds). This works well if you're targeting an older clientele.
- **Theme nights:** You can base themes on a type of food, movie, sport, or holiday, such as a garlic festival, Oscar night, Mardi Gras, and so on.
- **Menu item promotions:** Create a few special menu items for a limited time only and advertise them.
- **Family nights:** Pick a slow night of the week when kids eat free, and offer some small gifts for kids or other promotions for families.
- **Cross promotions with other businesses:** Pair up with a local video store or theater and do a dinner-and-a-movie promotion to offer discounts or coupons.

Generate Publicity with Little or No Money

Publicity is different from advertising. Advertising is an attempt to attract targeted consumers by calling attention to the desirable qualities of its products. Publicity, on the other hand, is a message designed to generate public interest, but it does not necessarily call attention to any desirable qualities.

Doing Your Own Public Relations

Publicity—either positive or negative—isn't something that you can necessarily control. Public relations, on the other hand, is the ongoing effort to create and maintain a strong public image. You can do a lot for your public relations just by running your operation well and treating your customers with courtesy and respect. But in a competitive business, you will likely need to do more to keep the momentum going. By making the effort to maintain public relations, you will be more proactive in contributing to your restaurant's image as well as making yourself more visible to the community.

Participating in the Community

Be active in your community. Contribute to charity events and fundraisers by donating services, food, or gift certificates to be auctioned. You can also volunteer your services in community development projects. Hold cooking demonstrations or teach cooking classes at local centers, or set up a booth at street fairs or community events. Let people taste a sample of your food. Don't forget to have a supply of business cards and copies of your menu handy! You can also put in a bid to cater charity events. You may have to take less money than you'd make normally, but you'll gain invaluable exposure.

Local media outlets usually give some coverage to special events, such as charity fundraisers, gallery openings, new music venues, and other happenings that may generate public interest. Not all charity and fundraising events will be given media attention. Still, you are establishing goodwill by being active for the sake of your community at the same time you are building relationships with the community and neighboring businesses.

Generating Word-of-Mouth Publicity

Word-of-mouth still ranks high in generating significant interest in restaurants. Every person who has come across your restaurant, whether he's visited it, seen an ad, or just heard good things about it, is likely to talk to others about it. Provide your customers a great dining experience so they can spread the word. You can also start the chain going by having your staff create the buzz. You and your staff can create a grassroots effort by talking up your restaurant to friends, neighbors, and relatives, and hopefully, keep that momentum going.

Dealing with Negative Publicity

The most common kind of negative publicity to impact restaurants is related to public-safety concerns, such as an outbreak of foodborne illness or a structural problem on the premises. You have to know your options in dealing with these situations if they occur. It is important to consult an attorney on legal issues, but in general, staving off bad publicity means being proactive in correcting a problem and making yourself accessible to the authorities, the press, and your customers. Make the public aware that you are taking the measures to correct the problem and ensure that it will never occur again.

ESSENTIAL

Negative reports or claims by your competition, the media, or even a food critic may sometimes call for a response. But choose your battles carefully. Look at your own operation first to be sure you don't need to make adjustments from within. While you should protect your image, you shouldn't take all negative opinions as a personal attack. Part of being successful is knowing how to handle negativity, regardless of whether it's fair.

Negative publicity can come from sources other than your restaurant. Outside sources that are linked with your restaurant can be the culprit. For example, in the early 1990s, a study came out that attacked the fat content of Chinese restaurant food, and subsequently, led to a significant drop in sales. But instead of waiting for the negativity to pass, owners of Chinese restaurants mobilized and responded. They pointed out that they were simply catering to their customers, who prefer large portions with lots of sauce (where most of the fat is). If customers wanted less sauce, they would accommodate them. They emphasized that people should not think that Chinese food was inherently fattening. In essence, these restaurant owners weren't going to let the study alter the public perception without a fight.

Prepare a Press Kit

Imagine this scenario: A nationally prominent food magazine e-mails you that your restaurant is being considered for an award for your region. In order to be considered, you need to submit information regarding your restaurant, including photos, owner and chef bios, press releases, awards, and community service—and you need to submit it in three days. But how can you put all this information together in three days and have it look professional? That is where having a press kit helps.

A press or media kit is a packet of information that serves somewhat like a resume for your restaurant. It isn't like marketing material in which you are trying to attract customers and build your brand. Mainly, it provides the media information about your establishment for press purposes, but it may also be used as an information packet for potential investors, vendors, and business partners. Like a résumé, it should make an impression on the intended audience. While a press kit may contain many items, here's a list of items that you should consider:

- **Pitch letter:** Cover letter describing the purpose of the press kit. It should include a short description of items enclosed and all contact information.
- **Company profile:** Description of concept, history, bios of owners, chefs, managers, etc.
- **Description of past and recent appearances:** In print, radio, and television. Include copies of publications in newspaper and magazines.
- **Photos:** Include your restaurant, dishes, and key staff.
- **Community involvement:** Include charitable work.
- **Awards and achievements:** Include prizes won by owners and key staff members.

Make sure that the information in the kit is accurate and up to date, and that it is clearly communicated. The press and media can misinterpret (or more often "spin") information to fit their angle, but if you do your part, you might make such instances less likely.

CHAPTER 17

Basic Accounting and Administrative Duties

Generating sales is only part of the restaurant's financial picture. You need to look at all the financial figures to find out if you are profiting from your business. Although an accountant will prepare your tax returns and periodic financial statements, you must do your part by maintaining good records and following the proper procedures of running a business. Set parameters to control your costs, so you can actually keep some of the money you take in.

The Daily Sales Report

A daily sales report is essential in maintaining good financial records. There are a number of ways you can format it to make the information easy to read. A daily sales report allows you to do a number of things, including the following:

- Create a sales history that is necessary for generating financial statements.
- Categorize your sales in various ways for analysis.
- Ensure that money in the register balances out with total sales of the day.
- Point out discrepancies that may require further investigation.
- Track sales for developing patterns and trends.

If you have a POS (point-of-sale) system, the computer software may have a function that creates reports with various sales analyses. If you don't, you'll need to create a template form so you can fill out the information every day. Different restaurants track their data differently, depending on how they choose to analyze their sales. Take a look at the following table for an example of a daily sales report.

▼ **SAMPLE DAILY SALES REPORT FOR THURSDAY, MAY 23**

	Lunch	Dinner	Total
Total Sales	$850	$1,500	$2,350
Food	$765	$1,300	$2,065
Beverage (alcoholic)	$85	$200	$285
Number of Covers	85	100	185
Check Average	$10	$15	$12.70
Check Average (food)	$9	$13	$11.35
Check Average (beverage)	$1	$2	$1.35
Credit Card Sales	$500	$800	$1,300
Cash Sales	$350	$700	$1,050
Cash Payouts	$5	$20	$25
Cash in Register	$443	$780	$1,125
Beginning Register	$100	$100	$100
Cash to Be Deposited	$345	$680	$1,025
Amount Over (short)	($2)	$0	($2)

Including information such as the weather, holidays, or special events in your daily sales report can be helpful in explaining sudden changes in business levels. A snowstorm, for example, can impact sales negatively for days and should be seen as an anomaly. However, a sudden boost in sales during several holiday weekends may indicate a foreseeable pattern for subsequent holiday weekends. Other information you may wish to enter includes sales by individual servers, sales by food categories, and food and labor costs—essentially, whatever you feel can help you analyze your business. A daily sales report is the beginning step to reviewing your sales data. You can't really tell how your restaurant is progressing by a single report. You have to review the reports over a period of time to track your progress as you try to achieve your goals.

The last line of the table shows a shortage of $2 after the register was counted and checked with total sales. A number of possibilities could explain the shortage, including giving out the wrong change, miscalculating the total sales, counting out the register wrong, and so on. It is important that all possibilities are examined before determining that money is actually missing.

ALERT

Missing money is a serious concern regardless of the amount, but don't immediately jump to the conclusion that theft is involved. While your employees may be accountable for the errors, honest mistakes do happen. Keep an eye out for recurrences of the problem, especially if it follows a pattern with the same employees. Close supervision is the best way to minimize such incidents.

Tracking Expenses

Just as you have to keep track of the money coming in, you also have to keep track of the money going out. Generating high volume of sales doesn't mean a whole lot if you don't know what you're buying and how much you're spending on it. Make a habit of logging these expenses, either with accounting software, a spreadsheet, or a detailed check stub. You'll need to have a record of all financial transactions for tax purposes. Not only that, tracking your expenses ensures that your bills are being paid on time.

Noncontrollable expenses are the costs to your business that you may be expected to pay regardless of how you run your business. Most noncontrollable expenses are fixed and may be paid in installments, perhaps monthly or quarterly. Create a timetable detailing when these expenses are due, and make sure that payment is sent on time whether you receive an invoice or not. These costs may include the following:

- Rent or mortgage on the property
- Equipment rental, such as dishwasher, refrigerators, and credit card terminals
- Real estate and personal property taxes
- General liability and business insurance
- Filing fees for incorporation or partnerships
- Local business taxes and license and permit renewals
- Insurance on building and contents
- Interest on loans and credit lines
- Depreciation

FACT

Depreciation is a noncash expense accrued from the purchase of fixed assets spread out over a period of time, usually five or ten years. "Assets" in this case usually mean furniture, fixtures, equipment, automobiles, and real estate the company may own. There are several methods of depreciating your assets for tax purposes. Your accountant should help you determine which method best suits your business.

On the other hand, controllable expenses are the kinds of expenses you may be able to control. These are the expenses that you want to pay particularly close attention to. Some controllable expenses include:

- Cost of sales, which includes food and beverage
- Payroll and employee benefits

- Direct operating expenses, such as paper supplies, linen rental, and utensils
- Music and entertainment
- Marketing, including advertising, public relations, and market research
- Administrative expenses, such as office supplies, postage, and consulting fees
- Repairs and maintenance
- Utilities, such as electricity, gas, oil, water, and waste removal

Payroll

In order to put your employees on the payroll, you must get the necessary information from them and fill out the proper paperwork, such as the I-9 and W-4 forms. If you have a large staff, you should consider keeping a separate bank account specifically for payroll expenses to make the restaurant's cash flow more manageable; this strategy can ensure that a portion of your revenue goes toward paying your employees. Fund the payroll account adequately, but resist putting too much money in it. After all checks for a pay period are cashed, you should not have much more than the minimum balance allowed by the bank. Never move funds from the payroll account to the master account.

Selecting a Pay Period

Most restaurants pay their employees every two weeks. Some choose to pay once a month. The period you choose is entirely up to you, as long as you pay your employees consistently—choose a pay period and stick to it. Your employee manual should indicate when you will distribute paychecks. Allot adequate time for you or a manager to perform payroll duties accurately. Most restaurants typically issue paychecks three or four days after a pay period ends.

ESSENTIAL

When opening a payroll account, make sure that the checks you receive are for payroll purposes. Each check should include two stubs (one for the employer, one for the employee) for entering information such as gross pay, tax withholdings, hours worked, and any other deductions.

Typical Payroll Duties

You'll need to find out the necessary tax withholdings and their rates from your accountant or the proper government agencies on the federal, state, and local levels. Accuracy is essential. Pay close attention to the numbers, and resolve any discrepancies. Accounting software with a payroll feature or a spreadsheet is helpful in making calculations faster with less chance of error, but you can perform the same tasks with a business calculator as well. Here are the usual steps involved:

1. **Check and tabulate time cards.** Add up employees' time cards yourself instead of having them do it. You should verify their hours anyway.
2. **Verify pay rates and collect tip reports.** Make sure your employees' pay rates are correct. Collect tip reports from tipped employees so that the money can be added to their gross pay.
3. **Calculate gross and net pay.** Calculate each employee's gross pay, tax, and Federal Insurance Contributions Act (FICA) withholdings. Deduct the withholdings (and tips) to come up with net pay.
4. **Write out the checks.** Include on a check stub details such as number of hours worked, gross pay, FICA, tax withholdings, and other deductions.
5. **Prepare for payroll deposit.** Total up the net pay of all employees to determine the amount you'll need to transfer. If both accounts are held at the same bank, you can likely transfer the funds over the phone or online.
6. **Issue checks to employees.** Distribute paychecks within the time frame promised in the employee manual.

More than likely, you or a manager will perform the payroll duties. If you have a large operation, you might consider outsourcing your payroll duties to an accountant or a payroll service. At the end of each pay period, you provide the employees' information such as hours and pay rate, and the payroll service will generally do the rest.

Analyzing Financial Data

Your accountant should take all your sales and expense reports to prepare your monthly financial statements. There may be other information and ways of analyzing information that will be useful to you. You may need to calculate your sales and expenses on your own in order to analyze specific areas and determine what adjustments are needed. The most efficient way to do this analysis is on a monthly basis.

Preparing the Monthly Sales Report

Your monthly sales report may look exactly like your daily sales report except it shows sales data for the entire month. If you have a point-of-sale (POS) system, you may already have a function that can produce reports on a monthly basis. Even without a POS system, the monthly sales report should not be difficult as long as you keep up on your daily sales report. If you're adept at using a spreadsheet, you can link all daily reports together to create a monthly report. You can also make it a little easier by doing a weekly sales report and then combining the weekly reports at the end of the month.

Preparing the Monthly Expense Report

The best way to organize and calculate your expenses is to use a spreadsheet or accounting software. Categorize your expenses as your accountant might, perhaps with even more specific categories. The following table presents a sample of monthly food expenses. It breaks down the purchases in categories of food types and shows the percentage of the total food purchases.

▼ **SAMPLE FOOD PURCHASES FOR MAY**

Food and Beverage	Amount	Percentage
Meat	$1,500	20%
Poultry	$1,100	15%
Seafood	$2,000	27%
Produce	$1,500	20%
Dry Goods	$1,000	13%
Beverage (nonalcoholic)	$400	5%
Total	$7,500	100%

Monthly Financial Statements

If you hire an accountant to prepare your financial statements, provide him with all sales figures and all payroll and operating expense transactions on a monthly basis. He will then record all business transactions in your general ledger and code them according to the restaurant chart of accounts. You should expect two monthly financial statements from your accountant: an income statement and a balance sheet.

Income Statement

Also known as a profit and loss statement, an income statement is a summary of your sales and expenses that shows your gross and net profit for the month. If your financial picture doesn't look as good as you expect, an income statement can point you to some areas of concern, but it won't necessarily pinpoint exactly where the problem lies. You will need to investigate further to find the areas of concern.

One area you should pay particular attention to in the income statement is the total cost of sales. This is the actual cost of your food and beverage that you've sold. To figure out your cost of sales, take inventory of your food and beverage supplies at the end of every month. The equation for determining total cost of sales is as follows:

Beginning inventory + purchases – ending inventory = total cost of sales

You can also show this number as a percentage by dividing it by your sales for the month. The following table shows an example.

▼ SAMPLE COST OF SALES

	Food	Beverage	Total
Beginning Inventory	$3,300	$5,000	$8,300
Purchases	$7,500	$2,000	$9,500
Ending Inventory	$2,100	$4,000	$6,100
Sales	$27,500	$9,100	$35,600
Total Cost of Sales	$8,700 (32%)	$2,000 (22 %)	$10,700 (30%)
Gross Profit	$18,800 (68%)	$7,100 (78%)	$25,900 (70%)

Your total sales minus your cost of sales equal your gross profit. This example shows a 70 percent gross profit in total sales. Before you start designing that new summer house in the tropics, remember that you still have your other operating expenses and depreciation to take into account before you arrive at your net profit, which is your true profit before taxes. But your gross profit and cost of sales are a direct reflection of how efficiently you are using your food supplies. You can break down the costs of sales even further by listing categories of items sold, as the table on this page shows. If the expenditure in certain categories doesn't look right, you may need to investigate how your supplies are being managed. If you're purchasing and managing your supplies correctly, you may need to adjust your prices.

The Balance Sheet

The balance sheet essentially shows the overall economic state of your business at any given time—in this case, at the end of the month. As the term suggests, a balance sheet should show that the value of your assets is equal to your liabilities and capital. When you look at a balance sheet, you have "Assets" in one section and "Liabilities and Capital" in another. The total of each section must equal the other, or else there is discrepancy.

Assets are divided into current assets and fixed assets. Current assets include cash in hand (or the bank), accounts receivable, inventory, and short-term notes to shareholders and employees. Fixed assets include buildings and land, furniture, fixtures and equipment, and long-term notes such as deposits for rent and utilities. Liabilities are also split. Current liabilities refer to the business' short-term debts, including accounts payable, taxes due, portions of loans and notes due in the next twelve months, or wages owed from previous work. Long-term liabilities are the business' long-term debts, including portions of loans due beyond the next twelve months. Capital simply designates the owner's (or owners') equity in the business, which includes the initial investment plus any earnings reinvested into the business. You may also refer to this as the restaurant's net worth because it is the difference between your debts and your assets.

One way to benchmark your restaurant's efficiency is to evaluate the inventory turnover. To calculate your monthly turnover rate, add the beginning and ending inventory and divide by two to get your average inventory. Divide your total cost of sales by your average inventory. Restaurants usually want a turnover rate of four. For example, if your cost of sales is $16,000, your average inventory should not be over $4,000.

ESSENTIAL

After the initial purchases when you first open (beginning inventory), you only need to take inventory once a month to calculate your total cost of sales. The inventory you take at the end of the month is your ending inventory for the first month, but it is also your beginning inventory for the next month. Following this cycle makes figuring out your cost of sales a little easier, as long as you do it consistently.

Developing an Operating Budget

Once your restaurant has been up and running for a few months, you should start seeing some patterns in your business levels. Your monthly income statements should allow you to compare how your income and expenses measure up to your financial projections in your business plan. Don't be disappointed if your figures don't meet your projected goals—very few restaurants do when they first start out. You must decide what adjustments will get you closer to your projections. Once you do that, you may want to develop an operating budget for the next few months to maintain some control over your costs and to keep your target profit on the right track.

Begin with Sales Projections

Speculate on your sales for the coming few months based on your monthly income statements. Ask yourself if the next few months will be busier, slower, or about the same. Consider your location, the season, and your market. Summer may be the busiest time of the year for you. On the other hand, if you're near a university and catering to a college crowd, summer may be a bit slower than when school is in session.

The following table shows a brief example of how Johnny's Steakhouse, a restaurant located near summer tourist attractions, projects its sales to budget its operation. After researching some local businesses to see how the summer months affect their sales, the owners figured that sales would increase by 30 percent in July and August and drop back to normal levels come September.

Budget Your Noncontrollable Expenses

Start your budgeting plan by accounting for your noncontrollable expenses. These are mostly fixed expenses you must pay just to stay open. The following table lists some of the noncontrollable expenses for Johnny's Steakhouse.

▼ **JOHNNY'S STEAKHOUSE**

Sample Sales Projections	July	August	September
Total Sales	$60,000	$55,000	$40,000
Food Sales	$40,000	$38,500	$26,800
Beverage Sales	$20,000	$16,500	$13,200
Noncontrollable Expenses			
Rent	$4,000	$4,000	$4,000
General Insurance	$350	$350	$350
Workers' Comp.	$600	$600	$600
Interest on Loans	$400	$400	$400
Equipment Leases	$200	$200	$200
Professional Fees	$150	$150	$150
Total	$5,700	$5,700	$5,700
Percentage of Costs	9.5%	10.4%	14.3%

Note that these necessary fixed expenses stay the same in terms of dollars, but the cost as a percentage of sales goes down. When sales go up, you have more flexibility in budgeting for your controllable expenses, including your inventory, payroll, and other optional expenses.

Budget Your Controllable Expenses

You should compare the expenses with the projected expenses in your business plan to determine if you need to control your costs more. Some of these costs may be fixed, while others may fluctuate dramatically. Investigate before you start to cut down on purchases and labor. Set the budget for the fixed controllable expenses. Set target percentages of cost for variable expenses based on your sales. Prioritize the expenses based on necessity. The following table shows Johnny's Steakhouse budgeting plan for controllable expenses.

▼ SAMPLE OPERATING BUDGET FOR JOHNNY'S STEAKHOUSE

	July	August	September	
Total Sales	$60,000	$55,000	$40,000	
Food Sales	$40,000	$38,500	$26,800	
Beverage Sales	$20,000	$16,500	$13,200	
Controllable Expenses				%
Food Cost	$10,800	$10,395	$7,236	27%
Beverage Cost	$5,000	$4,125	$3,564	25%
Total Cost of Sales	$15,800	$14,520	$10,800	26%
Utilities	$1,200	$1,100	$800	2%
Salaries and Wages	$21,000	$19,250	$14,000	35%
Direct Expenses	$2,400	$2,200	$1,600	4%
Benefits	$3,000	$2,750	$2,000	5%
Repairs/Maintenance	$600	$550	$400	1%
Marketing	$300	$250	$200	0.5%
Office Expenses	$600	$550	$400	1%
Controllable Expenses	$44,900	$41,170	$30,200	75%
Noncontrollable Expenses	$5,700	$5,700	$5,700	
Total Expenses	$50,600	$46,870	$35,900	
Net Profit Before Depreciation and Taxes	$9,400 (16 %)	$8,130 (15%)	$4,100 (10%)	

Remember that your operating budget isn't set in stone. It is a set of guidelines for allocating expenses based on speculation of your sales. Monitor your actual costs against your budget even if your sales are as projected.

Timely Tax Filing

As a business owner, you will have a number of tax returns to file throughout the year. Failing to file the proper returns on time can result in penalties and interests, which means less money in your pocket. If you have hired an accountant, she should prepare the appropriate returns for your particular business structure, whether you're a corporation, a partnership, or a sole proprietor. Your accountant should also alert you to when these returns are due, but ultimately it is your responsibility to know what types of tax returns to file and when to file them. Basically, you have to file various tax returns based on your payroll, sales, and income.

ALERT

Your accountant should alert you to new tax laws and changes in rates. If the changes are significant, you may need to adjust your budget. But the changes can also work in your favor as well in the form of higher permissible deductions and tax credits to businesses.

Employment Taxes

You will need to file tax returns on the federal, state, and perhaps the local level, depending on your municipality. The amount of your payroll will determine the taxes you have to pay for the following:

- **Payroll taxes:** These are the reported withholdings from your employees' pay on both the federal and state level. Some municipalities will also require you to withhold taxes for individuals residing in the area.
- **Social security (FICA) and Medicare:** Check with your accountant on the rates of withholdings from your employees' wages and contributions from your business.
- **Unemployment taxes:** This tax, known as FUTA, is paid on the federal and state level. It is also referred to as unemployment insurance.

You may pay these taxes once or twice a month. The IRS and the department of revenue in your state will determine the frequency of filing. Figuring out these taxes can be a daunting task. Aside from the complexities of the tax codes themselves, you also have to deal with an individual employee's tax status and make sure that you are withholding the correct amount. Marital and dependent status, work-visa status, and tax-free retirement plans can all affect the tax withholdings from your employees' paychecks. It is vital that you have a good accountant to advise you and make sure you are following the correct procedures.

Sales Tax

Sales tax is based on a percentage on your gross sales. In some states, certain goods and services are exempt from sales tax, but most states require restaurants to charge sales tax. Sales-tax percentages vary from state to state. A few states don't have a sales tax although a few municipalities within those states may charge a percent sales tax if you purchase goods or service in that area. Some municipalities may charge a different sales tax from the rest of the state. In some states, sales tax may be charged on food but not on alcoholic beverages. The system as a whole can be very diverse and complicated. The main thing you need to know is to charge the sales tax for applicable goods and services in your designated area and to file the sales-tax return for the appropriate amount when due. Check with your accountant or visit the website for your state's department of revenue for details.

Income Tax

Your accountant will prepare the appropriate federal and state income tax returns for your specific business structure. Depending on your location, you may also have to file a return on the municipal level as well. The returns are prepared annually, and the due dates may differ if your business operates on a different fiscal year. Most likely, you're operating on a calendar year and will have a due date of March 15 for corporate returns and April 15 for individual and partnership returns. Your accountant should provide you with the details concerning your business and individual tax status.

CHAPTER 18

Taking Care of Your Money

Before you open your doors to the public, you have to decide how you want to collect money from your customers. There was a time when nearly everybody paid with cash. But now, with credit cards, check cards, and debit cards, electronic payment has become the preferred payment for consumers. You need to decide what forms of payment are best suited for your business and how to set up the system to accept them. But first, you have to find the right bank to hold your money.

Choose the Right Bank

Although laws regulate the activities of financial institutions, each bank has different policies and criteria for products and services offered. You need a bank that handles business accounts, so shop around. Your choice of bank is a long-term investment, and you need to find a bank that services your needs and provides support as your business gets up and running. Several factors should guide your decision, including the types of services offered, the requirements and fees associated with those services, and convenience.

Business banking is very different from personal banking. Your business account balances may fluctuate more because you'll have significantly more activity. Business accounts need to be handled differently from personal accounts for accounting and tax purposes. Arrange a meeting with the bank's business-accounts' manager to show you the bank's range of services—most importantly, their checking account packages. Here is a list of features you may want to ask about:

- **Extra checking accounts:** Find out if there is a package that includes extra checking accounts. You may want one account for operating expenses and one for payroll.
- **Overdraft protection:** If you manage your business properly, you don't need this service. But if there's no charge for this service, it is worth having just in case.
- **Number of transactions per month:** Many banks allow a limited number of transactions per month without charge. After that, they'll charge a fee, usually per transaction.
- **Telephone and online banking:** The bank should have a dependable telephone system and a secure website where you can log in and monitor your account and transfer funds between linked accounts.
- **Business check card:** These are used like credit cards to make purchases, but the transaction is actually more like writing a check. This service should be free because the bank saves money on check processing and charges a merchant fee to the vendor.
- **Amount of cash deposits allowed:** Some banks set limits on the amount of cash deposits per month you can make for free. Since you're likely to have a lot of cash, make note of this.

- **Discounts and incentives:** Some banks offer higher interest rates on related interest bearing accounts, such as money markets and certificates of deposit (CDs), as well as free checks, discounts on term loans, and other incentives.

Let the business-accounts' manager know what your situation is, such as your projected cash flow and operating budget. She will be able to analyze your situation and recommend a package that best serves your needs with minimal risk of fees. How the bank relates to you and addresses your questions at this stage reflects how it values and assists small businesses.

Since you'll be going to the bank frequently to make cash deposits, proximity to your restaurant is a clear advantage—you want to reach your bank easily and quickly. But there are other conditions that may help you determine the convenience aspects of a bank. Take hours of operation, for example. While most banks have business hours between 9 A.M. and 5 P.M., some may open earlier, and some may stay open later. Having multiple branches in the area, too, can be a real plus when you have to make deposits and run other errands elsewhere. Drive-through windows are also attractive features that will make your trips to the bank easier.

FACT

Some banks may have night-depository boxes for making deposits after hours. You are better off keeping the cash in your safe rather than risking your own safety at night. If you have to deposit at night, take the proper precautions and have someone with you. Find out if the bank provides a locking, night depository bag, and scope out the area before making that first deposit.

Payment Options for Your Customers

Today's consumers pay their bills with credit and debit cards more often than cash. For most casual and fine-dining restaurants, accepting credit cards is not just an option, it's a necessity. Even fast-food operations, which for a long time only accepted cash, are now accepting credit and debit cards. With the popularity of debit cards growing, it is increasingly more difficult for a restaurant to compete if it only accepts cash. But some very successful restaurants do follow such a policy. Consider your concept and your customers, and decide what arrangement works best for your restaurant.

Cashing In on Cash Only

The biggest advantage of running a cash only operation is that you save money on the equipment necessary to run credit cards and on the processing fees that arise from card transactions. Cash is also immediate—you don't have to wait for payments to process before you receive your money. However, there is a higher risk of mishandling of money, whether it's an error in counting, bills sticking together, or worse—theft. Another downside to cash only is that you're limiting your customers' purchasing power. A customer with $10 cash can only spend up to $10, whereas if he could use his credit card, he might be inclined to spend more.

If you only accept cash, consider your customers' expectations. In a delicatessen or a fast-food restaurant, your customers probably won't be surprised by your cash only policy. However, if your casual restaurant averages $15 per entrée, your customers may expect you to take credit cards, so make customers aware of your policy before they step through the door.

Weighing In on Credit Cards

Credit cards are a fast and convenient way for your customers to pay their checks, but they also benefit the business by expanding your customer base. The purchasing power that credit cards offer makes your products accessible and affordable to more customers. In general, restaurants attribute about 60 to 70 percent of their income to credit card sales, which means there's less cash handling and, therefore, less chance of error and theft.

Credit cards do come at a cost. Your merchant-services company charges you various fees to set up your account and process the transactions. In addition, you have to acquire the credit card terminal for recording card and purchasing data to send for processing. After the merchant-services company processes the payments, you may have to wait two business days before the money is in your bank account. Most likely, the monthly processing fees will be taken out of your checking account during the following month. Don't let the percentages fool you; the fees can add up to 3 percent or more of your credit card sales. If your monthly credit card sales are $20,000, your fees for processing the charges may be as high as $600! Fortunately, you can shop around for merchant services and credit card terminals.

QUESTION

Is it a good idea to accept personal checks?
Accepting personal checks is never a good idea without the proper verification. Most restaurants don't accept them. However, e-checks, or electronic check conversions, may have lower processing costs than credit cards. With an electronic reader, restaurants can now verify checks instantaneously through a processing company with minimal risk of fraud or returned checks. Check with your local bank or merchant services for more information.

Debating Debit Cards

Debit cards as a payment method have been gaining popularity over credit cards. Although debit cards with the Visa or MasterCard logo (also called check cards) can be processed the same as a credit card, many businesses are now providing PIN (personal identification number) pads for customers to lower their processing cost. Your customers can punch in their PINs right on your card terminal, or on an external keypad, which you'll have to purchase. For a fast-food operation or a restaurant with a cashier counter, this may be a good way to go. However, this would not be practical for a table service restaurant. Wireless card terminals, which can be taken to a customer's table, are an option, albeit a more expensive one.

Handle Cash with Care

Despite the dominance of credit and debit cards, you will still generate significant cash sales. A POS system or a good cash register can eliminate errors in calculation and record purchases in detail, but cash still has to be counted and exchanged, and that poses a risk of mishandling and abuse. Establish some ground rules for cash handling, and create an environment that deters employees from stealing.

Minimizing Cash Handling Errors

Establish proper cash handling procedures for you and your staff to minimize errors in exchanging cash. Keep some of these suggestions in mind:

- **Limit cash handling to authorized employees.** Managers, waiters, bartenders, and perhaps the host may handle cash, but not bussers, food runners, cooks, or dishwashers.
- **Reconcile the cash drawer with the sales after every shift.**
- **Between shifts, take out the excess cash, leaving a beginning bank for the next shift.** Put the excess cash in the safe or deposit it in the bank right away.
- **Always keep the cash drawer balanced.** For example, if you put in a $10 roll of quarters, take $10 in bills out of the register.
- **Provide a moist sponge or pad near the cash drawer** for separating crisp bills more easily.

The best thing you can do to secure your cash is to hire good employees, train them well, and establish a positive work environment in which they are content and focused on their jobs. Maintain good records and investigate inconsistencies or discrepancies immediately.

Deterring Employee Theft

Employee theft is a common problem in the restaurant industry. Most employees are honest, but the few who do "skim off the top" can do so in ways that are hard to detect. Shortchanging the register, under ringing cash sales, and tearing up checks are among the common ways employees steal money. Some waiters, for example, may send a ticket order into the kitchen, serve the food, and later discard the check after the customer pays in cash. Bartenders have been known to steal cash by ringing in a lesser amount on the register while charging the customer full price. Here are a few measures you can take to protect yourself from theft:

- **Issue checks for your servers with the check numbers in sequence.** At the end of the shift, have servers surrender all unused checks so you can see if any checks are missing.

- **Some restaurants make the waiters hold onto all cash from their sales.** When their shifts end, they must payout their total cash sales recorded in the POS system.
- **If the register is coming up short consistently during certain shifts, switch your staff's schedule around** to find out where (or whom) the problem follows.
- **Never allow an order to be prepared without a ticket.**
- **Make note of suspicious behaviors,** such as an employee who goes into the register often for various reasons.
- **Beware of collusion among employees, including the manager.** A manager who does not address an existing problem is part of the problem.

These tips can deter employees who haven't stolen from becoming thieves and stop or eliminate those who are. But no protective measure is foolproof. The most you can do is to make your business less vulnerable by staying organized and alert. That is why many restaurants have gone with POS systems. A POS system that keeps details on all purchases and orders can reduce the risk of theft. However, someone will always try to find ways to get around the system. Your POS sales rep may be able to clue you in on how to detect these scams.

Select the Right Merchant Services

To accept charge cards, you will need an account with a merchant-services company to process the sales so the funds can be transferred into your bank account. Electronic-payment processing is a competitive industry, so shop around to find the service that best suits your business. The bank where you currently have your business accounts may offer incentives to sign up with its sponsored services, but make sure that there's not a better deal elsewhere.

Comparing Merchant-Services Providers

Since you'll be doing mostly high volume, face-to-face transactions, consider providers that cater to retail or hospitality businesses. When comparing services, you should consider the integrity of the companies. Make sure that the companies you're researching are sponsored by reliable,

FDIC-insured banks. Check out their websites for information regarding their fees and rates, customer service, and history. Some companies may charge lower fees and rates, but they may not offer the customer service you need. Don't compromise on service in favor of lower fees. Select a few companies, and call up their customer service numbers. Ask some questions about service. How long is the hold time? Is the telephone menu user-friendly? Are the service reps courteous and helpful? Is customer service available around the clock and on weekends and holidays?

The answer to the last question is paramount to your choice of provider. You're in a business that operates beyond typical business hours and days. Your provider's customer service should be available at all times to address your questions and help you resolve problems.

ESSENTIAL

Always keep a manual credit card imprinter and credit card slips around in case you experience technical problems with your credit card terminals. You should have phone numbers of credit card companies in case you need to call for authorization codes to verify charges.

Basic Fees and Terms

Most likely, you will meet with a merchant-services sales rep. Your sales rep should fully disclose all fees related to the service, but it's a good idea to know ahead of time what some of these fees and terms mean. Here are some terms that you may find relevant:

- **Discount rate:** The percentage discount that is deducted from the amount of the transaction. For example, a 2 percent discount rate on a $100 purchase will cost you $2.
- **Transaction fee:** The small fee charged in addition to the discount rate. The amount of the transaction does not affect the fee charge.
- **Application/set-up fee:** This fee covers the application process and set-up costs associated with a new account.

- **Chargeback:** If a customer disputes a charge on his credit card account, you'll have to provide proof of the approved sale, or the charge will be removed from your account.
- **Batch fee:** A fee for processing total card transactions for the business day that are saved in the terminal.
- **Average ticket:** The sum of all transactions divided by the number of transactions. Your average ticket may determine the discount rate.
- **Monthly service fee:** This is usually a flat fee charged monthly to pay for customer support, supplies such as printer ribbons and paper, monthly statements, and so on.
- **Authorization:** Process in which the financial institution issuing the card grants permission for the transaction.

Once you understand what some of these fees and terms mean, you'll have an easier time weighing the different costs. Different merchant services set up their pricing differently. Your sales rep should take into account your prices and volume to set up pricing. The discount rate, for example, depends on the range in which your average ticket falls. Estimate your average ticket fairly aggressively to see if you can get a lower rate. Multiply your check average (the average purchase of one customer) by average party size, about three or four. If you think you'll have high volume and a low average ticket, see how a lower transaction fee and higher discount rate would work for you. Keep in mind you may be charged additional fees for transactions that are keyed in rather than swiped and for processing corporate or foreign credit cards.

The Contract

Most likely, your merchant-services company will require a service contract. Review all the fees and rates on the contract to make sure they are what you and the sales rep had discussed. There are other issues besides the transaction fee and discount rate you should consider. Here are some questions you should ask the sales rep:

- How long is the contract, and what are its early termination fees? Be aware that early termination fees only apply if you switch merchant-services providers.

- How does the provider deal with chargebacks? What is the fee involved, if any?
- Is there a monthly minimum charge or transaction limit? The monthly minimum may vary, but as a restaurant, you should not have a transaction limit.
- How long will the funds take to transfer into the restaurant's bank account? If your account is with the bank sponsoring your merchant services, it may take only twenty-four hours.
- Negotiate for lower set-up or application fees, monthly service fees, and batch fees. These fees usually vary among companies, so you should negotiate for the best deal.

Before you sign any contract, read the fine print and make sure that all the issues you're concerned about are addressed. Your sales rep may not cover all the details of the contract with you, so take the time to go over the contract in detail.

ESSENTIAL

Check on the contract for a clause that includes a risk-free trial period (usually thirty days) during which you may cancel without penalty. If not, either request a trial run, or go with another company. If you are dissatisfied early on with the service, you should not have to stick with the company.

Your Credit Card Terminal

It's probably best to get your credit card terminal through your merchant-services company. They will preprogram your terminal to connect to their processing center and offer technical support through their customer service. If something goes wrong with your machine, your merchant services should provide you a replacement—for as long as you remain their client.

Choosing the Right Credit Card Terminal

As with most data-processing products, consider price, speed, and reliability. Get a terminal with a built-in printer—it takes up less space than a terminal with a printer attached and does not have a connecting cord getting in the way of other things. Printers can either be dot matrix, using ink ribbons to print on regular paper, or a slightly more expensive thermal printer, which uses heat to print on thermal paper. Thermal printers are faster, quieter, and usually more reliable. Other features to consider are the display screen and the keypad. If your restaurant has low lighting as part of the atmosphere, it is very important that the display screen be well-lit. The digits should be large and clearly visible. The keypad should be easy to use with numbers arranged in order like a business calculator.

Buy or Lease?

Conventional wisdom would say that if you have the funds readily available, you should purchase the credit card terminal outright. By leasing, you will end up paying much more for the terminal. However, don't count out leasing as an option, especially if you're on a tight budget. Leasing your machine frees up cash or credit that you may be able to put toward purchasing necessary restaurant equipment. Another advantage to leasing is that the lease is fully deductible for the entire year as an operating expense, which may lower your taxes. If you're considering leasing your terminal, pay close attention to the lease contract. Here are some of the issues and questions concerning whether to take on the lease:

- Avoid lease terms longer than thirty-six months. You may be paying slightly more monthly, but your shorter term gives a little more flexibility.
- Can the lease be canceled? What are the early cancellation penalties?
- Is there a late-payment penalty? Most contracts have a late-penalty fee, but if you default on your lease entirely, your credit will be negatively affected.
- What are your options at the end of your lease? Many leases contain a buyout clause, but if you want to own a terminal, buy a new one.
- Are there other charges besides sales tax? Look for other hidden fees, such as processing fees and administrative fees.
- If you have property insurance, your leasing company may require a certificate of insurance, or else they may charge you for insuring the terminal.
- Check for clauses that allow you to transfer your lease to a new owner in case you sell your share of the business.

ESSENTIAL

If you have a POS system, you may not need a separate credit card terminal. Many POS systems include card readers that you swipe through, just like a credit card terminal. The card information is stored in the system and processed through your merchant services. Be sure the POS system works with your provider.

Submit your monthly lease payment on time. More than likely, the leasing company will require you to personally guarantee the lease, meaning any default in payment may negatively affect your personal credit. You can authorize the leasing company to set up an ACH (automatic clearing house) debit from your business checking account every month to avoid late payments.

CHAPTER 19

Technology: Tools to Help You Run Your Restaurant

High-tech companies are constantly coming up with ways to make restaurant operation more productive and efficient. In many ways, large chain-restaurant operators are at the forefront of using the latest technology to provide better customer service, increase sales, and control costs. As a result, more restaurants are adopting technology to keep up with the competition. While technology will not guarantee you'll succeed, it is a valuable tool for you to use in running many aspects of your business.

Keep Space in Mind

Most likely, you'll need an office to keep your computer, printers, and other related equipment along with your files, safe, and other administrative materials. Think about how much space you want to allot for your office. The size of your office will depend on the size of your operation. To maximize on efficiency and profitability, most of your space should be used for the kitchen and dining room. Your office space may be limited to a small room near the kitchen or even just a desk in the dry goods storage area. If you want to go high-tech, make sure the area dedicated to the equipment isn't allocated at the expense of adequate kitchen and dining room space.

You'll also have to consider the space you'll need as your cashier counter, or point-of-sale, including your cash register or POS system, credit card terminals, telephones, and other electronic devices. When setting up space for your point-of-sale, keep some of the following in mind:

- If your bar generates significant sales on its own, get a separate POS system for it.
- Don't set up near a water station or anywhere moisture may exist. Keep water pitchers, beverages, and damp rags away.
- Avoid plugging blenders, microwaves, coffeemakers, and other high-wattage electrical devices into the same circuit as the POS equipment.
- Invest in a good uninterruptible power supply with a built-in surge protector in the event of a power outage or surge.
- Include a drawer, cupboard, or shelf to store some printer rolls and ribbons, pens, stationery, backup checks, and other office supplies.
- Have adequate phone jacks for the telephone system and credit card terminal or POS system.

Also consider the number of cash registers or POS terminals you may require, depending on the size of your operation. If your waitstaff consists of eight or more waiters per shift (not counting bussers and food runners), you should have at least two point-of-sale stations.

Point-of-Sale System

More and more restaurants today are switching from the traditional cash register to a POS system. With the right system, the restaurateur can have increased efficiency and control over his operation. A POS system, however, can be very expensive. Depending on the functions you want, the cost of equipment and software varies widely. Shop around for a system that best serves your needs at a price you can afford.

POS System Components

The POS system usually consists of several components. Much like your home computer, the main component is the central processing unit that runs the software that processes data and stores it in the hard drive. But here's where the similarities end. You may have a single station POS that contains all the software and data or multiple workstations with a main computer that serves as a database. The other key components of a POS system specific to the hospitality industry include the following:

- **LCD (liquid crystal display) touch screen:** You select what you want to view or perform by touching the screen. It is more user-friendly than a keyboard and allows you more control over options.
- **Keyboard and mouse:** You'll need these for at least one of the stations (preferably the main computer) if you have a networked system.
- **Receipt printers:** You may need one printer for each terminal to print out order tickets, customer checks, and credit card receipts.
- **Cash drawer:** For stashing cash as well as credit card slips, gift certificates, and other notes. Choose a sturdy cash drawer with at least 18-gauge steel casing.
- **Credit card readers:** Most POS software can process credit cards, but you may need to purchase an electronic reader if your system doesn't come with one.
- **Software:** Depending on the complexity of its software, the POS system can perform various functions, such as calculating checks, receiving orders, processing credit cards, tracking sales, and so on.

Choosing a POS System

You will most likely purchase a new POS system through a reseller, not the manufacturer. The costs of a POS system can vary greatly, so shop around and compare resellers—not just for their prices—but also for their services, experience, and technical support. Fortunately, you do have many options, but as with everything, you get what you pay for. Many restaurants purchase a system as a package, complete with all new hardware, software, training, and customer support—installed and customized for your business. This, of course, is the most expensive way to go. You may also opt for discount vendors who charge less but will not include the programming or the installation. To really save money, look in the newspapers or on the Internet for used systems. You may have to customize the applications or upgrade the software, so be sure that the system can perform what you need it to do.

POS Functions

Most restaurant-POS software should be able to perform a variety of tasks and reports. Here are some of the sales functions you should have with your system:

- **Cash register and payment processing:** Calculates and tracks order tickets, processes credit card payments, and reconciles cash exchanges.
- **Calculating sales reports:** Generates check averages, beverage and dessert sales averages, numbers of customers, and other reports for analyzing sales.
- **Categorizing sales trends:** Details how certain menu categories are selling in comparison to others; for example, how do chicken, beef, shrimp, or pasta compare.
- **Tracking of sales performance:** Reports sales categorized by certain shifts, sections, and employees.

Along with different sales reports, your POS system may also be integrated with your inventory system, scheduling system and labor hours, and even your reservation system with a designed floor plan. Having an all-in-one system that performs all these functions can help make your operation run very efficiently, but again, it will cost you. You should consult your POS vendor to see how much it costs to upgrade to these levels.

Computers and Accessories

Computers have become necessary tools for performing administrative and managerial duties. With today's user-friendly systems, anyone can easily perform fairly complex tasks with the right software. Although your POS software can provide many business-related functions such as tracking sales, inventory, and labor hours, you still need a computer to perform other tasks, such as communicating with staff, suppliers, and customers, menu planning and design, accounting and financial analysis, accessing the Internet, and so on. If you don't already have a computer system, it is worth the money and effort to purchase one that is properly accessorized to meet your needs.

Choosing a Computer System

Consider purchasing a laptop instead a desktop. A laptop saves space, and you may find its portability convenient in case you want to work in the dining or bar area or to take it home with you. In general, you should have a computer that runs on the same operating system as your POS, so that you can save some information onto a flash drive to work from your laptop. The computer should be fast and powerful enough to handle your software and have enough storage space to keep all the applications and data. If you want to read data using the POS software, you should check with your POS customer service rep to see how much speed and memory you need for your system.

Accessorizing Your System

Computers vary in speed and data storage space and usually come with certain kinds of accessories and software. You can also customize your computer to include features you want. The custom features, of course, are often reflected in the price. Aside from the monitor and keyboard, here are some important accessories and components that should go with your system:

- **Ethernet card:** If you are going to network with other computers or make a high-speed connection to the Internet, you will need this.
- **Sufficient USB (universal serial bus)/FireWire ports:** Most laptops come with at least two USB ports, and desktops may have more. Some devices require FireWire (IEEE 1394) ports for speedier transfers. You may also purchase an extra USB hub if you have other devices.
- **External-data storage:** You'll need a small, convenient storage device to transfer files from one computer to another. Most common forms are portable hard drive and USB pen or flash drive.
- **Printer:** Laser printers are the fastest and put out the highest quality documents, but color inkjets are also useful for menus, flyers, and other marketing material. Color laser printers are dropping in price, but the toner and ink can be costly.
- **Modem:** Most computers now come with a built-in modem. If you subscribe to a high-speed Internet service, the modem may be included.

Be sure that you have cables that are long enough to plug into your devices. If you have a laptop, you should consider purchasing an extra battery in case you want to work somewhere without plugging into an outlet.

Software That Makes Life Easier

You will need software to perform a variety of tasks, including protecting your computer from worms, viruses, and other harmful intrusions. Your computer may already come packaged with some software to perform some simple tasks. There are others you may download for free on the Internet. Be wary, however, when downloading free programs from the Internet. Make sure the program is coming from a reliable source. Your best bet is to purchase the software.

Word-Processing Program

With word-processing software like Microsoft Word, you can create menus, letterhead with your logo, memos, faxes, and other documents for your business. These programs are quite versatile, and they often include templates to do a variety of tasks, such as creating mailing lists and printing them on labels and envelopes. When you're running a business, it is important that your documents, mailings, and other forms look professional. Having a word-processing program can help you achieve that look.

Graphic Design and Desktop Publishing Software

If you choose to create a logo yourself and design your own menu and other marketing items, you'll need some graphic illustration and perhaps desktop publishing software. Adobe Illustrator and Photoshop are very popular graphic applications and fairly simply to use if you are computer savvy. You can use these types of programs to create illustrations or manipulate photos for marketing, to establish your restaurant's identity, and generally to design the look of your restaurant. Some common items you can design include flyers, posters, business cards, logos, T-shirt designs, and postcards.

If you're interested in creating menus, newsletters, or brochures with more complex layouts and designs, you should use a desktop publishing program. Adobe InDesign is one of the most popular. This program allows you to work with word-processing and graphic design programs to create a customized layout of your publication. For example, you can import images from a graphics application and place them in the background of some text from a document created from a word-processing program, or you can wrap the text around the image to create a smooth professional look.

Spreadsheet and Accounting Programs

Spreadsheets make it easy to organize and calculate financial data, inventory, and other information. With a spreadsheet application like Microsoft Excel, you can set formulas to calculate a number of figures such as total sales, taxes, payroll, purchases, and inventory. A spreadsheet program is essential if you do not have a POS system to track your sales and other data, or if your POS system is not integrated to do inventory, scheduling, or other tasks.

You may need an accounting program such as QuickBooks to manage your sales, write checks, and keep track of your accounts payables. Essentially, the accounting program is a glorified spreadsheet, with set formulas to help manage your financial data and to create analyses and statements.

It may take a little time to set up your accounts and organize your data, but once you're set up, the program is quite easy to navigate.

Phone Systems

Depending on the size of your operation and call volume, you may need several phone lines. If you accept credit cards, you should have at least two lines, one for communication, the other for processing credit cards. Your concept should also help you determine the number of phone lines you need. If you have a small bistro that focuses mainly on dine-in customers, you may only need one telephone line to take reservations or answer customers' questions. However, if you're running a busy pizza shop that depends largely on phone orders, you may want to have several lines for answering calls.

QUESTION

How many phones do you need in your restaurant?
It depends on the size. In general, for an operation seating seventy-five to a hundred people, you may want a phone at the host station, one at the bar, one in the office, and perhaps one in the kitchen. But if your operation seats fewer than fifty, consider having just one phone in the dining room and one in the office (if you have one).

For your fax machine, credit card terminal, and Internet connection, you can probably get by with just one extra phone line. With DSL (digital subscriber line) service, you can still use the Internet while the fax machine and credit card terminal share the line. Aside from these items, you should definitely include some, if not all, of the following items:

- **Long-distance plan:** The plan should cover all lines, not just the primary line. Set up a dial-in code to access long-distance service for protection against abuse.
- **Messaging system:** An outgoing message detailing your restaurant's information is essential. Set up a voicemail system for employees who have regular telephone business contacts.

- **Intercom system:** This makes paging someone in the kitchen much more efficient, especially if you have a large operation.
- **On-hold recording:** You can play music, a personalized message, or just a general recording. There are many different systems, so choose the equipment that can do what you want it to do.
- **Caller ID:** This is essential if you take a lot of phone orders. You may also be able to identify purveyors and other business contacts.

Find an authorized dealer to help you pick out a phone system that meets your needs, or check with your local phone company about business packages that do not require you to purchase additional equipment.

Other Technology Items to Consider

Most of the latest technology is being used in larger chain operations to accommodate their volume. While technology can help you manage your restaurant more efficiently, technology can neither replace great customer service nor motivate your staff to perform better. In fact, too many technological gizmos can take away some of the atmosphere you are trying to create. Consider the scale of your operation (not to mention your budget) and how you want to use technology.

Reservation Systems

If your restaurant accepts reservations, you might consider setting up a computerized reservation system. Your POS system may be able to integrate with the software, so ask your POS customer service rep to see what can be done. Or you may just purchase the package as a stand-alone unit. There are many different kinds of systems and software, and they may perform other functions in addition to recording customer's reservation information.

A very appealing feature of some systems is the ability to build a return client database. You can record certain kinds of information about your customers, such as their food and wine preferences, special occasions, and frequency of visit. That knowledge can help you tailor your service to your customers, making them feel special. You can also connect the reservation system to your website so your guests can make reservations online. Or you can subscribe to an online reservation service, such as *www.opentable.com*, to process the reservation for you.

As always, make sure you consider cost before committing to a reservation system. A reservation system pays off only if your customers make reservations often. If you are fortunate enough to be at a point where reservations at your restaurant are not just suggested but required, the system will definitely be a plus.

Paging Systems

Paging systems are popular at large restaurants with long wait times. Unless you have a large operation that generates long waiting lists, you don't need a guest paging system. Essentially, when the guest puts his name on the waiting list, he is given a pager. When his turn comes to be seated, the pager vibrates, beeps, or flashes, alerting the guest to approach the host stand. This system eliminates the hassle of calling out names or searching for the right party when guests are ready to be seated. Guests may also move to the bar area or wait at another part of the restaurant and not worry about getting skipped. This helps to reduce congestion in the front waiting area, which makes your space more appealing to people entering the restaurant or passing by.

If you are considering this system, keep your concept and your customers in mind. While this system may be more efficient for servicing many people, your guests may not like the idea of being paged. They may feel that this system is impersonal and not something they would expect from your restaurant. Consider your customers before going in this direction.

CHAPTER 20

How to Attract Repeat Business

Drawing customers to your restaurant with the right marketing is not enough for your business to be successful. You have to keep them coming back—again and again. As with any business, you need to build a loyal customer base by trying your best to exceed your customer's expectations. You also need to handle complaints properly to win back your customer's repeat business. You always like to draw new customers, but you also have to keep your regulars coming back.

Get to Know Your Customers

You already know your target market and how to attract them. Now you have to find out who your customers are in the flesh, what motivates them, and what you can do to keep them returning. Getting to know your customers means more than just knowing what they like to eat and drink and how much they spend. It means getting to know their interests, likes and dislikes, preferences, lifestyles, and activities.

Observing Your Customers

How do you find out what your customers are like? Talk to them! Ask them questions, and take mental notes of what they say and how they react to you. The best way to break the ice is to simply go up to them and ask them how everything is, as a server would do during their meal. Note what they are eating, and try to figure out their preferences. Are they vegetarians? Health-conscious? Do they like foods that are off the beaten path, or do they stick with familiar items? Compare your observations with the sales report categorized by menu items to see if there's a pattern.

ESSENTIAL

Customers love to chat it up with the owner because it makes them feel special. Some customers prefer to be more private, but they won't necessarily communicate that to you directly. Read their responses and body language. Simply ask them how everything is, and if they don't seem to be open for conversation, thank them and move on.

Aside from their food and drink preferences, find out your customers' lifestyles and activities. You can figure out a lot about your clientele just by observing them: their age ranges, families with children, couples, students, sports fans, business professionals, and so on. Know the customers who visit your restaurant regularly. Learn their names, and let them know that you recognize they're regulars. Get your customers talking about themselves, and make them feel that their opinions and their lifestyles are important.

Tailoring Your Restaurant toward Preferences

Use your observations to see who would most likely visit your restaurant on a regular basis, and tailor your services around their preferences. For example, if you want more families with children as customers, you may want to provide some placemats with puzzles and games and crayons to keep the kids entertained. Or if you're getting a lot of theatergoers coming in before a show, you may set up a pretheater prix fixe dinner at a special price and get them ready to go before the show starts. Just to give you some ideas, here is a list of how you can play up to what your customers want:

- **College/graduate students:** To attract a college crowd, offer a student discount and play the kind of music students like.
- **Health-conscious customers:** Promote more healthy choices on your menu. You can even list the nutritional information of each dish as a selling point!
- **Gourmet beer drinkers:** Expand your beer selections to include some more expensive imports and microbrews, and offer specials during the day or week.
- **After work hangout:** Set up a specially priced cocktails and food menu at the bar for people who may just want a drink and a light snack.
- **Theatergoers:** Offer a prix fixe dinner before show time at a special price to save them some time on decision-making.
- **People who eat alone:** Have a daily newspaper or magazines available for people who eat alone, especially during lunch or breakfast.

Remember, you want to tailor your restaurant to attract repeat business from a certain type of customer. Don't try to do too many things at once to increase your customer base. If you try to please everybody, you'll lose sight of your concept and along with that your preferred clientele. For example, don't shift gears and cater to tourists to take advantage of the tourist season if your steady customers are mostly from the neighborhood. These are the people who will keep you in business, so you have to continue to live up to their expectations.

Give Customers Value for Their Money

Value is what your customers perceive as getting from your product for the money they pay. Different people define value for a product in different ways. Some people may be willing to pay $18 for a hamburger at a famous restaurant frequented by celebrities and hip crowds. However, if a local burger joint charges even half that much, customers may just as easily deem your prices a huge rip-off, even if it is the best burger in town. Some people perceive value in large portions, while others see value in quality of ingredients and service. In this way, what is perceived as value for the money has everything to do with customer expectations. If your restaurant meets your customers' expectations, then your patrons will feel they are getting their money's worth, and their likelihood of becoming a regular clientele increases.

Gauging Your Customers' Expectations

Your customers will have expectations of your restaurant based on the kind of restaurant it is. They expect to spend much more money at an upscale French bistro, but they also expect to get top-notch food quality and service. Whether you run a casual family restaurant or just a hamburger stand, your customers will still have expectations, albeit different ones.

ALERT

No matter how popular your restaurant becomes, be grateful that your customers choose your restaurant over others. Never give your customers the impression that they should feel privileged to be dining in your restaurant. If your staff begins to adopt that attitude, step in and nip that attitude in the bud.

How do you gauge the level of your customers' expectations? For one thing, their expectations are probably not much different from yours when you go out to a restaurant. Think about your own experiences when dining out and look for ways to improve your own restaurant.

By the time your customers find out about your restaurant's existence, they already have developed expectations. The minute they enter your restaurant and experience the ambiance and decor, some of those expectations may or may not have been met. But decor and ambiance are rarely deal breakers for diners. That is why you and your staff should provide the best customer service you can offer—regardless of your concept. The formula seems very simple, but it requires a huge amount of attention to execute well day in and day out.

Greet your customers promptly upon their arrival. If there is a wait, give them a reasonable estimate. Never underestimate a time just to keep the customer around. Provide efficient service, and treat customers with courtesy. Exhibit knowledge of the menu and offer suggestions and explanations. Prepare the food up to or beyond the standards expected in a timely manner. Never make your customers feel rushed unless they are in a rush. Check with the customers often to make sure that they are enjoying themselves. Address any needs such as water, more bread, or more napkins. After their meal and dessert, present them with the check. Thank your customers for coming, and tell them you look forward to their next visit.

Exceeding Expectations

In a competitive business like the restaurant industry, meeting your customers' expectations sometimes isn't enough. You have to exceed those expectations to gain a competitive edge. You and your staff should aim to exceed the expectations of your target clientele without doing anything excessive or over-the-top. Sometimes the simplest things are enough to make an impression. Here are a few examples:

- Offer a small treat before or after dinner. Fine-dining restaurants usually offer an *amuse-bouche* (a small taste) before dinner. A few chocolate mints with the guest check are also a nice touch.
- Include your customers on your mailing list, and send them a small gift certificate on their birthdays.
- Offer a coat check service.
- Make note of your customer's individual preferences. For example, if you know that a customer likes his food spicy, bring him a bottle of hot sauce without his having to ask.

- Do a little something extra on special occasions. Offer a free dessert on birthdays, a rose on the table on Valentine's Day, or a small treat for Mom on Mother's Day.

There are many little extras you can do to make an impression on your customers, but the biggest impression they'll have is how you execute the basics: food quality, preparation, service, value—the overall experience. Doing the little things gives your restaurant that extra push that turns first timers into regulars.

FACT

Research done by marketing firms has shown that when a restaurant owner gets directly involved with a customer, there is an 83 percent chance for repeat business. While satisfaction with the purchase is strongly related to a new customer's buying again, attaining a steady loyal customer involves the customer's need to belong. Recognition from the owner makes customers feel they belong more than anything else can.

Build a Rapport with Your Clientele

Knowing your customers is certainly an important part of developing a steady clientele. But just as you want to get to know your customers, you should let them get to know you as well. As a restaurant owner, you are your own best host and public relations person. Customers love it when owners approach them to ask about the food and service, and they also love it when the owners share a bit about themselves—their families, their restaurant experiences, and their interests. Building this kind of rapport with customers can be an effective way of gaining repeat business. Don't be shy or overly modest, but be careful that you don't seem boastful or self-important. Try to relate with your customers and find some common ground.

Encourage your waitstaff to develop good relations with their customers as well. You and your servers should make your customers feel like they are an important part of your success. A customer who feels like a part of your restaurant will want to see you succeed, so they'll advertise for you through word-of-mouth to friends, family, coworkers, and other people they come in contact with.

Address Customer Dissatisfaction

Despite your best efforts to exceed your customers' expectations every time, you will occasionally have a customer who is dissatisfied. You may get a few customers whose complaints are dubious, but even then you must deal with them in a professional manner and not lose sight of legitimate problems that may exist.

Altering the Perspective on Complaints

Many restaurants view complaints as a disruption to their operation, and as a result of this negative attitude, they do not take the effort to correct the problems properly. Thus, they lose customers. Complaints should not be seen as bad news, but rather seen as a customer doing you a favor by pointing out a problem. In fact, most people don't verbalize their dissatisfaction— they simply won't come back. So treat complaints as a way to learn from your mistakes and improve your business.

Complaints also present you with the opportunity to rectify the problem and win over your customer. Customers sometimes complain because they like your establishment in general and care enough to let you know when there is a problem. If you handle the situation properly, chances are good your customers will recognize that and visit your restaurant again.

Identifying Dissatisfied Customers

Market research shows that only 4 percent of dissatisfied customers actually direct their complaints to the restaurant itself. Instead, most people never return to the restaurant and express their dissatisfactions to other people or post their opinions on the Internet. Those responses make for really bad word-of-mouth publicity! Of course, you should do your best to ensure your customers are satisfied, but problems sometime do arise. Most of the time your customers won't let you know, so it is important that you and your staff recognize when a customer has a problem. You can sometimes tell just by their body language or a lukewarm response like "Okay" or "Just fine." Always check to ensure that they are satisfied with the service and the meal.

ESSENTIAL

There can be a variety of reasons customers don't complain directly to you, but if you don't seem to care about your customer's opinion, he certainly won't bother to tell you, and he won't bother to come back. Getting feedback—good and bad—from your customers provides you with valuable insight on how to improve your business.

Dealing with a Dissatisfied Customer

Take responsibility for the complaint even if you think you've done nothing wrong. In the restaurant business, being "right" won't win you customers. When faced with a customer complaint, don't get caught not knowing what to do. Have a plan of action to make handling an uncomfortable situation with a customer manageable. The following steps provide a good approach in dealing with a customer complaint:

- **Hear your customers out.** Listen to what they're saying and what they want from you. Sometimes they may just be commenting on what needs improvement.
- **Apologize to the customer.** Don't just say it—mean it. Often a sincere apology is enough to make customers feel better about the situation.
- **Correct the present problem.** Do what it takes for your customers to get what they want. Compensate them (with a discount or free dessert, for instance) for the inconvenience if necessary.
- **Investigate the problem.** Determine if the complaint is a persistent problem or just a fluke. Find out the cause of the problem.
- **Find a long-term solution.** Take the proper measures to rectify the problem so that your customers can see you have addressed the issue.

Hopefully, you can fix the situation so that the customer will feel satisfied enough to give your restaurant another chance. But even if you can't win back that customer's business, your other customers will feel confident about how you deal with such situations.

FACT

Statistics show that 70 percent of restaurant patrons who complain will return if you handle the situation in their favor. If you resolve the complaint on the spot, the likelihood of your customers' returning goes up to 95 percent.

Create a Mailing List

Creating a mailing list is a great way of staying in touch with your customers and keeping your restaurant fresh in their minds. You can use the mailing list to announce special events and promotions, offer discounts and coupons, describe seasonal menus, and so on. If you get the right information from customers, a mailing list can be a tremendously useful market research tool as well. This information cannot only help you map out who your customers are and where they are from, but it can also tell you where customers aren't coming from so you can focus more attention on marketing to those areas.

There are different ways you can get customers on the mailing list. Plan to use at least two approaches to make it convenient for customers to provide you with information:

- **Comment cards:** You can include spaces for customers to put their names and addresses.
- **E-mail and website:** If you have a website, include a page where people can sign up to be on a mailing list or to receive e-mail updates.
- **Ask your customers:** When waiters deliver the check or while a host is taking a reservation over the phone, ask your customers if they would like to be on the mailing list.
- **Business card drop box:** Some restaurants have boxes where customers can drop their business cards for a chance to win a free business lunch.
- **Frequent customer program:** You can start a frequent customer program by having your customers fill out a form with their information.

Sometimes people may comment on the restaurant by postcard or letter. Regardless of whether the comments are good or bad, use the return address on the envelope to respond, and then put them on the mailing list.

Your mailing list should have at the least your customers' names and addresses, but there is other information that you might find useful as well:

- **Special dates, such as birthdays and anniversaries:** Many restaurants acknowledge their customers' birthdays or anniversaries by sending them a coupon or gift certificate.
- **Company address:** Some customers may be interested in mailings about business-related events, catering information, and business-lunch specials.
- **E-mail address:** E-mailing your customers is faster and costs less than creating and mailing out newsletters, brochures, and coupons. Just remember that not everyone has an e-mail address.
- **Phone number:** Privacy has become more of an issue, and customers may be less inclined to give their numbers out. Respect your customers' wishes if they do not wish to provide such information.
- **How customers heard about you:** From friends? Newspaper? Food website? Magazine? This information is useful in strategizing for future marketing plans.
- **Preferred method of contact:** Ask your customers how they'd like to be contacted. Although mail and e-mail are usually what most people prefer, you can list the phone as an option as well.

There may be other information you want to request, such as preferences and interests, but you shouldn't go into too much detail. Getting customers on the mailing list should be a simple procedure and not like processing an application.

ALERT

Protect customer information—let only certain authorized employees, such as your manager or marketing director, have access to it. You do not want this kind of information in the wrong hands, especially if your customers use credit cards at your establishment.

Other Strategies to Win Customer Loyalty

Winning and maintaining customer loyalty is an ongoing challenge for today's restaurants. Many restaurants can start out being the hottest and hippest place to be, but few can keep their customers interested and coming back once the novelty wears off. You have to keep your restaurant innovative and fresh, but at the same time, you must maintain the identity that made you successful from the start. This means coming up with new strategies to give your customers incentives to come back again and again.

Promoting Themes and Special Events

Themes and special events include anything restaurants do to mark a difference from the everyday operation—whether it's a special occasion, holiday, charitable event, or a theme planned around food or beverage. There is no limit to what you can do. Remember the objective is to raise your customers' interest and to keep them coming back, so come up with a theme or an event that they'd be interested in and that matches your concept. For example, if you're a German restaurant serving different kinds of German lagers and ales, you should consider having a special Oktoberfest event promoting seasonal beers and a special menu. Other popular holiday themes include St. Patrick's Day, Mardi Gras, and Cinco de Mayo.

But you don't need a special holiday to promote a theme. You can run promotions on any theme you feel will get your customers' attention. For example, if you run an Italian restaurant that does mostly pasta, you can do a special risotto once a week. Or when tomatoes are in season, you can feature a menu that focuses on tomato as a key ingredient. Be creative, but consider your repeat customers. Don't run themes or promotions that would exclude or not interest them.

Establishing a Frequent Customer Program

Frequent-buyer programs of all kinds are popular now, whether it's with an airline, a hotel, a video store, or grocery store. Restaurants have issued similar programs with variations, but the principal incentive is the same. For every purchase you make, you get closer to getting something for free. This strategy is a good way to give incentives for customers to come back again and again. Some fast-food restaurants offer a punch card system. Higher-end restaurants may have membership programs that offer special perks, which may include preferential seating, discounts, and complimentary drinks. Many programs offer prizes and gift certificates as well as other incentives if you accumulate a certain amount of points from your purchases. The more the customer spends, the more points are awarded.

If you're only going to print simple punch cards, the cost of starting up and maintaining a frequent customer program may be relatively low. The point system might require some costlier computer software or equipment to keep track of the points customers accumulate. Keep in mind that a frequent customer program may not be right for every concept. It is important that you know who your customers are and determine if this kind of promotion is necessary or even beneficial to your business.

CHAPTER 21

Staying on the Path of Success

Operating a restaurant is more than just setting up shop and watching the people come in and spend money. You must consistently monitor your restaurant's performance over time so that you can sustain a profitable business. You'll need to evaluate how your restaurant does financially and how efficiently your operation runs. But numbers and charts don't tell the whole story. Customer and employee feedback also provides a useful analysis on the state of your restaurant as well as changes in the current market.

Review Your Restaurant's Finances

In any business, it's important to review your finances regularly. If the numbers don't seem right, you have to find out the discrepancy and resolve it. The accuracy of the final financial picture depends on how well you organize your sales and expense figures. It is essential to make a good habit of keeping your books updated and to address any errors or discrepancies when they appear.

Analyzing Your Sales History

In order to assess your sales history accurately, you need to maintain your daily sales report consistently. Over time you'll be able to compare numbers by the days, weeks, months, and years and determine if any patterns develop and where your sales have grown or shrunk. Charting your figures on a graph is a good way to look at the overall picture, but you also need to analyze specific areas to see where improvements need to be made. Your sales history won't give you any specific information on what the problem is, if any, but it will pinpoint an area of concern that is in need of further investigation. Here are some areas you may want to look at more closely:

- **Sales volume over time:** Has volume increased, decreased, or stayed the same over time? For example, are sales on Monday of this week better or worse than previous Mondays? Are weekends in January usually slower than in June?
- **Check averages:** If the check averages on a certain day of the week are consistently lower than other days, you'll need to find out why.
- **Significant drop or rise in sales:** There will be days when you'll experience a significant drop or rise in sales due to weather, holiday, special events, and the like. Note these occasions so you can make adjustments for the future.
- **Customer counts:** If the number of customers served per shift or day is significantly lower on some days of the week, see what you can do to get people in for those days.
- **Sales volume by individual servers:** Some waiters are better at selling than others. Adjust the schedule to put your best servers on the busiest days, and provide additional training for those who are lagging.

- **Food/beverage mix:** If your food sales are increasing over time, but your bar sales are dropping, you may have a problem. You may need to revamp your beverage selections, or, worse, determine whether theft and free drinks are involved.

It may take a few months before you can establish any kind of pattern in your sales. Different restaurants establish themselves in different ways. Some restaurants may be huge hits the moment their doors are open and level off after the initial buzz is gone. Other restaurants start off slow, but their sales increase steadily over time as they establish themselves in the market and more people become aware of their presence. So if your sales aren't meeting your expectations during the first month of operation, don't start retooling what isn't broken. Before making any significant adjustments, give your restaurant a chance to pick up momentum.

ESSENTIAL

If you have a POS (point-of-sale) system, you may be able to track your sales history in various categories just by installing the proper software. Check with your POS sales rep to see if your system has such a feature.

Analyzing Your Cash Flow

Your cash flow refers to the movement of money in (as sales) and out (as expenses) of your business. You must keep a close eye on the cash you have on hand at any given time and the amount of money you owe in the coming days to make sure that you are ahead. Your accountant may be able to map out your cash flow on a monthly basis. A cash-flow statement is different from your income statement in that you are only dealing with cash items, not credit items and noncash deductions such as depreciation; you are also including cash at the beginning of the month and the cash at the end of the month. To maintain adequate cash flow in your business, try the following ideas:

- Set up a consistent payment schedule for noncontrollable expenses, such as loan payments, rent, insurance, and equipment leases.

- Deposit cash from sales every day. Credit card sales may take one to two business days to process, but cash should show up immediately in your account.
- Avoid over purchasing, regardless of the volume discount. Don't tie up cash in excess inventory if it's not going to bring a return soon.
- Set up a budget plan for utilities such as gas and electric. Spreading your payments out over the year can help you maintain consistent bill payments.
- Don't let bills pile up. Pay them off slowly but in a timely manner so you won't get penalized.
- Make sure that you have enough cash in your account to cover payroll after each pay period.

If you're not comfortable with your current cash flow, reducing your inventory may be a good way to start. If reducing your inventory is not enough, you need to rethink your pricing or marketing strategy before you start cutting down payroll or other expenses.

Looking at the Bottom Line

The bottom line in any business operation is profits. No matter how popular your restaurant is or how many awards you win, without profit, your restaurant will not last long. Review your profits regularly on your income statement. Your income statement shows your net profit minus depreciation and interest from loans. It lists your sales and expenses in a detailed manner so that you may spot areas of concern that need addressing. If your sales are meeting your expectations, but your profits are not where you would like them to be, then investigate where the money is going. Perhaps you are taking on too much inventory or payroll. Perhaps your projections were not accurate. There can be a variety of reasons, but your income statement is the place to begin your analysis.

Break Down the Sale of Menu Items

Aside from reviewing your restaurant in financial terms, you have to evaluate your operation's efficiency and profitability. Not only do you need to keep track of how much money your business is generating, you should review which items are selling and which aren't and, more importantly, how much you are profiting from each item. To do that, you have to break down your total sales according to the number of each items sold.

Menu item sales in a single day are broken down to give you a basic idea of how this analysis can be done. Look at the sales over a longer period of time to get a more accurate assessment of how your menu items are selling. Furthermore, remember that seasonal changes may also affect how people eat. You may see more salads and lighter meals sold in the summer, while more steaks and stews are sold in the winter. The following table illustrates how you can organize your menu items sales for analysis.

▼ **SAMPLE BREAKDOWN OF DAILY SALE OF MENU ITEMS**

Menu Item (Price)	No. Sold	Total Sales	Food Cost	Gross Profit (% of Total)
NY Strip ($17.95)	10	$179.50	$52.00 (29%)	$127.50 (20%)
Spaghetti ($9.50)	18	$171.00	$34.20 (20%)	$136.80 (22%)
Shrimp Scampi ($18.95)	7	$132.65	$42.45 (32%)	$90.20 (15%)
Fried Chicken ($11.95)	15	$179.25	$38.00 (21%)	$141.25 (23%)
Pork Chop ($12.50)	13	$162.50	$38.00 (23%)	$124.50 (20%)
Total	63	$824.90	$204.65 (25%)	$620.25 (100%)

According to this table, the most popular item is spaghetti, but the item that brings in the most revenue is the New York strip steak—even though it ranks next to last in popularity. On the other hand, shrimp scampi is the most expensive and the least popular, and it brings in the least revenue. The food cost of the shrimp scampi is also very high, at 32 percent, but it does bring in $12.90 in gross profit for every one sold, better than any of the other dishes. The item that sells very well and has a high-profit margin is the fried chicken. Not only does it bring in significant revenue, second only to the steak, it also grosses the most profit at 23 percent, bringing in $9.42 per item sold. However, spaghetti, the most popular dish, only brings in $7.60 per item sold.

After studying this example, you would probably want to increase the sales of shrimp scampi and the New York strip steak because they bring in the most profit per item sold. But why are they the worst performers? If some of your menu items aren't selling well, investigate further on the reasons before making any adjustments. Here are some situations you may want to explore:

- **Pricing point:** Are you charging too much for the items? Dropping the price will decrease the profit, but if the margin is high already, it might be worth doing.
- **Preparation and quality:** Are the items prepared well? Is the quality up to standard? Perhaps customers who have ordered these items before aren't ordering them again.
- **Menu descriptions:** Do the menu descriptions need to be more appealing? Adding a little more zip may just be the answer to low-selling, high-profit margin items.
- **Menu layout:** Are your more expensive items placed prominently on the menu to attract customers' attention? Think about reformatting your menu for an easier read.
- **Fear of the unknown:** Customers may be reluctant to try items they know little about. Train your staff to sell the items in terms customers can understand.
- **Item not matching rest of menu:** Consider dropping it or modifying it to match the menu. If you're a seafood restaurant, and you have steak on your menu, consider making it a surf-and-turf dish.

ESSENTIAL

Most POS systems and even some cash registers include a feature that tracks sales of individual items. You can use the information and create a spreadsheet to do the calculations for you so you can analyze the data more easily. Keep track of this information on a daily basis. That way, you can compare over time how items sell during different periods.

You should consider raising the prices of popular items to increase the profit margin, but beware you don't price yourself out of the competition.

Evaluate Your Inventory Efficiency

There are two factors to look at when evaluating how efficiently you are utilizing your inventory. The first factor is your cost of sales, which is your actual food cost percentage. The second, which is related to your cost of sales, is your inventory turnover rate. Both these factors can help you pinpoint where problems may lie if your bottom-line profit is not meeting your expectations.

Reviewing Your Cost of Sales

You now know how to determine your cost of sales. You may feel you are purchasing properly and pricing your menu items appropriately, but if your gross profits are affected because your cost of sales is above what you expected, you need to look into why that is. There may be a variety of reasons. Perhaps your kitchen staff isn't storing your fresh ingredients properly, and they become spoiled. Perhaps your cooks are portioning out too much food. And the reasons are not just limited to your food costs—the bartender may be pouring too much liquor per cocktail or not cleaning the taps properly to fully empty the beer kegs. Whatever the cause, you need to find it out.

It is important that you break down your costs of sales by category: food, wine, beer, liquor, and so forth. This makes pinpointing problems much easier. For example, if your cost of sales for liquor is disproportionately higher than other alcoholic beverages, you know where to start looking.

FACT

Different restaurants have different benchmarks for their cost of sales. Typically, a profitable restaurant may have a food cost of sales between 28 percent and 35 percent. Some high-end restaurants may have a higher food cost percentage due to the superior quality of their ingredients. However, they maintain a good profit margin by pricing their items high.

Calculating Your Inventory Turnover

Your inventory turnover rate refers to the number of times your purchases are used up and restocked in a given period, usually a month. To calculate your turnover rate, you must first determine your average inventory, which is theoretically your inventory on any given day: Average inventory = (beginning inventory + ending inventory) ÷ 2.

Next, take your cost of sales and divide it by your average inventory. Take a look at this example:

- Beginning inventory = $3,300
- Ending inventory = $3,000
- Cost of sales = $8,700

Your average inventory in this case is $3,150. Divide the cost of sales ($8,700) by this number, and you get 2.762, meaning you turn over your inventory about three times a month. Normally, in the restaurant business you want a monthly turnover rate to be around four. Therefore, if your cost of sales is $8,700, your average inventory, or inventory at any given time, should be around $2,175. Remember, this number represents your inventory in theory. In the real world, your inventory will fluctuate depending on your purchases. This is a benchmark that you can set for yourself so your purchases can efficiently be used to make a profit. In the previous example, you may decide to cut down on purchases during the month to bring the ending inventory down to around $2,500.

Respond to Customer Feedback

Customer feedback can be positive or negative, and in either case, it can be a valuable source of information for you on improving your business. Don't rely on your customers to approach you and let you know what they think. Make every effort to find out what they think and how you can respond.

Getting Feedback from Comment Cards

Offer a comment card that customers can fill out and drop off in a box at the host station or leave on the table. You can format your questions in a number of ways, such as using a ratings system, or providing space in which customers can write down their comments. You may include some general questions regarding the service, food, and atmosphere in a ratings format (such as a scale of one to five, one being poor, five being excellent). However, you should also include questions that request more specific answers. That way, you can gauge your restaurant's performance in a general sense while making note of comments that may provide specific ways for you to improve your business.

ESSENTIAL

Go to several restaurants and collect their comment cards to use as models. You can shape the questions to find out what you want to know from your guests. Be sure to ask for a customer's name, address, phone, e-mail address, date of visit, number of people in party, the frequency of visits, the server's name (if known), and whatever information you find to be helpful to you.

Make your comment cards as clear and concise as you can. Your customers are offering their time and effort to help your business, so you should make it easy for them. Don't rest on your laurels based on the good marks you get from your customers. Pay particular attention to their negative remarks. Investigate them, and respond to the customer in a timely manner.

Getting Feedback in Person

You can easily get some great feedback from customers just by stopping by their tables and chatting with them. In most cases, customers love it when the owner approaches them to ask how everything is. Here are some ways you can get some good specific information from your customers:

- Don't ask yes-or-no questions, and be specific. Instead of asking "Is everything all right?" ask, "How is your steak?"
- Know your regulars by name, and let them get to know you. Your rapport with them will make them more comfortable telling you what they think.

- If you notice that someone doesn't like a meal, find out what's wrong and fix the situation. Prepare the dish again correctly or offer something else.
- Find a reason to approach customers for conversation. Refill their water glass, or take away a dirty dish. Make a comment about the food they're eating, and see the response.
- Get feedback on the service. Good questions include "Did you get everything you ordered?" or "Is your server taking good care of you?"

There are instances in which you want to leave your customers alone—people who are having a serious private conversation, for example, or who seem obviously emotional. Remember, just because a customer doesn't openly express his opinion, it doesn't mean he won't be a good customer.

Getting Feedback via the Internet

You can see what people are saying about your restaurant on the Internet just by typing in its name in a search engine. Facebook and Twitter allow your customers to interact with you directly and offer feedback. Besides Facebook and Twitter, there are a number of consumer review sites, food blogs, and dining sites that may offer you some insight as to how the public perceives your restaurant. Urbanspoon and Yelp, for example, are two of the most popular that allow users to post reviews of restaurants. Urbanspoon lets users "like" or "don't like" your restaurant and shows the number of votes, the percentage of "likes", and your restaurant rank. Yelp employs a five star system for its users and offers breakdowns on the reviews based on the number of stars.

ALERT

Read all the reviews written about your restaurant on these dining sites in chronological order. Are the reviews getting worse or better over time? Are they getting fewer or increasing over time? It may be difficult to judge if you haven't had that many. But then, the question becomes: why aren't there more reviews? These questions are all issues to consider when coming up strategies to win customers back.

Food blogs also do restaurant reviews. Some of these food blogs are popular enough that they can be as influential (positively and negatively) as press reviews, especially in larger cities. Most of these blogged reviews also allow readers to comment, so if you've been written up, you can actually get some idea about the people who have been to your restaurant and what they think.

Listen to Your Employees

Your employees may also provide some valuable feedback concerning the restaurant's operation. Keep the lines of communication open with your staff, from your chef down to your bussers. Here are some ideas on how to get feedback from your employees:

- Meet with individual employees occasionally to get their perspective. Get their opinion on how they see the operation in general and what they need to perform their job better.
- Hold meetings on a regular basis with the entire staff as well as with different sides of the house. Front-of-the-house employees generally have a very different perspective from those in the back.
- Involve your staff in finding solutions to problems. Keep a log of incidents that indicates potential problems, and see how your staff can help resolve them.
- Encourage your staff to e-mail you or leave you notes if they are afraid to speak up during meetings or bring suggestions up in person. Keep your communication confidential if that's what your employees want.
- Create a survey form for your employees to review the restaurant's operation and offer suggestions. You can keep the survey anonymous so your employees can be more honest.

Remember that your employees' opinions are just that—opinions. They present just one version of reality. You still have to look deeper into an issue to get a better picture of the real situation. Ultimately, you are the one who weighs all the suggestions coming in and decides how to go about fixing or improving a situation.

Take Notes on Restaurant Reviews

Restaurant reviews written or broadcast in local media can have a positive or negative effect on your business in the short run, but they aren't going to make or break you. Take all reviews, positive and negative, in stride. If you are fortunate enough to receive a good review from a restaurant critic, don't rest on your laurels just yet. A positive review will likely help your restaurant draw new customers, but they will come with raised expectations from reading or hearing about the review. You must still exceed those expectations to keep them coming back. The restaurant review is only one opinion. The members of the general public will form their own opinion once they give your restaurant a try.

Always capitalize on anything positive written about your establishment and any honors or distinctions you, your chef, your bartender or any other employee receives. If your chef is featured in a national food magazine, cut out the article and frame it for everyone to see. If the local newspaper has voted you the best new restaurant, advertise that. Not only are you taking advantage of good publicity, the posting is also a huge morale booster for your staff, who will be proud of being a part of your establishment.

ALERT

Restaurant reviews, good and bad, fade fast. If you receive a good review, you may experience an increase in sales for a little while. However, if you don't follow through with your best effort, your success will not last long. On the other hand, you can turn a negative review into something positive by working out the problems and doing your best. Remember, there's always a chance that another one will be written.

Even if you receive a less-than-stellar review, don't be disheartened. Look at the details of the criticism and see if there's any validity to them. Treat this as an opportunity to examine your operation, and try to improve on areas that the critic mentions in the review. You can't control what restaurant critics are going to write. They are entitled to their opinion. The best thing that you can do is to run your operation well every day and provide the best service you can for every customer who walks into your restaurant.

CHAPTER 22

Some Strategies for Future Developments

After your restaurant has established itself as a community fixture, you may want to re-evaluate the goals you set at the time you began your planning. Refer to your business plan and see how your business stacks up to your expectations. With that in mind, you may want to start thinking about how to grow your business. There are many directions you can go, but do some extensive research before deciding on a route.

Ways to Expand Your Business

Successful entrepreneurs are always looking for ways to expand business to increase their profits and overall worth. Although some restaurant owners have expanded their operations quite successfully, there are many others who have done so with less than adequate results. Restaurateurs commonly enlarge their operations in one of two ways, either by increasing the size of the current location or adding other locations. While both means of expansion hold the potential for success, they also have limitations.

Increasing the Size of Your Current Location

Increasing the size of a current location depends on the right set of circumstances. There must actually be space available for expansion, the structure must be right for expansion, and there can be no legal impediments due to local building ordinances or other laws.

A larger operation means greater operating expenses, with no guarantee that sales will increase significantly enough (if at all) to cover the extra costs. After putting up the capital for expansion, you may find yourself in the financial hole again.

Nevertheless, if you plan well and all the pieces fit together, you may be able to accommodate more people and expand the possibilities of your restaurant space. You can, for example, set up banquet facilities, a music venue, a lounge area, or even a game room. Consider the use of the space most appropriate for your market.

ALERT

Before you decide to expand, ask yourself whether you have the management capacity to operate a larger restaurant or additional locations. Don't spread yourself so thin that you can't handle it all.

Adding Another Location

More commonly, restaurateurs expand by adding another location. The new spot may have the same concept, or it may have a totally different concept altogether. If you're starting a whole new concept, you'll have to start from square one in the planning process. If you're keeping the same concept, you may just need to find a location that has good market potential and figure out how to finance it. The following list provides a few pointers:

- If you started in a developing neighborhood, you might want to add a location in a more established neighborhood to further build your brand identity.
- Focus on areas from which you are not currently drawing customers and research the market potential in those areas. You can do that by checking your mailing lists and comment cards.
- Neighborhood development associations are always seeking new businesses for their areas. Contact them and see what kind of assistance and support they can offer.
- What other demographic groups can you target? If your current target group is professionals from twenty-five to thirty-five-years old, can you tweak your concept to reach eighteen to twenty-five-year-olds?
- Keep an eye out for up-and-coming neighborhoods that appeal to young professionals looking for a place to settle.

The concept at another location may be similar in some ways and very different in others. For example, you may be operating a successful establishment, but you'd like to open a more casual version of your restaurant. You may have a different style of service, a similar menu that's also less expensive, and a more laid-back atmosphere. The foundation of your concept is pretty much the same, but you're revising it to target a different market.

ESSENTIAL

Whether you're expanding at a current location or opening another restaurant, prepare a business plan. If you're increasing the size of your restaurant, include how the current operation is doing, what changes you're proposing, how much they will cost, and how expansion will increase sales. If you're opening another location, explain how adding another location increases your market share. In both cases, project realistic financial data to serve as goals for your efforts.

Diversify Your Services

Investors in the stock market diversify their portfolios so they can have a balanced return in different areas of industry. Similarly, you should consider diversifying your services to meet the other needs and wants of your market. You can expand upon other areas of food-and-beverage service and market these services as a way to increase your revenue. Here are a few examples of ways to expand on your services:

- **Delivery service:** It used to be that deliveries were limited to pizza and Chinese food. But now many restaurants use delivery services or are delivering themselves.
- **Off-site catering/event planning:** Catering events means big money, but the catering business can be very different from a restaurant— you'll likely need different marketing kits, contracts, and so on.
- **Selling food to other vendors:** Sell some of your food (soups, pasta salads, cakes, pies) in volume to gourmet delis, cafés, or other vendors.
- **Lunch truck:** You've probably seen these near colleges and office buildings. It's like having a separate takeout restaurant, except it comes back to your restaurant!
- **Private parties:** You can close the restaurant for private parties during slow nights if the money is worth it.

You'll have to market these services the same way you market your restaurant. People need to be aware that you offer more than just a pleasant dining experience and that you can fulfill some of their other needs as well. Consider the types of advertising media to best reach them. For example, if you have a lunch truck serving the local university campus, you can advertise in the school's newspaper. Be sure that you have the appropriate marketing materials, such as brochures and flyers, available for your customers.

Can You Franchise Your Concept?

In some respects, growing your business by franchising your restaurant has many advantages over adding another location yourself. The biggest advantage is that as a franchiser (the one who sells the franchise) you do not have to bear the start-up costs of opening a new location. It is the franchisee (the one who buys the franchise) who takes on those responsibilities. The franchisee is also the one who signs the leases to the premises and equipment as well as various service contracts, so your risk of liability is greatly reduced. Furthermore, you get a percentage of the gross sales, not profit, which relieves you of the issues of cost control and staff monitoring.

Franchising sounds like a surefire strategy, doesn't it? Before you start drawing your logo all over a road map, you have to determine, first of all, whether your concept can work as a franchise. Also, just because franchising your concept may incur a lower cost than opening another location yourself, it doesn't mean there's no cost.

Does Your Concept Meet the Criteria?

There are literally hundreds of franchised concepts available for purchase, from fast-food operations to high-end restaurants. What determines whether a concept can be franchised? First of all, your concept must have good management in place and a proven track record. It has to have a good public image and a marketable brand. It must have uniqueness and, to use a marketing cliché, "sizzle" with a sustainable competitive edge.

Your concept must also be replicable, teachable, and easily systematized. If your menu requires hard-to-find ingredients and a highly skilled chef, you probably want to grow your business in another way. In order for a franchise to work, you must have a great system already in place, including an operations manual, a comprehensive training program, quality control checklists, policies, hiring procedures—essentially everything your franchisees will need to operate the restaurant.

Most importantly, you'll need to convince prospective franchisees that your concept will bring in an adequate return on their investment. Since you'll be taking a percentage from their gross sales, you need to show how there's an attractive profit potential even after the adjustment. Potential franchisees will scrutinize your business's financial data carefully, so your numbers must be accurate and representative of a well-managed organization.

Do as much research as you can about franchising before you embark on this road. Read magazines like *Entrepreneur* or *Franchise Times* to get some insight on starting a franchise. There are also a number of books on the subject that can give you some details on how to go about it and where to look for help. Also check out *www.franchise.org* for some valuable information.

The Costs of Franchising

Although franchising may incur a lower cost for expanding your business than opening another location, the cost is still significant. As with most businesses, a failure to invest adequate capital is the chief reason new franchisers fail. Here are the major costs associated with franchising:

- **Legal expenses:** You'll need a franchising specialist to walk you through the legalities of this area, consult on contracts, and file the proper documents.
- **Documentation and registration fees:** These fees may include trademark protection, licenses, state registrations, and an offering circular (Federal Trade Commission requirement).
- **Quality control:** You'll need a highly developed system of quality control, including operations and training manuals, checklists, policies and procedures.
- **Marketing materials:** Brochures, videotapes, marketing kits, and anything else that can be used to help sell franchises.
- **Sales team:** If you are expanding quickly through your franchising, you may need a good sales force to keep the momentum going.

While the costs associated with opening a franchise fall mainly on the franchisee, remember that franchising is about marketing to and servicing your franchisees—you need to package your concept, attract the right prospects, and make your franchisees successful.

Merchandising Strategies

You see them just about everywhere, in one form or another—in grocery stores or gourmet shops, on T-shirts and hats, coffee mugs and shot glasses. Successful restaurant concepts branch out through merchandising to strengthen their brand identities. It may even become a significant source of revenue. As successful as your restaurant may be, you have to continue to reach out to more potential customers. Merchandising may be a good way to build your brand identity and develop another source of income.

What to Merchandise?

You can put your name and logo on just about anything, but if you want to merchandise your brand effectively, you need to figure out what consumers want to buy. T-shirts, for one, are a popular merchandising strategy for restaurants because they are relatively inexpensive to produce and are a good way to gain exposure for your restaurant—not to mention that people love buying them. This may be a particularly good strategy if you're located in a big tourist area, where out-of-towners are always looking for nice souvenirs. Design is the key here. If your T-shirts are cleverly designed, people may buy them even if they've never heard of your restaurant. You can use jokes, puns, cartoons, or just something simple like your logo. You can also produce hats, mugs, shot glasses, golf balls—you name it. Just be sure to choose products your customer base will buy.

Packaging Your Food for Retail

Your customers may often ask if they could buy a particular dish, such as a jar of sauce or condiment you serve to take home. Consider fulfilling that need by packaging your products for retail sale. Packaging your product for retail, however, is quite a complicated process. This may be a costly investment, so you must have a good plan for the entire process. Here are a few tips to get you started:

- Choose food items that have a long shelf life, low pH (acidic level to reduce risk of food pathogens), and that are easily processed. These include sauces and soups, dry goods, and items that freeze well and require little preparation.

- Determine the market potential for items. Your customers may love your salsa, but do they love it enough to buy a jar of it in a store?
- You may have to adjust the recipes to conform to Food and Drug Administration guidelines, but you still have to find a way to produce a product that matches your restaurant's quality.
- Decide whether to choose a co-packer or license your brand to a manufacturer. Do extensive research on the route you choose and consult an attorney if necessary.
- Decide on a design package for your items. You may need the help of a designer in this case, but your co-packer might have some good input also.
- Figure out what vendors are most suitable for your items. Look for some good food brokers to help distribute your food for retail sales.

Remember, the process is complicated, and there is much more involved than what's listed above. But selling merchandise can be done, and it may prove to be a worthwhile investment. You're marketing your restaurant on another level. Not only are you attracting customers to come to your restaurant, you're also enticing them to take a piece of your restaurant home with them!

QUESTION

What is a co-packer?
A co-packer manufactures and packages foods for other companies to sell in the retail trade. Restaurants don't have the facilities to produce the food items on a massive scale, and costs for such facilities are enormous. A co-packer facilitates the production efficiently, making it possible for the restaurateurs to sell their goods without the hefty start-up costs.

Selling Your Restaurant for Profit

You've worked hard to create a successful business, established a good name for yourself in your community, and made a good living doing what you love, so why would you want to sell your business? There may be a variety of reasons—some may have do with the business itself or your partners—while some may be more personal. Perhaps you're ready to retire or move onto something different in your life. It's your restaurant— you can do as you please. If you do decide to sell your restaurant, you must evaluate its worth and research the market to find out how much you can get for it.

Before you evaluate your restaurant's worth, you have to decide on what you want to sell. Do you want to sell your concept as the whole package, meaning the menu, the name, logo, all the equipment, liquor licenses, and such? Or do you want to sell your restaurant solely as a food-service facility, in which the new owner will have to come up with his own concept? Your decision depends upon your reason for selling and the value of your concept. If you're selling because you want to use the concept somewhere else, then you certainly don't want to sell your concept. Another factor to consider is whether prospective buyers are interested in your concept. More than likely, potential buyers will already have their own concepts in mind and are searching for locations.

Evaluating your restaurant's worth is not an easy task. On the one hand, you have your tangible assets, such as your equipment, liquor licenses, property, and cash in bank, all of which factor into your restaurant's net worth in accounting terms. On the other hand, you also have intangible assets (frequently called goodwill), which may include the restaurant's name and reputation, location, lease terms, built-in designs, and other characteristics that the buyer may benefit from in the sale.

There are several formulas based on the restaurant's earnings that appraisers use to determine a restaurant's worth. Ultimately, the value of the business is dependent upon what the market bears. For example, even a marginally profitable restaurant can get top-dollar if it's in a hot location or if the market for restaurants is strong. Nevertheless, you need to base your valuations on some tangible grounds. Arbitrarily setting a price for your restaurant is never a good strategy. You need to know on some concrete level where your restaurant stands and weigh the different factors, including market conditions that may affect its value.

Remodeling Your Restaurant

After your restaurant has been up and running for a number of years, it may be necessary to update some of the equipment and replace older fixtures. One decision you may also need to make is whether your restaurant needs remodeling. Some restaurants go through a change of look every few years while others try to maintain the same decor and atmosphere they've always had for years. Ultimately, you have to decide what's best for your operation and whether or not it is even in your budget to make changes.

Should You Remodel?

The decision of whether to remodel depends on a number of factors. The most crucial factor in your decision is affordability. Remodeling your restaurant may require you to close your restaurant for a period of time. Not only would the cost of remodeling set you back, but you'd also lose significant revenue as a result of your restaurant's not operating. If the remodeling requires several weeks to complete, you may have to lay off some employees for a short period of time with no guarantees they'll be back. Furthermore, you still have to pay your rent, insurance, utilities, and other overhead.

Consider also the history of your establishment and the effect remodeling may have on your clientele. Will they be receptive to the changes? They may very well find the changes refreshing, but they might also find them dismaying. There's a good reason why your regulars come in as often as they do. They know what they're expecting and feel comfortable in the environment you've provided them. These are factors you need to consider. Ask yourself what you would gain from remodeling? Would you likely gain new clientele? Would you lose some of your regulars? Will the restaurant's identity change along with the remodeling?

Deciding on How to Remodel

If you decide on remodeling your restaurant, you must plan it out in detail and do it efficiently and promptly. To get you started on your planning, answer these questions for yourself:

- **Why are you remodeling?** Maybe you want to update the look and feel of the restaurant, make the space more efficient, or reconfigure the use of the space.
- **What is your budget?** The cost of renovation will largely depend on your existing decor. Certainly, you're not going to downgrade your design efforts with your new look.
- **Has your clientele changed?** Demographics shift. Tastes change. You may have to redefine your target customer's preferences before you remodel.
- **How much of the restaurant will you change?** Maybe all you need is a new paint job, or hardwood flooring instead of that old carpeting.
- **How will remodeling serve your target customer better?** Perhaps you want to improve the flow of traffic for more efficient service.
- **Will your renovations match your location?** Be sure that your remodeling still fits in the neighborhood, especially if the neighborhood has changed.

You may want to consult an interior designer or an architect to help you design the new look you want for your restaurant. Just make it clear what you want the design to accomplish and, more importantly, how much you're willing to spend. Give the designer a time frame in which you want everything to be finished. Remember, you will be required to close your restaurant while renovations are taking place. Each day late means less money in your pocket, so stick to your schedule!

Become a Restaurant Consultant

Owning and running a restaurant consumes a lot of time and energy. As detailed early in this book, the business is demanding and can weigh on your lifestyle should any changes occur in your personal life. If you'd like to distance yourself from the day-to-day demands and have earned a reputation as a successful restaurateur, you might consider becoming a consultant.

Consultants use their expertise and connections to help potential and existing restaurant owners with all aspects of the business—concept development, menu planning, interior design, web design, financing, training, and so on. As a consultant, you are paid for your advice and assistance without taking on the financial risks. Your biggest asset is your knowledge and contacts, and your financial overhead is minimal, save for typical office and communications expenses. You can choose your clients, set your own schedule, and focus on projects you want to do. Your overhead costs are minimal. And as a consultant, you can have your holidays free for the most part, unlike in running a restaurant where you might be working during New Year's Eve, Mother's Day, and Valentine's Day.

QUESTION

Can you be a restaurant consultant and own a restaurant?
There's no law saying you can't be both, though you risk conflict of interest issues from potential clients if you both are competing in the same market. One way to avoid the issue is to consult in another market, i.e., different neighborhood, region, or even state.

That being said, consulting is like any other independent contract work—the work and cash flow are unpredictable. You may do a lot of work competing for an account and then lose out to someone else. You may not have the same out-of-pocket risks as in owning a restaurant, but you may run the risk of clients not paying you on time or worse, not at all. In other words, it's running a business, just a different business.

APPENDIX A

Additional Resources

BOOKS

Baraban, Regina, and Joseph F. Durocher. *Successful Restaurant Design, 3rd Edition.* (Hoboken, NJ: John Wiley and Sons, Inc., 2010)

Birchfield, John C. *Design and Layout of Foodservice Facilities.* (Hoboken, NJ: John Wiley and Sons, Inc. 2008)

Khan, Mahmood A. *Restaurant Franchising.* (New York: John Wiley and Sons, Inc., 1999)

McVety, Paul J., Bradley J. Ware, and Claudette Leveque. *Fundamentals of Menu Planning, 3rd Edition.* (Hoboken, NJ: John Wiley and Sons, Inc., 2008)

Neumier, Marty. *The Brand Gap: How to Bridge the Distance Between Business Strategy and Design.* (Indianapolis, IN: New Riders Publishing, 2003)

Sandler, Corey and Janice Keefe. *Performance Appraisal Phrase Book.* (Avon, MA: Adams Media Corporation, 1992)

TRADE MAGAZINES

Nation's Restaurant News (New York: Lebhar-Friedman, Inc.), *www.nrn.com*, is a weekly trade publication that features news, current trends, and events. Subscription includes access to website.

Restaurants & Institutions (New York: Reed Business Information), *www.rimag.com*, is a twice-monthly publication providing information on trends, industry outlook, concepts, and recipes. Free subscription offer for restaurant operators.

Restaurant Business (New York: VNU Business Media, Inc.), *www.restaurantbiz.com*, is a twice-monthly trade magazine similar to *Restaurants & Institutions*, with coverage and analysis of industry trends, labor, special interests, and supplier resources.

Flavor & the Menu (Tigard, OR: Media Unlimited, Inc.), *www.flavor-online.com*, is a quarterly publication that features analyses of taste trends and patterns of menu development in the restaurant industry

GOVERNMENT AGENCIES AND BUSINESS ORGANIZATIONS

United States Department of Commerce, *www.commerce.gov*, provides statistics about certain industry sectors and regional economic developments.

United States Department of Labor, *www.dol.gov*, provides important information regarding labor laws and practices, including minimum wage, benefits, and unemployment insurance.

United States Patent and Trademark Office, *www.uspto.gov*, provides information on the process of trademarking your name and logo, including the application and fees.

Small Business Administration, *www.sba.gov*, sponsors many programs assisting small businesses with various issues, including financing, site location, start-up, and management.

Internal Revenue Service, *www.irs.gov*, provides a great deal of information concerning your business' tax structure, downloadable tax forms, and other online features.

National Restaurant Association, *www.restaurant.org*. has long been considered the industry's premier association; NRA sets out to educate, promote, and offer restaurant owners helpful tips and research.

Service Corps of Retired Executives (SCORE), *www.score.org*, is a nonprofit organization with a network of experienced entrepreneurs who offer advice to small businesses in all stages of development.

GENERAL BUSINESS WEBSITES

www.allbusiness.com provides small business owners with advice, business directories and products, forums, news, and downloadable sample business forms and plans.

www.bplan.com provides guidance on writing business plans with feature articles, tips and advice, and sample business plans.

www.entrepreneur.com covers various issues of the entrepreneurial business, from financing to management to marketing.

FOOD AND BEVERAGE INDUSTRY WEBSITES

www.restaurantowner.com is a subscription-based service that gives you access to articles and downloadable tools to help you run your business.

www.restaurantreport.com is a free website providing tips and articles on the restaurant industry on many different issues, with an invitation to users to respond.

www.foodservice.com is an all-inclusive site for the food-service industry with news, sources, directories, and discussion boards with industry pros.

www.beveragenet.net is a source of information for the alcoholic beverage industry featuring forecasts, trends, and news.

FOOD AND BEVERAGE SOURCE WEBSITES

www.epicurean.com is a great gourmet food-and-beverage site with feature articles, book reviews, recipes, and discussion forum.

www.chow.com contains recipes, articles, discussion boards, and generally everything about food and cooking.

www.vino.com is a great site for information for learning about wine including buying guides, reviews, and feature articles.

www.beeradvocate.com features information on beer basics, reviews, events, and discussion boards.

www.eater.com is a national blog site about restaurants, bars, and clubs.

Sample Business Plan

This appendix presents a simple business plan for a fictitious casual restaurant. Your business plan will most likely be different in tone, organization, format, and length. The facts, figures, and analyses used in the sample plan is intended to illustrate the structure and some key elements of a typical business plan and should not be construed as complete or accurate in the real world. Any likeness to people, organizations, and concepts, real or fictional, presented in this plan is purely coincidental.

Ama-Zen:
"The Restaurant That Cares about Your Body, Mind, and Spirit"
100 Elderbrook Avenue
Phillytown, PA 15555-5555
Business Plan
Jennifer Ho and Matthew Cornelius Kirkland
1100 Karma Road
Phillytown, PA 15555-5511
1-412-555-1989
E-mail: jho@ama-zen.com

Table of Contents

1.0 Executive Summary

Ama-Zen is a unique concept that approaches casual dining in a whole new light, blending Eastern philosophy and cuisine with the emphasis on nutrition and serenity as the path to well-being. Eastern practices have emerged as very effective ways to combat the stress of modern life. People may now practice yoga, read about feng shui, get Thai or shiatsu massages, eat brown rice, or drink tea green to improve their health and well-being. Yet, when it comes to dining out, many health-conscious consumers find their options to be very limited. Most restaurants may offer a few "healthy" selections, but these are seen as alternatives to the main cuisine being offered.

At Ama-Zen, nutrition and well-being will be the primary focus, not the alternative. Ama-Zen will answer to the needs of the consumers who care about their bodies but are tired of the healthy alternatives when dining out. Health-conscious consumers will know that everything on the menu is prepared with quality organic ingredients from local farms and with the utmost attention to nutritional details. Whether the customers have had a long day of shopping or just a long day, or they are getting a break from work or rewarding themselves after a workout, they will feel relaxed in the simple, serene atmosphere that is free of cluttered decor, point-of-sale ads, and over-the-top service.

Ama-Zen's unique approach will fulfill the needs of an emerging market in Phillytown, a market that is more concerned about its health and environment. Fast-paced cities such as New York and Los Angeles have restaurants with similar concepts appealing to consumers who yearn for an environment that takes them away from the noise and chaos of city life but remains urban and hip. The key to Ama-Zen's success will be reaching its target market and delivering its message, which is "a restaurant that cares about your body, mind, and spirit."

1.1 Mission Statement

Ama-Zen aims to serve healthy, tasty food made with high quality, locally sourced organic ingredients in an atmosphere that enhances the experience by promoting serenity, simplicity, and well-being.

1.2 Statement of Purpose

Jennifer Ho and Matthew Cornelius Kirkland, partners, are seeking financial contributions of $120,000 in addition to their $120,000 personal investment. The funds will be used for all expenses relating to start-up including: deposit for leases and utilities, building improvements, permits, fixtures, furniture, equipment, starting inventory, and other costs as detailed in this business plan. The partners are confident that the business will show a profit in the first year, and increase in profit in subsequent years, producing an attractive rate of return.

2.0 Industry Analysis

Although the food-service industry is becoming more and more competitive, the market for new concepts continues to be strong. Changes in lifestyle have caused people to have less time and fewer resources to cook for themselves. Furthermore, people nowadays prefer to eat out more due to the numerous choices available to them in terms of both food variety and price.

2.1 The Restaurant World—Present Day

Forty years ago, dining out was an event. Restaurants were fewer, and people mostly ate at home unless it was a special occasion. Today, the food-service industry is one of the largest industries in the country, accounting for over $300 billion in sales per year. According to industry reports, Americans spend on the average 15 percent of their income on meals prepared outside the home. In the past five years, the restaurant industry has outperformed other industries by 40 percent.

2.2 Industry Outlook

Industry reports estimate that the demand for meals prepared outside the home will increase by 30 percent over the next five years. The industry outlook for restaurants remains strong in the short- and long-term. New restaurants are opening every day nationwide, and still more are needed to meet increasing demand.

3.0 Business Concept

Ama-Zen will be a moderately priced, casual restaurant featuring a variety of Eastern cuisines, such as Indian, Chinese, Tibetan, and more. Zen is the meditative philosophy of purity and simplicity, and therefore, purity and simplicity are the recurring themes in all aspects of the restaurant.

3.1 Menu

Ama-Zen will feature a variety of Eastern cuisines made from scratch using fresh, organic ingredients from local farms. Ama-Zen will feature a rotating monthly menu that focuses on seasonal availability of fresh produce, but will also contain several perennial signature dishes. Though most menu items will be vegetarian to emphasize the organic, low-fat, and nutritious theme of the menu, a few meat options will be available, depending on the season. Some sample menu items include:

- Eggplant and lamb casserole with soy béchamel.
- Green tea soba with chilled tamari-dashi broth.
- Steamed tofu with ginger, garlic, and scallion soy sauce.
- Spicy lentil stew with yams and jalapeño pepper.
- Potato and chickpea salad with coriander.
- Free-range Cornish hen stuffed with rice pilaf, pine nuts, and raisins.

3.2 Decor and Atmosphere

Ama-Zen will adopt a minimalist approach to decor that is similar to the designs of some high-end restaurants and retail stores in cities such as New York and Los Angeles. The ambiance will promote serenity and peacefulness: white walls accented with simple design; muted, soft-colored lighting with hues of blue and yellow; bleached wood tabletops and white café chairs; and ambient, meditative music playing softly in the background. Bonzai trees and bamboo plants will highlight various parts of the dining room. The design of the fixtures will be sleek yet simple, with little ornamentation: brushed aluminum ceiling fans; hanging lights with parchment shades; bleached wood counter and frosted glass shelving on the wall behind it, showcasing large stainless-steel canisters of various green tea leaves and tea ware.

3.3 Service

Ama-Zen will be a full table service restaurant, although it will accommodate takeout orders at the counter. While the decor may suggest a hip or high concept ambiance, the service and attitude here will be casual and down-to-earth. The servers will display a working knowledge of the menu and styles of the cuisine, in order to educate and accommodate requests from customers. Servers will be required to wear the company uniform, a white T-shirt with the Ama-Zen logo near the shoulder. While Ama-Zen would like to be a destination spot for customers, it must also appeal to the cultural district shoppers who would like to drop in for a quick lunch or decide to stay for dinner on the fly. Therefore, reservations will not be necessary so we can accommodate more walk-ins.

3.4 Pricing Strategy

Because Ama-Zen will use mostly locally grown and organic ingredients, the pricing will be slightly higher than the nearby competition, but the perceived value for customers will be much greater due to the quality of the ingredients and unique methods of preparation. In order to maintain reasonable pricing points, no menu item will be priced more than $16.95. To keep food costs manageable at 32 percent and sustain adequate return on investment, we will monitor our purchases carefully and maintain reasonable portion control.

3.5 Size of the Restaurant and Hours of Operation

Ama-Zen will have fifteen tables, carrying a total seating capacity of fifty guests. It will be open for lunch and dinner six days a week. Lunch will be served Monday through Saturday from noon to 3:00 P.M. Dinner will be served Monday through Thursday 6:00 to 10:30 P.M., Friday and Saturday from 6:00 P.M. to midnight. The restaurant will open for tea service only between the hours of 3:00 and 6:00 P.M. so that the kitchen can make meal period transitions and change staff.

4.0 Market Analysis

Ama-Zen will be located at 200 Elderbrook Street, Phillytown, PA. The location is in the heart of the cultural district with more than 100 retail businesses and restaurants combined in a quarter square mile area. During the day, the area is a destination for consumers who seek an alternative to the typical retail stores found in malls, including fashion boutiques, cosmetics, furniture and lifestyle stores, hair salons, jewelry designers, a fitness center, and art galleries. At night, many people go to the restaurants and bars in the neighborhood. The customer base can be broken down into three major categories:

- **Local population:** The cultural district is centrally located in an affluent neighborhood and is a short drive from two other, more affluent neighborhoods.
- **College and universities:** Two major universities within walking distance from the cultural district have a combined population of more than 50,000 students and employees.
- **Suburbs:** Consumers from outlying suburbs head to the cultural district to shop in retail stores and go to the kinds of restaurants and bars that their local area doesn't offer.

4.1 Target Market Demographics

The concept of Ama-Zen will appeal to the following customer profiles:

- Women between the ages of eighteen and forty, with incomes over $35,000 or coming from households with combined incomes over $50,000.
- Women who are either in college or have college degrees.
- Consumers who are health-conscious and concerned about body image. They work out regularly (yoga, Pilates) and adopt a low-fat, healthy diet.
- Customers who read magazines such as *Vogue* and *Elle* to keep up with the latest fashion trends, buy designer clothing and accessories, and maintain an active social life.
- Customers who are environmentally conscious and are willing to pay more for higher quality, local, organically grown produce and grains.
- Customers who enjoy a diversity of cuisine, whether Thai, Indian, French, or Italian.

This demographic group will be the most likely market for Ama-Zen to target. The ambiance and menu will appeal to their desire for healthy, light food in a serene yet down-to-earth atmosphere.

4.2 Market Outlook

Although the population of Phillytown has decreased for the last decade, the percentage of college-educated women has either remained steady or increased during that span. Women working in the professional fields have also steadily increased, along with their incomes.

- About 50 percent of the students and employees at the two nearby universities are women, 85 percent of whom are between the ages of eighteen and forty.
- Median income for working college-educated women between the ages of twenty-five and forty who live in the surrounding neighborhoods has increased from $33,000 to $35,000.
- Some 35 percent of the women between the ages of eighteen and forty come from households with incomes over $65,000.

Industry reports predict that this trend will continue to grow, and businesses in the retail and food-service sectors have increased efforts to market to this group. The majority of the women who shop in the cultural district fit into this demographic. Close to 75 percent of the retail businesses in the area target higher income women. Since these consumers are willing to pay considerably more for what is perceived to be higher quality and design in fashion, cosmetics, and other products, they may be willing to pay a little more for higher quality food and a serene atmosphere.

5.0 Competitive Analysis

There are over a dozen restaurants in a small, concentrated area that have a similar or lower pricing structure. Few restaurants in the cultural district are priced above $15 per entrée. Although penetrating this market is obviously a challenge, Ama-Zen will make a successful entrance because of its unique concept and approach to reaching its target market.

5.1 Direct Competitors

There are five restaurants serving Asian cuisine within a three-block radius. All have a similar or slightly lower pricing structure and provide service and atmosphere that match their respective concepts. No single competitor can match the diversity of cuisine of Ama-Zen, but they may offer a few items that may appear similar to Ama-Zen's menu. All five restaurants are well-established and generate significant sales volume. Each has been at the same location for at least five years. The following list presents a brief description of each restaurant and the main point of difference that sets each apart:

- **Thai House:** Authentic Thai cuisine with ethnic decor, reasonable portions, targets urban professionals and neighborhood families; operating for fifteen years; numerous awards and recognition; prices higher than other Thai places—$8.50 to $20.00 per entrée.
- **China Wall:** Over 100 menu items, large portions, family atmosphere; food generally heavy with sauces; Chinese food interest has decreased slightly in favor of Thai; entrées range from $7.95 to $14.95.
- **Sushi Palace:** Sushi and Japanese cuisine; focus on fresh sushi; popular with market targeted by Ama-Zen; ambiance trying to capture similar feel as Ama-Zen, but service is suspect; average sushi platter for one: $18.95.
- **Thai Won Down:** Another Thai concept capitalizing on a hot trend; a funkier, laid-back version appealing to a younger, hip crowd; small space can be uncomfortable when crowded; food quality is average; entrées range from $6.50 to $10.95
- **Bistro Bombay:** Indian cuisine with French influences; point of difference is on fusion menu in an elegant modern setting unlike other Indian restaurants, and the prices reflect that; entrées range $17.00 to $24.00.

Because Ama-Zen will use organic produce and meats in its food, some items on the menu will be priced slightly higher than comparable items competitors may have. However, shoppers in the cultural district pay considerably more for items they perceive to be a better brand and design. Therefore, they will be willing to pay more for better quality ingredients that they know cost more than conventional products. Yet, the company is aware of the pricing points and will maintain a competitive pricing strategy.

5.2 Competitive Advantages

Because Ama-Zen is tailoring its concept around the needs and preferences of its target market, it has a number of distinct advantages over its competitors:

1. **Focus on health.** All menu items will be prepared specifically with consumers' health awareness in mind. Competitors may have "healthy" options, but they do not market their restaurant as such nor focus specifically on them.
2. **Diversity of cuisine.** Ama-Zen will present a sampling of different Eastern cuisines with exotic dishes for the more adventurous patrons and familiar dishes for the more conservative ones.
3. **Focus on quality, not quantity.** Ama-Zen will use only organically grown produce and meats on the premises. We will list some of our suppliers by name on the menu to show customers our commitment to the quality of our ingredients.
4. **Focus on atmosphere.** The simple decor and ambiance will promote a serene, but cosmopolitan atmosphere that reflects the attitude and approach to the food.

The servers will also work to reinforce the customer's experience with their knowledge of the menu and down-to-earth attitude. The primary focus of the product and service is the target market's tastes and preferences that aren't being met by the competitors. Portion size and prices aren't the chief concern. The overall experience of the restaurant will determine the perceived value for this market.

6.0 Marketing Strategy

Ama-Zen will have high visibility. The cultural district is busy year round with heavy foot traffic during the day and evening, and Ama-Zen is right in the epicenter of activity. Neighborhood residents are always excited about new restaurants in the area, so Ama-Zen will likely draw a lot of attention from them. The company is considering a budget of $3,000 for preopening marketing. Efforts will focus on reaching the target market in areas where they are likely to go and through media they are likely to see and hear. Advertising should be a mix of cross promotional efforts through both local businesses and local print media.

Marketing efforts will use the following strategies:

- **Social Media:** Utilize Facebook, Twitter, Urbanspoon, and other websites.
- **Print Media Advertising:** Seek out local newspapers, city magazines, and weekly arts and entertainment publications.
- **Public Relations:** Send media kits and press releases to various media as well as nearby hotel concierges, day spas, and museums.
- **Direct Mail:** Create a mailing list of area residents, businesses, and subscribers.
- **Cross Promotions:** Exchange point-of-sale marketing materials, like postcards and business cards with area businesses such as hair salons, the local fitness center, art galleries, and local bed-and-breakfasts.
- **Grass Roots Efforts:** Encourage word-of-mouth referrals from a well-trained staff as well as friends and neighborhoods.

The message in all marketing efforts will convey Ama-Zen to the target market as "the restaurant that cares about your body, mind, and spirit." It will emphasize freshness, nutrition, taste, serenity, and simplicity.

7.0 Management Team

The restaurant's day-to-day operation will initially be managed by the founding partners themselves in order to control the overhead and maintain adequate staff. As such, the management team will include the two co-owners: Jennifer Ho will serve as president and executive chef. Jennifer was a chef at Vendage, a restaurant located in the world famous Laurel Highlands health resort, Mannolin. For ten years, she has developed creative, healthy, tasty menus that feature organically grown produce and meats. She has received awards as one of the best chefs in the state from several magazines and associations. Jennifer has gained valuable experience in the cuisine of several countries during her six-month study in Asia. Matthew Cornelius Kirkland will act as vice president and manager. Matthew has fourteen years of experience in restaurant management. He holds a bachelor degree in business administration and an associate degree in culinary arts. For the past five years, Matthew has managed the Phoenix, a high-end French Lebanese restaurant, in Phillytown, PA. While under his management, the Phoenix has consistently won accolades from the media and clientele and has averaged 20 percent in net profits.

Once fully operational, Ama-Zen will seek to add an assistant manager and sous chef, who will report to their respective managers.

8.0 Facilities and Operations

The restaurant space for Ama-Zen is approximately 2,000-square feet. It was formerly a dance studio with open space, and therefore would need total renovation for commercial food service. Although the building does not need to be rezoned, building permits and final approval by city inspectors will be necessary. All new furnishings and equipment will need to be purchased and installed by a licensed contractor. However, there are two handicapped-accessible restrooms and central HVAC already installed on the premises.

8.1 Employee Training

Employees will have an orientation period in which they will learn the policies and procedures as written in their employee and operation manuals. They will not only receive practical, hands-on training to perform specific duties, but they will also learn to uphold the philosophy, attitude, and standards promoted by the concept.

8.2 Food Production

All food items will be prepared from scratch on the premises. Most food items will be made to order. Some will be prepared ahead and properly stored until ready to serve. Because Ama-Zen will use only organically grown produce, the kitchen staff must maintain high standards of sanitation and storage to ensure the food is safe.

8.3 Purchases and Inventory Control

The founding partners will personally oversee all purchases and control over inventory. Because of the abundant use of fresh ingredients, inventory will be kept low initially and adjusted to the business in order to ensure that products are used efficiently with minimal waste. The partners will also personally negotiate with local purveyors to establish delivery dates and times.

9.0 Start-Up Requirements

The partners have determined the start-up requirements for the operation as follows:

▼ START-UP REQUIREMENTS FOR AMA-ZEN

Deposits (rent, utilities)	$7,000.00
Building Improvements	$50,000.00
Legal and Consulting Fees	$1,500.00
Licenses and Permits	$1,000.00
Fixtures, Furniture, and Equipment	$100,000.00
Liquor License	$25,000.00
Starting Inventory (food, beverages, supplies)	$15,000.00
Initial Marketing Expenses (business cards, menus, advertising, PR)	$3,000.00
Insurance	$3,500.00
Preopening employees' payroll	$4,000.00
Reserve Operating Capital	$30,000.00
Total	$240,000.00

Details of building improvements and fixtures, furniture, and equipment are listed in the appendices.

10.0 Financial Projections

While Ama-Zen is expected to operate profitably during its first year, the partners have kept the financial projections conservative to take into account the current economic climate. The immediate objective is to generate sufficient cash flow to pay for all expenses, as the projected cash flow analysis will illustrate. The goals will be accomplished through a combination of strategic and efficient use of marketing, effective purchasing, and cost and inventory control. Every attempt will be made to maintain a cost of sales level below 32 percent. However, because of the concept, which emphasizes the use of fresh ingredients, at times the costs may surpass that level.

10.1 Projected Annual Sales

Sales are expected to grow steadily at a 10 percent rate during the first three years of operation. The number of customers and check averages for each day of the week are as follows:

▼ **PROJECTED CUSTOMER COUNT AND CHECK AVERAGES**

	Lunch	Ck. Avg.	Dinner	Ck. Avg.
Monday	35	$8.00	5	$15.00
Tuesday	40	$8.00	55	$15.00
Wednesday	50	$8.00	55	$16.00
Thursday	80	$10.00	100	$18.00
Friday	90	$10.00	120	$20.00
Saturday	110	$12.00	120	$20.00
Average	67	$9.33	86	$18.00

From the figures, the partners calculate the revenue to be:
Average daily sales: $2,214.00
Projected monthly sales: $53,000.00
Projected Annual Sales: $642,000.00 Year One; $706,200.00 Year Two; $776,820.00 Year Three.

Sales volume is expected to be the highest during the summer months, in which several events occur including a week-long arts festival that brings roughly 350,000 people to the area. Sales are expected to level off during the fall months, picking up again after Thanksgiving Day, the start of the Christmas shopping season, then leveling off again.

10.2 Projected Monthly Operating Expenses

The average monthly expenses necessary to maintain operation are estimated as follows:

▼ **AVERAGE MONTHLY OPERATING EXPENSES**

Cost of Sales (food and beverage)	$17,000.00
Payroll (salaried, hourly wages, benefits)	$13,900.00
Direct Operating Expenses	$2,000.00
Music and Entertainment	$75.00
Marketing	$3,000.00
Utilities	$1,500.00
General and Administrative	$600.00
Repairs and Maintenance	$200.00
Occupancy Costs (rent, taxes, insurance)	$7,500.00
Leased Equipment Expenses	$350.00
Depreciation	$1,000.00
Interest on Loans	$300.00
Total Expenses	$47,425.00

Operating expenses are expected to fluctuate on a month-by-month basis, depending on the sale volumes and price of food and other supplies.

Appendix 1—Furniture, Fixtures, and Equipment

▼ **LIST OF FURNITURE, FIXTURES, AND EQUIPMENT**

Quantity	Item	Cost
1	Walk-in Cooler	$8,000
1	Commercial Dishwasher with Sink and Table	$7,000
2	Reach-in Stainless-Steel Freezers	$6,000
1	36-Inch Charcoal Gas Grill	$550
1	Chinese Wok Range with Three Burners	$5,000
1	Six-Burner Restaurant Range	$1,800
1	Stainless-Steel Cold Station	$3,000
6	Chrome Shelving Systems	$500
2	Reach-in Coolers, (39 cu. ft. stainless steel)	$3,600
3	Stainless-Steel Work Tables	$1,200
2	Hutches for Stainless-Steel Work Tables	$800

Quantity	Item	Cost
1	Ice Maker with Storage Bin	$4,000
2	Sandwich Prep Reach-ins	$5,000
1	20-Quart Food Processor/Blender	$900
1	Stainless-Steel Hood and Exhaust System	$11,000
1	Point-of-Sale System with Software	$4,000
1	Liquid Fire Protection System	$4,000
1	Stainless-Steel Three-Bowl Sink	$1,500
1	Mini-Hand Sink	$150
3	Stainless-Steel Single-Basin Sink and Mop Sink	$1,000
1	Three-Door Reach-in Beverage Cooler with Glass Door	$3,500
10	Bleached Wood Tabletops with Bases, Two Seats	$2,500
5	Bleached Wood Tabletops with Bases, Four Seats	$1,500
55	Bleached Wood Café Chairs	$2,800
1	Bleached Wood Counters	$6,000
2	Brushed Aluminum Ceiling Fans	$800
12	Track Lighting	$500
2	Bleached Wood Shelving Systems	$1,000
1	Hot-Water Dispensing Unit	$300
1	Water Filtration System	$500
4	Large Decorative Vases	$200
1	Three-Bowl Bar Sink, (stainless steel)	$1,500
	Misc. Smallware and Supplies	$300
1	Leather Sofa Set	$3,000
1	Office Furniture	$500
1	Fireproof Safe	$500
	Computer Equipment and Communications	$5,600
	Total Cost of Furniture, Fixtures, and Equipment	$100,000

Appendix 2—Building Improvements

▼ **BUILDING IMPROVEMENTS**

Electrical	$12,500
Plumbing	$15,600
Structural Changes and Built-Ins	$15,900
Heating, Ventilation, Air-Conditioning	$6,000
Total Cost of Building Improvements	$50,000

Appendix 3—Financial Statements and Analyses

▼ **PRO FORMA INCOME STATEMENT**

	July	Aug.	Sept.	Oct.	Nov.	Dec.	Total	% of Revenue
Income								
Food	$60,300	$60,950	$61,480	$52,360	$50,300	$61,354	$346,744	89.15%
Beverage	$5,699	$9,484	$7,888	$8,383	$7,373	$3,388	$42,215	10.85%
Other income	0.00	0.00	0.00	0.00	0.00	0.00	$0	0.00%
Total	**$65,999**	**$70,434**	**$69,368**	**$60,743**	**$57,673**	**$64,742**	**$388,959**	**100.00%**
Expenses								
Food Cost	$19,296	$19,504	$19,674	$16,755	$16,096	$19,633	$110,958	28.53%
Beverage	$1,824	$3,035	$2,524	$2,683	$2,359	$1,084	$13,509	3.47%
Total Cost of Sales	**$21,120**	**$22,539**	**$22,198**	**$19,438**	**$18,455**	**$20,717**	**$124,467**	**32.00%**
Payroll								
Salaries	$11,000	$11,000	$11,000	$11,000	$11,000	$11,000	$66,000	16.97%
Hourly Wages	$5,400	$5,600	$5,800	$6,000	$5,900	$5,899	$34,599	8.90%
Benefits	$500	$500	$500	$500	$500	$500	$3,000	0.77%
Freelance/ Contract	$0	$0	$0	$0	$0	$0	$0	0.00%
Total Payroll	**$16,900**	**$17,100**	**$17,300**	**$17,500**	**$17,400**	**$17,399**	**$103,599**	**26.63%**
Operating Expenses								
Direct Operating Expenses	$2,000	$2,000	$2,000	$2,000	$2,000	$2,000	$12,000	3.09%
Entertainment	$300	$200	$200	$200	$200	$200	$1,300	0.33%
Marketing	$3,000	$3,000	$3,000	$3,000	$3,000	$3,000	$18,000	4.63%

Utilities	$2,000	$2,000	$2,200	$1,510	$1,500	$1,800	$11,010	2.83%
Administrative	$600	$600	$600	$600	$600	$600	$3,600	0.93%
Repairs & Maintenance	$100	$299	$300	$300	$209	$299	$1,507	0.39%
Total Operating Expenses	**$8,000**	**$8,099**	**$8,300**	**$7,610**	**$7,509**	**$7,899**	**$47,417**	**12.19%**
Gross Operating Profit	**$19,979**	**$22,696**	**$21,570**	**$16,195**	**$14,309**	**$18,727**	**$113,476**	**29.17%**
Other Expenses								
Rent	$7,000	$7,000	$7,000	$7,000	$7,000	$7,000	$42,000	10.80%
Real Estate Taxes/ Insurance	$500	$500	$500	$500	$500	$500	$3,000	0.77%
Equipment Leases	$100	$100	$100	$100	$100	$100	$600	0.15%
Insurance	$800	$800	$800	$800	$800	$800	$4,800	1.23%
Total Other Expenses	**$8,400**	**$8,400**	**$8,400**	**$8,400**	**$8,400**	**$8,400**	**$50,400**	**12.95%**
Adjusted Gross Profit	**$11,579**	**$14,296**	**$13,170**	**$7,795**	**$5,909**	**$10,327**	**$63,076**	**16.43%**
Interest from Loans	$300	$300	$300	$300	$300	$300	$1,800	0.46%
Depreciation	$900	$900	$900	$900	$900	$900	$5,400	1.39%
Net Profit/ Loss	**$10,379**	**$13,096**	**$11,970**	**$6,595**	**$4,709**	**$9,127**	**$55,876**	**14.37%**

▼ **PRO FORMA CASH-FLOW ANALYSIS**

	July	Aug.	Sept.	Oct.	Nov.	Dec.	Total
Cash Flow from Operations							
Cash Receipts	$65,999	$70,434	$69,368	$60,743	$57,673	$64,742	$388,959
Cash Disbursements	$54,720	$56,438	$56,498	$53,248	$52,064	$54,715	$327,682
Net from Operations	**$11,279**	**$13,996**	**$12,870**	**$7,495**	**$5,609**	**$10,027**	**$61,276**
Cash on Hand							
Opening Balance	$0	$10,279	$20,275	$27,146	$29,641	$30,250	
New Loan	$0	$0	$0	$0	$0	$0	
Capital Contributions	$0	$0	$0	$0	$0	$0	
Sale of Fixed Assets	$0	$0	$0	$0	$0	$0	
Net Profit from Operation	$0	$0	$0	$0	$0	$0	
Total Cash Available	**$11,279**	**$24,275**	**$33,146**	**$34,641**	**$35,250**	**$40,276**	
Other Disbursements							
Debt Reduction	$1,000	$2,000	$2,000	$2,000	$2,000	$2,000	
New Equipment and Fixtures	$0	$0	$0	$0	$0	$0	
Profit Distributions	$0	$2,000	$4,000	$3,000	$3,000	$5,000	
Total Cash Paid Out	**$1,000**	**$4,000**	**$6,000**	**$5,000**	**$5,000**	**$7,000**	
Ending Cash Position	**$10,279**	**$20,275**	**$27,146**	**$29,641**	**$30,250**	**$33,276**	

MONTHLY BREAK-EVEN ANALYSIS

	July	Aug.	Sept.	Oct.	Nov.	Dec.
Monthly Expenses	$34,500	$34,799	$35,200	$34,710	$34,509	$34,898
Monthly Cost of Sales	$21,120	$22,539	$22,198	$19,438	$18,455	$20,717
Required Revenue	**$55,620**	**$57,338**	**$57,398**	**$54,148**	**$52,964**	**$55,615**
Average Daily Sales	**$2,139**	**$2,205**	**$2,208**	**$2,083**	**$2,037**	**$2,139**

▼ PRO FORMA BALANCE SHEET AFTER ONE MONTH

Assets		
Currrent Assets		
Cash	$40,279	
Accounts Receivables	$0	
Inventory	$17,100	
Deposits/Rent	$7,000	
Prepaid Expense	$1,700	
Total Current Assets	$66,079	
Fixed Assets		
Building	$50,000	
Less Depreciation	$400	$49,584
Furniture, Fixtures, and Equipment	$100,000	
Less Depreciation	$500	$99,167
Vehicles	$0	
Less Depreciation	$0	
Liquor License	$25,000	
Total Fixed Assets	$173,751	
Total Assets	$239,830	
Liabilities and capital		
Current Liabilities		
Accounts Payable	$2,500	
Sales Taxes Payable	$0	
Payroll Taxes Payable	$0	
Accrued Wages Payable	$0	
Unearned Revenue	$0	
Short-Term Notes	$0	
Short-Term Bank Loan	$300	
Total Current Liabilities	$2,800	
Long-Term Liabilities		
Long-Term Notes Payable	$120,000	
Mortgage Payable	$0	
Total Long-Term Liabilities	$0	$120,000
Total Liabilities	**$122,800**	
Capital		
Owners' Equity	$105,751	
Net Profit	$11,279	
Total Capital	**$117,030**	
Total Liabilities and Capital	**$239,830**	

Appendix 4 – Floor Plans

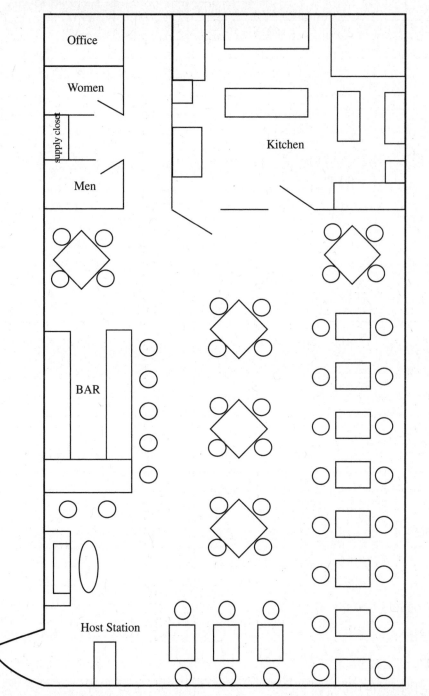

Ama-Zen Floor Plan

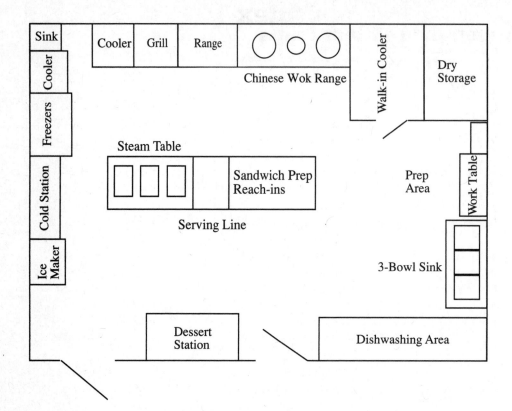

Kitchen Floor Plan

Index

We Have
EVERYTHING®
on Anything!

With more than 19 million copies sold, **the Everything® series** has become one of America's favorite resources for solving problems, learning new skills, and organizing lives. Our brand is not only recognizable—it's also welcomed.

The series is a hand-in-hand partner for people who are ready to tackle new subjects—like you!

For more information on the Everything® series, please visit *www.adamsmedia.com*

The Everything® list spans a wide range of subjects, with more than 500 titles covering 25 different categories:

Business	History	Reference
Careers	Home Improvement	Religion
Children's Storybooks	Everything Kids	Self-Help
Computers	Languages	Sports & Fitness
Cooking	Music	Travel
Crafts and Hobbies	New Age	Wedding
Education/Schools	Parenting	Writing
Games and Puzzles	Personal Finance	
Health	Pets	